LIEUT. COLONEL
WILLIAM WILLIS BLACKFORD C.S.A

WAR YEARS WITH
JEB STUART

Arcadia Press

CONTENTS

WAR YEARS WITH JEB STUART

INTRODUCTION

Every line of this narrative by Lieut. Col. William Willis Blackford has the "feel" of the cavalry Corps of the Army of Northern Virginia. Authenticity is stamped on each paragraph. The historical evidence is that of an eye-witness. First as Adjutant of "Jeb" Stuart's command and then as chief engineer and a member of the staff at cavalry headquarters, Blackford observed from his commander's side nearly all the operations of the mounted troops from June, 1861, to the end of January, 1864. He had Stuart's full confidence and he probably knew more of what prompted the moves of the "Beau Sabreur" than did any other staff officer who ever wrote of Stuart except H. B. McClellan and John Esten Cooke. In some respects, Blackford was a closer witness than either of these men. McClellan, an invaluable historical authority, did not join the staff until April, 1863. Cooke was a professional writer whose sketches of Stuart in *Wearing of the Gray* are the accepted, full-length literary portrait, but Cooke's duties as inspector frequently kept him away from headquarters when events of interest were occurring. Besides, Colonel Blackford loved the life of a soldier. Cooke did not, and in his diary said so with complete and characteristic honesty. If, then, a reader wishes a sympathetic and intelligent close-up of Stuart and the interesting young men around him, here it is in Blackford's memoirs.

Regret will be felt, of course, that Blackford was not with Stuart at Yellow Tavern, when Lee's most renowned cavalryman fought his last battle. Compensation for this is offered by the transfer of Blackford to most important service as second in command of the First Virginia Engineer troops. His immediate superior became Col. T. M. R. Talcott, a former member of the personal staff of Gen. R. E. Lee, and a son of Andrew and Harriet Hackley Talcott, the "beautiful Talcott" of Lee's early days as an officer in the United States Army. Under the admirable leadership of Talcott and Blackford, the regiment deserved all that Colonel Blackford said of it. His narrative, in fact, is the only one that describes by examples and day-by-day report what the Engineer Troops accomplished. Colonel Talcott wrote in the *Photographic History of the Civil War* a brief account of the countermining at Petersburg; but the Colonel devoted most of his other articles to the defense of his "great captain" Lee and not to the glorification of his regiment or of his own service. Colonel Talcott long outlived his Lieutenant Colonel and did not come to the end of his days until 1920. In his old age he was a beautiful figure of gentility and modest scholarship.

Of his relations with Colonel Talcott, the author of these memoirs writes appreciatively. That was characteristic of him and of his able family. Colonel Blackford was one of five brothers in the Confederate service. They inherited capacity and had from youth the environment that shaped firmly their character. Their father was William M. Blackford, one-time editor of the Lynchburg *Virginian* and later cashier of the Exchange Bank of that city, a man of solid strength and dependable judgment. Mrs. Blackford was born Mary Berkeley Minor, daughter of Gen. John Minor of Fredericksburg, an officer of the Virginia Line in the War of 1812 and an eloquent, efficient lawyer. Nearly all the Minors of this line were exceptional in capacity and in diligence. The best known of them, a cousin of Mary Berkeley Minor Blackford, was John B. Minor, for a half a century professor of law at the University of Virginia and undoubtedly one of the foremost law teachers of his generation. Had he followed letters he would have won eminence because he possessed a style of vividness, vigor and subtle rhythm. Some passages from his published *Institutes of Common and Statute Law* have genuine majesty.

William Willis Blackford, inheritor of this same gift of words, was born in Fredericksburg, Virginia, March 23, 1831 and was the eldest of the sons of William M. and Mary Berkeley Minor Blackford. The second son of this union was Captain Charles Minor Blackford, a member of the Second Virginia Cavalry until 1863 and then, because of partial disability, Judge Advocate of the Military Court of the Second Corps, Army of Northern Virginia. Third among the sons was Benjamin Lewis Blackford, a private in the renowned Eleventh Virginia Infantry, Samuel Garland's regiment. Subsequently he was a Lieutenant of Engineers and was stationed at Wilmington, North Carolina, where he had a love affair that fulfilled perfectly all the requirements of the romantic literature of the time, except that it did not lead to marriage. The fourth son was Launcelot M. Blackford, a private of the Rockbridge artillery, then clerk of his brother Charles's military court and later Adjutant of the Twenty-fourth Virginia Infantry, William R. Terry's Brigade, Pickett's Division. Launcelot Blackford became, after the war, the head of the Episcopal High School, near Alexandria, Virginia, where his influence was particularly stimulating to those who studied under him Shakespeare and the English Bible.

Youngest of the soldierly Blackfords was Eugene, Major of the Fifth Alabama Infantry and, in all but formal commission, its Lieutenant Colonel. His service, which was full of interest, carried him farther from Lynchburg than most of his brothers had to go.

Major Blackford's letters, Benjamin Lewis Blackford's fervid account of his courtship, and hundreds of papers equally exciting appear in the Blackford correspondence, which is almost unique. Mrs. William M. Blackford, mother of the five Confederate soldiers, must have spent much of her time in writing them. Her husband was not backward, either, in sending his boys the news of home. They responded with frequency and zest and gave their parents a verbal picture, rich in detail of camp and court and war on many fields. Scarcely any of the letters from "the boys" were lost during or after the war. The whole body of Colonel Blackford's letters to his parents from youth to middle life has been preserved. Some of the letters of Charles M. Blackford and the diary of his father were edited by Mrs. Charles M. (Susan Leigh Colston) Blackford and were published in 1894-96. Unfortunately these *Memoirs of Life in and out of the Army in Virginia during the War Between the States* were issued in so small an edition that they have been accessible to few readers, though several of the letters are thrilling. Captain Blackford's account of Appomattox, in particular, is one of the most moving of all narratives of April 9, 1865. It is quoted briefly in 4 *R. E. Lee*, 146 ff. Letters from the other sons have been copied and bound but never have been published. The most informative of them, with a reprint of some of Charles M. Blackford's, would make an interesting supplement to these memoirs of Colonel W. W. Blackford.

The Colonel himself might have continued to hold the interest of readers had he carried his narrative through the long post-bellum period, of which there are few portrayals in the autobiography of informed Southern men and women. For two years after the war, Colonel Blackford was Chief Engineer of the Lynchburg and Danville Railroad, now a part of the main line of the Southern Railway. Then he went to Louisiana to develop a sugar plantation given him and his children by his father-in-law, Ex-Governor Wyndham Robertson. In a flood of 1874, Colonel Blackford lost overnight the labor of years and all the improvements he had made to the property. Dauntless, he returned to his native State and accepted in 1880 a professorship of Mechanics and Drawing at the Virginia Polytechnic Institute. In two years, larger professional opportunities led him to resign, but not until, as superintendent of grounds and buildings, he had completed a design for the beautification of the site. This plan, faithfully executed, gave to the large campus of V. P. I. many of its trees and much of its present dignity. From Blacksburg, the Colonel went into the service of the Baltimore and Ohio Railroad as one of its construction engineers on the line to Philadelphia. When that was completed, he assumed charge of the location and building of the railroad from Lynchburg, Virginia, to Durham, North Carolina. In June, 1890, when he was in his sixtieth year, he retired from his profession, purchased a farm on Lynnhaven Bay, Princess Anne County, Virginia, and engaged in oyster planting. His end came from apoplexy, May 1, 1905, when he was 74 years of age.

The date of the writing of his military memoirs is not given, but internal evidence shows that the work was taken in hand prior to the death of his mother, which occurred in 1896. In general, the precision of statement and unpremeditated clarity of detail suggest a date of composition considerably prior to 1896. If the matter becomes one of importance to any historical investigator, it may be possible to approximate the date more closely by comparing the several manuscript copies in family hands.

Subsequent to the completion of his memoirs, Colonel Blackford undertook the correction of some of the mistakes he, like every other observant writer, had found in his text. The publishers state that this has presented some editorial puzzles which they have not felt they should undertake to solve. Such contradictions as exist in the text are not of major importance. Nor are Colonel Blackford's errors serious. When he passed in his honest narrative from fact to opinion, he usually took pains to point out the transition. In a few instances he spun theories that historians may not be willing to accept, as, for example, when he stated that an attack of diarrhoea probably incapacitated General Lee for command at Gettysburg. It is prudent for the reader to consult on these occasional questions of doubt the witnesses who were nearer than Colonel Blackford was to the men of whom he wrote. To be specific, none of Lee's staff officers mentioned any illness on the General's part during the Gettysburg campaign, though they wrote in exhaustive detail of July 1-8, 1868. Episodes concerning which Colonel Blackford unintentionally gives disputable testimony do not number half a dozen in the whole body of his memoirs and they in no way discredit his admirably valuable narrative. He will be read and respected as a citizen-soldier of honest mind, exceptional intelligence and just judgment, a "gentleman unafraid."

DOUGLAS SOUTHALL FREEMAN
Westbourne
Richmond, Virginia
June 17, 1945

PREFACE

The traveller who wishes to write a book about a country he has visited, and to present the subject in a clear manner, must present maps, give statistics of population and resources, etc., etc., and an outline of its history. All this is necessary, but this alone is not sufficient to convey a full idea of the people and country to the reader. He must speak of the thoughts and feelings and mode of life of the people, and bring their habits before the reader just as he saw them.

The historian is the traveller, the past is his country — but he must get his material, not from personal observation, but from the writings of those who lived then and who were actors in the events. Abundant supplies of statistical matter already exist and I shall not attempt to add to the amount in these reminiscences but shall try to give just what I saw and felt. I do this not from egotism but because I consider myself only a representative of the thoughts, feelings and actions of thousands of others at that period, and may thus furnish sketches that may be useful to the future historian, and I hope entertaining to the general reader should they ever find their way into print.

WM. W. B.

I — EARLY YEARS

My mother has urged me for some years to write my reminiscences of the war between the States, 1861-1865, for the benefit of my children, and for possible publication after my death; and I have concluded to do so: but before beginning about the war I will give a brief outline of my previous life.

My father, the late Hon. Wm. M. Blackford of Lynchburg, Va., was born in Maryland. His father, Mr. Benjamin Blackford, was a New Jerseyian by birth, who was largely engaged in the iron business, first in Pennsylvania and then in Maryland. He then purchased iron property near Luray, Va., and built the Isabella Furnace, named after his wife, who was a Miss Arthur, and there he lived the greater portion of his life, a prosperous and highly respected man; as noble in his appearance and bearing, as he was upright and pure in character.

On Oct. IS, 1825, my father married Mary Berkely Minor, the only daughter of the late General John Minor of Fredericksburg, Va., and settled in Fredericksburg as a lawyer. When the Revolutionary War broke out my Grandfather Minor was a student at William and Mary College and, at the age of fifteen, ran away from there and joined the army as a private soldier in Nelson's troop of Light-horse, a part of Lighthorse Harry Lee's command, in which he served through the war. In 1783, soon after becoming of age, he was elected to the General Assembly of Virginia, and served in either the Upper or Lower House a number of years. He became a lawyer and made a considerable fortune by his profession. When the War of 1812 broke out he was commissioned Brigadier General. He married Lucy Landon Carter of "Cleve" in King George County, a lady celebrated in her day for her beauty and grace of mind and person … General Minor died while yet in the prime of life, leaving his widow the sole management of his estate and the care of a large family of young children; a trust she nobly fulfilled.

In 1841, my father was appointed by President Tyler Chargé d'Affaires to New Granada in South America. Owing to the destruction of the steamboats, by a recent war, on the Magdalena River, the difficulties of travelling were so great that my father concluded to take only me with him at first and to bring out the rest of the family at a later period.

We sailed from Norfolk in 1841 on board the U. S. sloop of war, *Falmouth*, Captain McIntosh. The ship belonged to the West India squadron, and the Captain had orders to land my father at any port in South America he might desire. On the way, the Captain was at liberty to touch at any of the islands he liked. My father and Captain McIntosh became great friends and he was glad to show us all the ports he could. We spent some days at St. Thomas's and there were fortunate in securing a capital servant — a Frenchman who spoke both English and Spanish. While we were in port Lord Elgin and his family arrived on their way to Canada where he had been appointed Governor-General. My Lord's French valet, afterwards our man, Pierre, and my Lady's English maid had had so violent a quarrel that at St. Thomas's Pierre had to remain, though with good recommendations from his Lordship as to character and qualifications. We found him invaluable to us during the two years he was with us in South America. We touched at La Guayra, and then with a party composed of officers of the ship visited Caracas, the capital of Venezuela and the scene of the great earthquake some years before; a large part of the place was still in ruins. We called on General Paiez, then President of the Republic. He was one of the most distinguished of all of Bolivar's officers during the war which freed them from the Spanish yoke. The palace was built by the old viceroys of Spain, and was surrounded by beautiful gardens filled with tropical trees and plants, cool shady walks and fountains. General Paiez, I remember, kissed me as we took our leave and plucked a pomegranate and gave it to me.

We next touched at the Dutch islands of Curação and spent a couple of weeks. We got information which determined my father to leave the *Falmouth* here and go over to Maracaybo in a small vessel, the bar not admitting the *Falmouth*. Crossing the lake and ascending the river Zulia a short distance, we began our 500 mile ride on mules to Bogota via Pamplona and Tunja, through the Andes the greater part of the way, and occupying a month of hard labor.

Bogota is the capital of New Granada, now The United States of Colombia, situated on a plain 60 by 30 miles and 9,000 feet above the sea, and though very near the equator the climate is cool enough for winter clothing all the year. The thermometer is at 62° almost all the time. The population was then 60,000.

The society of the place was very agreeable. There were several native families we liked very much, M. Paris and Señor Santa Maria and Senor Cordovez; the two latter had some lovely daughters. But it was among the foreigners of course we found most agreeable company. When we first got to Bogota the Honorable Mr. Stuart M. P. was British Minister, and we were a great deal at his house. Mrs. Stuart was a charming woman. Hetty, her daughter, and Dick, her son, were about my age. Mr. Stuart died in about a year and was succeeded by General O'Leary, who had married a Spanish lady. He had a lovely daughter almost grown, that is about fifteen years old, with whom I fell very much in love. We took drawing lessons together one hour every other day and then generally spent the rest of the day together, riding, reading, playing battledore, or sketching. "Meme" was the pet name she was known by in the family, and I don't remember her real name. We loved each other, we thought, forever. But Ellena Cordovez won me away from her towards the last. We were spending a week or two in the Tierra Caliente at a pretty little watering place and Meme was not there. Ellena used to sit with me out in the moonlight, and once she asked if that was the same moon that shone in "el norte" — Well! I suppose they are all grandmothers now.

Mr. Rainsford, the British Secretary of Legation, was my father's special friend; he was a Scotchman and one of the most charming men I ever knew. He used to ride very fine horses, which to me was a great point of admiration at that time. Mr. Stuart and General O'Leary both rode superb horses. Dick Stuart and myself used to spend a good deal of our time in the stables at the British Legation, and the English grooms were to us oracles of wisdom. The horses were all stallions. All genteel people rode stallions there. Mrs. Stuart's saddle horse was one of the most beautiful I ever saw, his mane reached below his knees, and his forelock below his nose. The horses in that country are descended from the barbs the Spanish knights brought from Spain, and they were pure Arabians. Mr. Constantine was an attaché and also had fine horses in the stable.

When we first got to Bogota Baron Gros was the French Minister, but he was recalled and M. de Lisle succeeded him. He, Mr. Rainsford and my father were together all the time. M. Guise was the French Secretary of Legation, a lively pleasant fellow, but not such a man as M. de Lisle, who had nothing Frenchy about him. They both spoke English perfectly. I soon learned to speak Spanish with ease.

Then there was Mr. Wilson, the head of a great English branch of a commercial house. He was a bachelor, and kept a splendid house with several of his assistants. There was a dinner-party there almost every day. Mr. Wilson kept some fine Newfoundland dogs and gave me the dog, Maynard, that I brought home with me. Mr. Gooding was an American and the manager of the copper mines of Velez, three days' journey from Bogota. He kept a house in the city and we occupied it for the first two or three months. Then when we took a house Mr. Gooding always stayed with us when he came to town every few months. He was an excellent man.

My father rented an elegant house, ready furnished, that belonged to a wealthy gentleman who took his family to Europe to be educated. It had twenty-two rooms, built in Spanish style, in hollow squares filled with flowers. For two years Pierre was our butler, but he got spoiled and was discharged.

I had a fine horse and my great occupation and delight was going out on the plain two or three times a week to some of the haciendas to lasso wild cattle and horses. The llaneros took great pleasure and pains in teaching me the wonderful skill they possessed, and I became as skillful as any of them. There is no finer school for horsemanship in the world, and as a sport it is unrivaled in thrilling excitement. It was many and many a day before I caught my first animal in full career, and after that a long time before I could throw my horse back on his haunches at the right time to roll my capture over on the ground. They would get off with my lasso in spite of all I could do, and then a llanero would dash forward, pick up the dragging lasso, at full speed, and throw the animal over.

The election of James K. Polk as President terminated our stay in Bogota. The boats on the Magdalena not having been started, my father never could take out his family. There was great sorrow expressed at our leaving, and a cavalcade of fifty gentlemen escorted us a couple of leagues across the plain. We returned down the Magdalena, from Honda, in champans (covered, poled boats) to Carthagena, and then to New York, reaching there on Feb. 12, 1845, after a three years' absence. A man-of-war had been waiting for weeks, at Carthagena, for my father, but had to leave for rations; a man named Dickson, who had been sent with dispatches, had fallen sick on the river, and hence the delay. We had to return in a merchant brig, the *Chares*, and were nearly wrecked in a great storm off the North Carolina coast.

Soon after his return, my father became the editor of the *Lynchburg Virginian* and we moved to Lynchburg, and after some years he was made cashier of the Exchange Bank in which he remained until the time of his death, universally beloved and respected. He died in 1864 from the care and anxiety of the war, in which he had five sons, and from overwork in his business.

After receiving a school education at a private school my father had for his boys, for which he employed the teacher and then limited admission from others to eight or ten, I adopted as a profession civil engineering, and began as rodman at seventeen, and after three years had made enough to send myself to the University of Virginia for two years. I was then with Mr. Charles B. Shaw and he agreed that I should go, and come back to duty in the vacation; so in the three months' vacation I made two hundred dollars clear as leveler on the surveys for the railroad from Covington by the White Sulphur to New River, now the route of the C. & 0. Railroad.

After leaving the University I took a trip through the northern states and Canada, and then became Resident Engineer on the Va. & Tenn. R. R., under Col. C. F. M. Garnett, Chief Engineer, at a salary of eighteen hundred dollars per annum, where I remained until the completion of the road, and for a time, after Colonel Garnett's resignation, was acting Chief Engineer.

While stationed on this work I married Mary, the eldest daughter of Governor Wyndham Robertson, on Jan. 10, 1856, in Richmond. The family lived in Richmond at that time, but spent the summers at "The Meadows" near Abingdon. After the completion of the railroad I went to Buena Vista, Washington County, to live, and became a partner of Sir. Robertson in the mining of plaster at his mines there; and was living there when the war broke out.

The war found me, at the age of thirty, a prosperous man with a lovely young wife and four sweet and beautiful children, engaged as a partner with my father-in-law, Governor Wyndham Robertson, in mining Plaster of Paris from his mines in Washington County, Va. I was surrounded by every attraction of family affection and interest and, until the mighty war tempest arose, considered myself settled for life. Looking back to those days, and with the lights then before me, I should do the same again, but it was a great and terrible sacrifice to leave it all and go into the army.

We read much in the papers about the excited political feeling in Kansas upon the slavery question; and there was the usual supply of inflammatory gas exhaled from the so-called representative men, on both sides, in Congress — all of which was read by the businessmen of the country about as they read of horse races and prize fights, and with about as little idea that such folly could involve the country in war, in the one case or the other.

We have all seen a half drunken crowd quarrelling around a bar-room door by the hour, and cooling down when their senseless gabble ceases to attract attention from passers-by — but let a blow be struck, by even the most worthless vagabond of the lot, and a general fight ensues. This was what happened at Harpers Ferry, Oct. 16, 1859. In all human probability the election of Lincoln would have been accomplished without serious results but for the spark applied to the inflamed public mind, at that time, by John Brown's crazy attempt at instigating the negroes of Virginia to servile insurrection.

So far as the negroes were concerned the attempt was a perfect failure, and Brown was caught and hung as he deserved; but what was the surprise of the people of the South to see his course endorsed by a large portion of the northern people — to see requiems over the death of the "martyred hero," as they called him, from pulpit, press and rostrum, and bells tolling from steeples in almost every large city in the North, the day he was hanged. When we reflect what negro insurrection meant, as Brown wished it to be, we can readily understand the revelation this evidence of feeling in his behalf was to our people. That a large part of our countrymen should allow themselves to sympathize with a plot involving the indiscriminate rape of innocent women, their subsequent murder, and the murder of all children, before the men of the country could collect to prevent it, is a stain forever upon our country. That all this was the inevitable sequence of successful negro insurrection no one who has ever taken the trouble to look into the history of such events in other countries can deny. The abolition fanatics had worked themselves up into the belief that the negroes had a grievance and that opportunity was all that was lacking to make them rise and rid themselves of it. But unfortunately for this theory the negroes *had* no grievance — they were happy and contented with their lot, and the plan failed. Throughout the four years of war, when whole counties were left with scarcely an able-bodied white man, in not one single instance in all the slave states was there the slightest hostile demonstration made by the slaves. Can any stronger evidence be wanted of the kindly feelings existing between the races? And could such feelings have found place under a yoke felt to be oppressive by those who wore it?

I am heartily glad that slavery is gone on my children's account, though they would have inherited a goodly number, and on account of the white race of the South, because I think they are better without them. But, when time removes the fog of fanaticism that has surrounded the subject, the world will see that never before were labor and capital brought together under circumstances more advantageous to the development of the laborer — nor was there ever a greater blessing bestowed on the negro race. If it was not a blessing, but an evil, then logically it should not have been. Now can any unprejudiced person, who wishes the negro well, wish them to have remained in heathenism and barbarism as they were when slavery rescued them from it?

After the John Brown affair I was so firmly convinced that there might be trouble that I took active steps to raise a cavalry company in Washington County. There was living not far from me a gentleman who had, some years before, resigned his commission as Lieutenant in the U. S. cavalry service and was a frequent visitor at my house, Mr., afterwards Maj. General, Wm. E. Jones. I conceived the idea of raising a cavalry company and making him the captain. He agreed to it provided I would take all the trouble of getting it up. At that time I knew nothing of cavalry tactics and thought his instruction was absolutely necessary, though as it turned out, he took little interest in either raising or drilling the company and almost the whole burden fell upon me.

I canvassed for it and then called a meeting in Abingdon. Jones did not attend but we elected him Captain. I became 1st Lieutenant, Reese B. Edmondson 2nd Lieutenant, and George Victor Litchfield 3rd Lieutenant. We named the company The Washington Mounted Rifles. I procured a copy of Hardee's tactics and studied it intently, drilling the men every court day. At first only a dozen or so took interest in it but during the winter of 1860-61 many more joined.

The Harpers Ferry affair occurred on the night of the 16th of October, 1859. Lincoln's election followed; the cloud thickened and darkened. State after state seceded with a shock like the bursting of sail after sail on a ship in a mighty tempest. Then with the flash and the thunder from the bombardment of Fort Sumter the war burst upon us.

I was opposed to secession and voted against the secession candidate to the convention, Ex-Gov. John B. Floyd. I thought that Lincoln, though a sectional candidate, was constitutionally elected and that we ought to have waited to see what he would do. But when he called for troops from Virginia and we had to take one side or the other, then of course I was for going with the South in her mad scheme, right or wrong.

The country was red hot with excitement. In every county from the mountains to the sea, men were preparing for war. Long trains on the railroads, loaded with troops, came from the South to join the army assembling at Manassas, and at every station they met an ovation.

Going to Abingdon one day a short time after the Virginia convention passed the ordinance of secession on April 17, 1861, and expecting to return that night as usual, I found the place in a blaze of excitement, and it was years and years before I saw my home again. We went into barracks and a few weeks after marched off to the seat of war, a company one hundred strong and superbly mounted. The most of this time our Captain was in Richmond trying to get higher rank, but failing in this he returned and took command of the company a short time before we started. After taking command, however, he made a very efficient officer. John S. Mosby, the future brilliant partisan leader, was a private soldier in our company. He was a lawyer, living at Bristol at the time. There was nothing about him then to indicate what he was to be — he was rather a slouchy rider, and did not seem to take any interest in military duties. He had been but seldom at our drills before starting, and we all thought he was rather an indifferent soldier. I remember there was another man in the company who everybody said was an acquisition, and would make a splendid fighter — he was a noted bar-room bully, and fist fighter; but the very first time we were under fire this fellow ran away, and by pretending sickness got on a hospital detail and was never seen again, while Mosby distinguished himself in every affair we had.

My dear wife came down to the "Meadows," her father's country residence near Abingdon, to be near me for the few weeks we were still to be together, and devoted herself nobly to the cause in which I was embarked, and to my encouragement in the many trials it involved. The day of parting came at last. The company halted in town for the men to take leave of their friends. Mary and the children were at Mrs. Trigg's watching with streaming eyes the martial array pass by, and there I found her when the halt was made. There was not a dry eye to be seen on the crowded street as the flower of the county marched away — many of them never to return.

We marched to Richmond where we remained a few days and drew a supply of fine Sharp's carbines, breechloaders; we were then at the camp of instruction at Ashland a week or two; and were then ordered to join the 1st Regiment of Virginia Cavalry under the command of Lieut. Col. J. E. B. Stuart, operating with Gen. J. E. Johnston's army in the valley of Virginia, near Shepherdstown. Upon reaching our destination we had marched altogether five hundred miles. We had drawn, in Abingdon, a supply of sabres, and many of us had Colt's army pistols, five shooters, so we were well armed. The march was a continuous ovation — ladies lined the streets of the towns and showered flowers upon us — every delicacy the country could afford was spread before us, and we imagined ourselves heroes. The only care we felt was the dread that the war would be over before we got there. It is amusing now to recall how general this feeling was — every one seemed to think one battle would settle it, and those in authority, who had brought on all the trouble, who ought to have known better, unfortunately thought so too. In Richmond I saw for the first time Gen. R. E. Lee and a handsomer man than he was, mounted on a superb bay stallion he then rode, I never saw. I also saw President Davis in church. Walking along the street one day I happened to be behind a lady as she reached a cross street. A negro boy was coming along the cross street mounted on a beautiful blooded horse which he was, after the manner of his kind, when unobserved, fretting and jerking to make him prance. The lady burst out into a fury of invective, the like of which I never before heard from lady's lips, and made the groom dismount and lead the horse away. It was Mrs. Jeff Davis and the groom and horse belonged to the President's stables. Richmond was overrun with people from the Cotton States connected with the new Confederate government, and some of them were rather a shock to the refinement of Richmond. The tone of society in Richmond has never recovered from this inroad.

Just as the sun was setting one evening in June, 1861, we came in sight of Colonel Stuart's camp at Bunker Hill, nine miles north of Winchester — the first troops we had seen engaged in actual warfare. We had seen plenty of camps around Richmond and Ashland, but they had the air of holiday parade about them — tents handsomely furnished and the men's trunks around the walls inside, after the fashion of the volunteer of that period of the war — but here all looked like business. The camp was in a little valley — between the rows of company tents picket ropes were stretched, to which were haltered the horses, while over a detached group of tents on a little rise near by floated the headquarters flag. Before these tents some forty or fifty horsemen were drawn up for inspection, and the young officer in a U. S. undress uniform was Lieutenant Colonel Stuart. He was giving the men their final instructions for the night, for this was the guard going out for the relief on the picket posts. This was the man whose fame was afterwards to rank with that of Lee and Jackson and who will probably be regarded in history as the greatest cavalry leader of modern times. He was a little above medium height, broad shouldered and powerfully built, ruddy complexion and blue-gray eyes which could flash fire on the battlefield, or sparkle with the merry glance which ladies love.

Stuart was then about twenty-nine years of age and our Captain was very much his senior in age; so, true to the spirit of the average West Point man, he regarded our Colonel with intense jealousy when placed under his command, a feeling which ripened afterwards into as genuine hatred as I ever remember to have seen in my experience in life. The feeling finally led him into such a flagrant piece of official insolence that even Stuart's magnanimity could stand it no longer. He was tried by court-martial and sentenced to receive a reprimand from General Lee. This was given personally and soon after Jones was sent elsewhere. This occurred after he became a Brigadier General, in 1863, I think it was.

When we joined Stuart's command he had already attracted some attention by his connection with the capture of John Brown, and by some brilliant little cavalry affairs in the valley. With our fine company he had about 500 men, well mounted and of the best material the state could afford. I remember with what interest and respect I looked at those men going out on picket duty that night in the presence of an actual enemy — people they might kill like game if they could.

Colonel Stuart received me very cordially, and then began the friendship between us which lasted until his death, without a break. It so happened that in one or two little affairs soon after this, I had opportunities of eliciting his commendation and he appointed me his Adjutant, making my commission date the twenty-first of July in compliment of my services in the battle that day, though I had been appointed a few days before. The first of these affairs occurred the first night I went on picket. I took twenty men to a post eight miles from camp in a little village at a crossroads two or three miles from the enemy's lines. By the time I had examined the front I was to cover, and had relieved the men on duty at the outposts, it was dark. After chatting with the people in the place until bedtime, I spread my blanket on the floor of the porch of the store at the corner and stretched out for a nap. Just then came the sound of the clatter of a horse's hoofs away up the turnpike, and presently the peremptory order to halt from the vidette, and the corporal of the guard brought in a citizen. He was a man left in charge of an estate half way between us and the enemy, whose owner was a refugee, and he had come to tell us that a cavalry scouting party of the enemy had just arrived at his house and that he had barely made his escape.

I sent the man on to Colonel Stuart with a note saying that I would investigate the matter and report later. After getting some citizens as guides I took ten men and started, keeping a vidette in front and my main body ready to charge instantly if we met the enemy, knowing that in the dark they could not tell how small our number was, and that we could throw them into confusion, ascertain their force and withdraw before they recovered from their surprise. But we reached the vicinity of the house without meeting any one. I sent a couple of men, dismounted, to reconnoitre. Presently they were halted and an explanation followed. It was a party from our own regiment. They had been vigilant enough to discover our approach and the officer in command had withdrawn his party from the house, where they had made arrangements to pass the night, until our status could be ascertained. We all then went in and had a good supper, while I sent a report back to Colonel Stuart. As it was now past midnight I determined to join my late supposed enemy in a night's rest upon the floor of the beautiful parlor of this elegant country house, and we all slept there. Colonel Stuart was much pleased with the whole affair and complimented both myself and the officer commanding the other party for our vigilance and for not getting into a mess by firing into each other out there in the dark.

A week or two after this another little matter occurred which seemed to please our Colonel. We were out on a scout and the Colonel had his whole command dismounted in an apple orchard behind a hill half a mile from the enemy's lines. He was watching an opportunity to make an attack, after getting reports from some spies he had sent in, and we were all grazing our horses or dozing in the warm sunshine. It seems that the man of the house nearby was a "Union man," not an unusual thing around that part of the valley, and he had gone over to their camp and told them of our presence. They formed a column of infantry, and with a battery of artillery, dashed across towards us at the double quick. Having no artillery then attached to the cavalry and being greatly inferior to them in numbers, the only thing to do was to get out of the way. Stuart was on the hill watching and saw them start; he galloped down to us, laughing, and gave the order for each company to get back to some woods, half a mile in the rear, as fast as possible. There was no time lost, but before we got out of the orchard their battery was in position on the hill above us and pounding away at our fleeing troopers. The companies being separated saved us from much loss but it was the first time any of us had been under artillery fire and most of the command were a good deal demoralized. Our company was the only one which came off in perfect order, due in a large measure to my efforts, as I brought up the rear. Some of them stampeded utterly and did not stop for miles. When we halted in the woods I found I had lost my pistol — pistols were hard to get in those days, and I remembered exactly where it must have fallen out of my belt as I jumped "Comet" over a fence; so I applied for leave to go back for it. The shelling was still going on and Stuart looked at me with a surprised and pleased expression as he gave permission, but I knew it was a long way from their battery and there would be small chance of their hitting me at that distance. I found the pistol exactly where I thought it was and returned, the shells all passing high over my head. These incidents led no doubt to his appointing me his Adjutant not long after.

*

The enemy threatened us from two points — from Alexandria and from the lower valley. Our forces under Beauregard were at Manassas confronting the Alexandria column, and those under Joseph E. Johnston were confronting the other. McDowell commanded their advance from Alexandria, and Patterson in the valley. Our plan was for Johnston to hold Patterson in check, and at the last moment to come over to Beauregard's assistance, if possible without letting Patterson find out he was gone. To affect this Stuart drew a curtain of cavalry across the valley, -cutting off all communication until Johnston's army crossed the Blue Ridge, and then by rapid marches followed, leaving enough cavalry, however, to keep up a thin line to hold the enemy in check. The road was full of infantry and artillery and we had to pass through the fields. All night long they marched forward, and we were compelled to encounter the fatigue of constantly crossing ditches and fences and the uneven ground on the side. Hundreds of men from the infantry, who had slipped out of the road to sleep, were scattered about everywhere and we had constantly to be on the lookout to keep from riding over them in the dark. The first day our wagons did not meet us and we were without rations; I was famishing when we halted for rest, but just then a man passed by with a huge bullfrog he had caught in a creek we had crossed and told me I might have it if I liked, as he would not eat one for the world. It was but the work of a few moments to kindle a fire, dress the frog and broil him, not the hind legs only but the whole body; it was delicious, and quite enough to serve as a pretty good meal.

In passing Mill Wood Mrs. Randolph was at the door of her house and I stopped to speak to her. She asked me to take some money to her grandson, Randolph McKim, who was a private soldier in a Maryland infantry regiment and was then a mere boy. She sent him five dollars which I found a chance to hand him a few days after the battle.

The morning of the day we reached Manassas, the irregularity of diet, loss of sleep, and the march all the night, brought on a severe attack on my bowels, and to my intense mortification I found myself scarcely able to keep my saddle. Colonel Stuart had just appointed me Adjutant of the regiment and it was dreadful to think of being taken sick the day before the great battle; it would look so suspicious — so much like the battle had brought on the attack. I never shall forget the look our Colonel gave me when I applied for leave to drop out of the column and catch up when I was able, and the meaning glance of his eye when he said, "Yes, but remember there is going to be a battle tomorrow." Just then we came in sight of a pretty country house, barely visible in the early dawn, half a mile from the road and I rode over to it and aroused the inmates. I had been in the saddle all the day before and all night, and without food during that time except the bullfrog; this together with my attack of sickness made me so weak that I could scarcely walk across the front yard of the house to knock at the door. Some charming girls in wrappers, aroused from their slumbers, appeared at the upper windows and after hearing my tale hastened to dress and come down. They received me most cordially and, with the assistance of their mother, who soon appeared also, seemed ministering angels. A basin of cold water fresh from the well and snowy towels refreshed me inexpressibly, for the roads were suffocating in dust. Then a delicious breakfast, hot strong coffee in a huge cup, seemed to bring new life into my bones. Then two hours profound sleep, by the watch, on the sofa in the sweet cool parlor with the birds to sing me to sleep, and the softest little hand to fix my pillow; how could I help kissing it? and all the while Comet running his nose up to the eyes in a great trough full of oats, and a darky, earning the half dollar I promised, rubbing him for dear life. What a haven for a sick and weary soldier to drift into! After many heartfelt thanks to my kind friends I mounted and pushed on my way, finding to my inexpressible relief that health and strength had returned to me. I am sorry I cannot remember the name of this family, but all records of that period, in the shape of my frequent letters to my wife, were destroyed by fire when my office in Lynchburg was burned, when I was Chief Engineer of the Lynchburg and Danville R. R. in 1867.

But I must now tell who Comet was, for to a cavalry officer in active service his horse is his second self, his companion and friend, upon whom his very life may depend. A few days before leaving home the horse I had showed symptoms of weakness about the eyes and I had to look around for another. The supply of good animals in the county had been much diminished by the pick having been bought up by the members of our company, so my father-in-law, Mr. Robertson, agreed to let me have Comet, an animal of his own rearing, and I executed my note @ sixty days for his price; but after the horse bore me so gallantly in the battle of the twenty-first, he canceled the note and sent it back to me, asking me to accept Comet as a present from him. Comet was by Mr. T. L. Preston's horse Hamlet, out of a daughter of Prima

Donna, belonging to Mr. Robertson, and was consequently of the best blood in Virginia. He was a dark mahogany bay, almost brown, with black mane, tail and legs and a small white star in his forehead — great eyes standing out like those of a deer, small delicate muzzle — delicate ears in which you could see the veins, and which were constantly in motion with every thought which passed through his mind — small and beautiful feet — and legs as hard as the bone itself. He was compactly and powerfully built — his action superb — head and tail carried high in air, and he had a way of tossing his head and champing his bit, and tossing the foam over his breast that set your blood to tingling in sympathy with his spirit. When we halted in towns people would collect around to admire his beauty, and one evening when Colonel Stuart and myself were riding out together, after a brisk gallop he watched the horse for some time, and then said, "Well, Blackford, that is a perfect model of a war horse." A fence as high as his withers he would take me over like a bird. His beauty and strength were equaled by his mental and moral qualities; Comet was a horse of high order, and as gallant a gentleman in his feelings as ever wore a horse's hide. The winning ways he had, the ease with which he would learn anything, and his strong attachments were very remarkable. When other horses were crowding around an exhausted pump, or hydrant trough, awaiting the scanty flow, Comet would put his mouth to the spout and drink his fill. When I would be eating on the march his eyes would watch me, and if I did not soon lean forward and hand him a taste, he would stop deliberately and reach his mouth up for his share; nothing seemed to come amiss; bread, crackers, meat, sugar, and fruit, all seemed to be relished. I could tie the halter strap to my leg and lie down to sleep while he would graze around, step over me or lie down by me without ever treading on me. Sometimes when he would lie down he would lay his head in an affectionate if uncomfortable manner upon me, and though it was disagreeable I could never have the heart to push it off. I had taught him to pull my handkerchief out of my pocket or take my hat off to look for sugar, and the trick amused people who did not know what he was after, which was a secret between Comet and me. The horse of one of the members of the company, Gilbert Greenway, formed an alliance, offensive and defensive, with Comet and when the horses of the regiment were turned out to graze, these two trotted about to select a choice piece of grass and, planting themselves there, would attack furiously any intruder. In cold, rainy weather, when the other horses would be drawn up and shivering, Comet attracted the attention and applause of the whole regiment by his plan for warming himself, and the cheers of the men seemed to be fully appreciated. He would begin by pawing with one fore-foot as fast as he could do it for five minutes; then the same with the other fore-foot; then with both hind feet, for a like time, he would kick as high in the air as he could get, and with a vigor and rapidity that was laughable; and wind up by a toss of the mane and tail and loud snorts, while the steam came pouring from him in the restored warmth and glow his exercise had produced. A year after this time poor Comet was desperately wounded and I rode him no more during the war.

After leaving my kind friends I pushed on to overtake the command, which I did before they reached Manassas that evening. Manassas Junction, on the evening of the 20th of July, 1861, presented a busy scene of martial preparation. Troops were arriving by the cars and marching out to the lines along Bull Run, six miles away. Great trains of wagons were hauling supplies of food and ammunition. Great crowds of men stood around everywhere, who seemed to have nothing to do, and among them, pushing their way regardless of imprecations showered upon their heads, rode orderlies, quartermasters and commissaries with the pompous gravity of those who believed the cares of the nation rested upon their sleek, well-greased heads. The clouds of suffocating dust, the bustle, and the knowledge of what it was the preparation for, made all this an impressive scene to us, whose eyes were yet unaccustomed to such sights.

As we marched by Gen. Joseph E. Johnston's quarters, he and his staff came out to see us pass. I stopped to speak to Capt. T. L. Preston, of General Johnston's staff, who was there, and also shook hands with the General, whom I had known in Abingdon. We went into bivouac before sundown, about a mile from the stone bridge over Bull Run. We had been thirty-six hours in the saddle and were very tired and hungry, but plenty of rations for man and horse were sent us from the Junction, and the tall thick broomsedge grass furnished a luxurious couch to sleep upon, and to some it was to be their last in this world. I had often read of the feelings of a soldier on the night before a battle, and particularly his first one, but after a hearty supper, stretched out on my blanket on the soft grass smoking a pipe of excellent tobacco, I must say I felt pretty comfortable, and before the pipe was finished the stars above melted into dreams of profound slumber.

As Adjutant of the regiment I no longer had my quarters with my company but had joined the Colonel's mess and lived at regimental headquarters. In marches I always slept next the Colonel so as to be within reach of his hand if wanted during the night. The next morning was Sunday, the eventful 21st of July. About daylight I was awakened by Colonel Stuart's springing up and exclaiming, "Hello! What is that?" It was rapid musketry firing away off several miles on our left near Sudley Mills in an entirely different direction from that we expected. They had crossed Bull Run at Sudley and were coming down on our left flank. The horses were fed and we took breakfast, and wishing to know something of the country, our Colonel then took us on a scout across the Bull Run. Our route lay through open fields and woodland without a commanding point from which to see around for any distance, just such a place as a cavalry command might fall into an ambuscade. Our Colonel halted and told me to take twelve men and push on until I found the enemy and then come back and report. I cut them off from the head of the column and trotted off, throwing out an advance guard of two, and a right and left flanking party of two each; retaining six as a reserve. The outriders were to hold up their hands if they saw anything, and no firing was to be done without special orders from me. We had not gone far when I saw the advance guard pull up and begin peering about over a hill, and I joined them. They said they thought they had caught sight of a man with a musket through an opening in the woods. I then rode about carefully, keeping the crest of the hill before me until at last I caught sight of a skirmisher, and then another and another about one hundred yards off and then about twenty more. My men were armed with rifled carbines and were capital shots and I did long to take a crack at them, but the Colonel's orders were positive that we must avoid attracting attention; so without making them aware of our presence by a little reminder of that kind, we galloped back and reported. It not being a part of Stuart's plan to make an attack, he recrossed the Bull Run and dismounted the regiment near where we spent the night, and here we remained until about two o'clock that evening. Most unfortunately, as it turned out, Stuart was ordered to make a detachment to serve in another place and had to send two of his companies away under Swann, our Major, and under such a commander of course they did nothing.

The Warrenton pike, by which the enemy had advanced from Alexandria, passes through Centreville and a few miles southward crosses Bull Run at the Stone Bridge obliquely, Centreville being nearer Bull Run at its nearest point than it is to Stone Bridge. From Stone Bridge to where Bull Run empties into the Potomac its valley is bounded by abrupt hills, the fords are few, and the line is strong for defence. Above Stone Bridge the valley rises more nearly to the level of the country, the fords are more frequent and the line is not so strong defensively as below. Our line of battle had been drawn along the lower reaches, with strong outposts at Sudley, some miles above Stone Bridge, and at Stone Bridge. On the 18th the enemy had made a demonstration at Blackburn's ford opposite Centreville. Fully appreciating the difficulties of this crossing after their repulse on the 18th, the enemy had moved a large force during the night by a wide circuit up to Sudley, intending to sweep down rapidly on our side of Bull Run, uncover Stone Bridge, march their remaining force across there, and attack the flank of our main body below, on ground of their own choosing.

The plan was well devised and well carried out up to their reaching Sudley but sufficient allowance had not been made, from there on, for the part we were to play in the game. Instead of sweeping all opposition away at Sudley and coming right on, as they expected, they encountered stubborn resistance from the small force there, which slowly retired down towards Stone Bridge, affording ample time for reinforcements from below to reach them there. We can now understand what Stuart meant when he exclaimed, "Hello! What is that?" Our position as before stated was about opposite the Stone Bridge; as the morning advanced the firing from Sudley approached nearer and nearer and troops from below were seen hurrying up to meet them, and it soon became apparent that the battle was to be fought just opposite us — and all we could do was to await the time when the cavalry could come into action with effect, for the infantry and artillery of course would have to meet the main shock of the conflict.

The duty of cavalry after battle is joined is to cover the flanks to prevent the enemy from turning them. If victorious, it improves the victory by rapid pursuit. If defeated, it covers the rear and makes vigorous charges to delay the advance of the enemy — or in the supreme moment, in the crisis of the battle, when victory is hovering over the field, uncertain upon which standard to alight — when the reserves are brought into action and the death struggle has come, *then* the cavalry comes down like an avalanche, upon the flanks of troops already engaged, with splendid effect.

A skirt of woods hid the battlefield from our view, but occasionally a shell would burst high in air, and sometimes the wind wafted the clouds upward above the trees, the roar of the conflict becoming louder and louder. Stuart was uneasy for fear that he would not be called into action; so every time a body of troops appeared he sent me over to tell the commanding officer that he was there and to ask him to let him know when he could be of service with the cavalry. He also rode over several times to the field to confer with the generals and watch the progress of the action. On one of my trips to a large body of troops moving into action, which one of the men told me was commanded by Colonel Jackson, I pushed on to the head of the column and found Colonel Jackson riding along holding up his hand which was wrapped in a bloody handkerchief, for his finger had just been shot off. This was the man who had just been christened "Stonewall" in the baptism of fire. I gave him Colonel Stuart's message and request, and his stern face lit up with a smile and he said, "That's good! That's good! Tell Stuart I will. That's good!" and rode on into action. "That's good!" was his favorite exclamation at anything which pleased him. Once during the morning, to our horror, we saw a great crowd of fugitives come pouring out of the woods and fleeing across the fields until they were out of sight. My heart seemed to stand still — was the battle lost? But presently they ceased coming — they were some South Carolina troops.

The battle roared louder and louder but still in the same spot. It was about two o'clock: Stuart was striding backwards and forwards in great impatience. Presently we saw a staff officer dash out of the woods and come spurring towards us. The men all sprang to their feet and began tightening their saddle girths, for we had a presentiment he was coming for us. The supreme moment had come at last. Colonel Stuart stepped forward to meet the officer. He reined up his horse and asked if that was Colonel Stuart and then, with a military salute, said, "*Colonel Stuart, General Beauregard directs that you bring your command into action at once and that you attach where the firing is hottest.*"

The bugle sounded "boots and saddles" and in a moment more we were moving off at a trot in a column of fours in the direction indicated plainly enough by the firing. It was our fate, however, to pass through a sickening ordeal before reaching the field. Along a shady little valley through which our road lay the surgeons had been plying their vocation all the morning upon the wounded. Tables about breast high had been erected upon which screaming victims were having legs and arms cut off. The surgeons and their assistants, stripped to the waist and all bespattered with blood, stood around, some holding the poor fellows while others, armed with long bloody knives and saws, cut and sawed away with frightful rapidity, throwing the mangled limbs on a pile near by as soon as removed. Many were stretched on the ground awaiting their turn, many more were arriving continually, either limping along or borne on stretchers, while those upon whom operations had already been performed calmly fanned the flies from their wounds. But among these last, alas! some moved not — for them the surgeons' skill had not availed. The battle roared in front — a sound calculated to arouse the sublimest emotions in the breast of the soldier, but the prayers, the curses, the screams, the blood, the flies, the sickening stench of this horrible little valley were too much for the stomachs of the men, and all along the column, leaning over the pommels of their saddles, they could be seen in ecstasies of protest.

Upon reaching the edge of the wood a view of the battle burst upon us, and Stuart halted to take a look. Smoke in dense white clouds lit up by lurid flashes from the cannon wrapped the position of the artillery; while lines of thin, blue, misty vapor floated over infantry, pouring out their deadly hail. At one moment all beneath would be invisible — at another the curtain, lifted by a passing breeze, revealed the thousands of busy reapers in the harvest of death. Colonel Stuart and myself were riding at the head of the column as the grand panorama opened before us, and there right in front, about seventy yards distant, and in strong relief against the smoke beyond, stretched a brilliant line of scarlet — a regiment of New York Zouaves in column of fours, marching out of the Sudley road to attack the flank of our line of battle. Dressed in scarlet caps and trousers, blue jackets with quantities of gilt buttons, and white gaiters, with a fringe of bayonets swaying above them as they moved, their appearance was indeed magnificent. The Sudley road was here in a deep depression and the rear of the column was still hid from view — there were about five hundred men in sight — they were all looking toward the battlefield and did not see us. Waving his sabre, Stuart ordered a charge, but instantly pulled up and called a halt and turning to me said, "Blackford, are those our men or the enemy?" I said I could not tell, but I had heard that Beauregard had a regiment of Zouaves from New Orleans, dressed, I had been told, like these men. Just then, however, all doubt was removed by the appearance of their colors, emerging from the road — the Stars and Stripes. I shall never forget the feelings with which I regarded this emblem of our country so long beloved, and now seen for the first time in the hands of a mortal foe. But there was no time for sentiment then. The instant the flag appeared, Stuart ordered the charge, and at them we went like an arrow from a bow.

As we were in column of fours it was necessary to deploy, and our gallant Colonel waved his sabre for the rear to oblique to the left, "on right into line," so as to strike the enemy in "echelon" and this they did. While a Lieutenant in my company, I had carried a Sharp's carbine slung to my shoulder and this I still wore; I also had my sabre and a large sized five-shooter. In the occupation of the moment I had not thought which of my weapons to draw until I had started, and as it does not take long for a horse at full speed to pass over seventy yards, I had little time to make the selection. I found in fact that it would be impossible to get either my sabre or pistol in time, and as the carbine hung conveniently under my right hand I seized and cocked that, holding it in my right hand with my thumb on the hammer and finger on the trigger. I thought I would fire it and then use it for a crushing blow, in which it would be almost as effective against a man standing on the ground as a sabre.

Half the distance was passed before they saw the avalanche coming upon them, but then they came to a "front face" — a long line of bright muskets was leveled — a sheet of red flame gleamed, and we could see no more. Capt. Welby Carter's horse sprang forward and rolled over dead, almost in front of Comet, so that a less active animal would have been thrown down, but Comet recovered himself and cleared the struggling horse and his rider. The smoke which wrapped them from our sight also hid us from them, and thinking perhaps that we had been swept away by the volley, they, instead of coming to a "charge bayonet," lowered their pieces to load, and in this position we struck them. The tremendous impetus of horses at full speed broke through and scattered their line like chaff before the wind. As the scarlet line appeared through the smoke, when within a couple of horse's lengths of them, I leaned down, with my carbine cocked, thumb on hammer and forefinger on trigger, and fixed my eye on a tall fellow I saw would be the one my course would place in the right position for the carbine, while the man next to him, in front of the horse, I would have to leave to Comet. I then plunged the spurs into Comet's flanks and he evidently thought I wanted him to jump over this strange looking wall I was riding him at, for he rose to make the leap; but he was too close and going too fast to rise higher than the breast of the man, and he struck him full on the chest, rolling him over and over under his hoofs and knocking him about ten feet backwards, depriving him of all further interest in the subsequent proceedings, and knocking the rear rank man to one side. As Comet rose to make the leap, I leaned down from the saddle, rammed the muzzle of the carbine into the stomach of my man and pulled the trigger. I could not help feeling a little sorry for the fellow as he lifted his handsome face to mine while he tried to get his bayonet up to meet me; but he was too slow, for the carbine blew a hole as big as my arm clear through him.

Just beyond their line was a fence, and Comet, exasperated to frenzy by the unusual application of the spur, was almost beyond my control, and entirely beyond the control of one hand; so I had to drop the carbine in its sling, and use both hands to swing him away from the fence which he seemed bent on clearing: the field beyond was filled with their troops and if he had gone over, there would have been small chance for return. With both hands I managed to turn the horse enough to bring him up to the fence so obliquely that even he did not like to attempt it, and he came round.

We now charged back, taking their line in the rear at another place, but they had begun to break and scatter clear down to the Sudley road before we reached them; all order was gone and it became a general melee or rather a chase. I might have put in some effective work with my revolver but it got hung in the case at my belt, and as I wanted to try the effect of a downward blow with the barrel of the carbine when swung high in air, I caught it up again; but the fellows dodged or parried every blow I got close enough to attempt, and I accomplished no more than chasing some of them back into the road where the rear of the regiment stood, and where I had no disposition to follow. This regiment — they say it was the Fire Zouaves — was completely paralyzed by this charge, and though their actual loss in killed and wounded was not very great, their demoralization was complete. The arrest of their dangerous move upon the exposed flank of our main line of battle was a result of the utmost importance and, I shall always think, saved the day. We had only two companies, commanded by Capt. Welby Carter and Capt. J. B. Hogue, actually engaged. Our loss was nine men and eighteen horses killed — the number of wounded is not recorded. It seemed strange that the fire from five hundred muskets, at thirty yards, should not have been more effective, but they had to shoot in a hurry and they were no doubt a little nervous at seeing the dreadful "Black Horse," as they then called all the Southern cavalry, coming down on them in that style, and I don't wonder at it. The mistake they made was in lowering their pieces to load; if they had come to a "charge bayonets," even with only two ranks, they would have given us trouble. But going at the speed we were, we could not have stopped after we got through their smoke, and would certainly have broken through, though with greater loss. The bayonets would have stuck so deep into the first horses that they could not have been recovered in time to meet the others, and the death struggle of the first horses falling into their line would, of itself, have broken it a good deal.

My duty as Adjutant of the regiment was now to re-form it, back of the woods from which we had charged. In the charges all formation was of course lost and in the return each man got back as he saw fit. The men had behaved well in attack but when the time came for withdrawal some of them did not want to stop at all, short of Manassas. I rallied about half of them back of the wood, and then found that the other half were going on down the road; so I dashed off after them, calling on all I overtook to return. When I stopped in front of them, they halted, but when I went on after more, they followed. As soon as I found out this I pushed on as fast as I could until I got ahead of all of them, and then halted them as they came up, until there was a squad of a dozen or so, and these I marched back, sweeping up all we met. When I got back, Colonel Stuart laughed in his jovial way and said as I met him, "Bully for you, Blackford."

He had been a little scandalized at what had happened, but he was so brave a man himself that he never seemed to attribute unworthy motives to his men, and this was one of the secrets of his great influence over them in action. They were ashamed to be anything but brave where he was. I had the names of one or two officers who had refused to return, but he would not let me prefer charges against them, saying they would be all right next time, and with one exception sure enough they were. Colonel Stuart came up to me a little after this and told me he would make my appointment as Adjutant, dated that day — a compliment I felt quite proud of.

It was now all-important that the efforts the enemy were making to extend their lines so as to outflank us should be frustrated until the reinforcements, which were coming from down Bull Run, could arrive. Stuart had secured a couple of guns under Lieut. R. F. Beckham, from a battery attached to the infantry, for at that time we had no horse artillery with the cavalry, and as soon as the men were formed, he moved forward to a hill across the Sudley road, from which a full view of the field could be had, at a distance of about five hundred yards from their right, and somewhat in their rear. Here he masked the guns behind a clump of pines, the foliage of which so entangled the smoke that they did not find out where we were for a long time; and behind these trees the cavalry support was also hid.

Beckham soon got the range, and then worked his pieces as fast as they could load them, with terrific effect upon the dense masses so near. Their lines were enfiladed by this fire; the fuses were cut long and the shell went skipping along through as round shot as far as we could see, and then did what execution they could in bursting. It was a grand and exciting spectacle. In their passage the shot opened a gap from end to end which remained open for an appreciable instant like the splash produced by striking the surface of water with a stick. This appearance was caused not only *by* the fall of the men struck by the shot, but from the involuntary dodging of those close to its path in opposite directions on each side. Their batteries were so closely engaged that they took no notice of us whatever, indeed from the way our guns were masked by the pines it is quite probable they never discovered our position at all. The effect of our fire was none the less destructive and materially delayed the extension of their flank at a time when delay was of vital importance. But for our charge and the fire of these guns, there can be no question that the flank of Jackson's "stone wall" would have been turned before Early arrived with his brigade, in which case the day would have been lost.

I now found myself almost perishing from thirst from the intense heat and the violence of my exertions during the charge. It seemed that water I must have or die, and Comet was suffering as much as his master. In rear of the enemy there was a small branch and to this I determined to venture. Its banks were lined with the enemy's wounded who had crawled there to drink, and many had died with their heads in the water, the dark blood flowing into and gradually mingling with the stream. I looked for a clear place in vain, and at last, driven to desperation, had to lie down and watch for the blood stains to pass, then drink until others came, lift my head for them to pass, and drink again. It was a long time before I could get Comet to touch it, but at last, succeeded, and after much snorting, pawing and tossing of head he drank his fill, by following pretty much my plan when the stained water floated by. Then drawing a long breath he turned and looked me full in the face, as much as to say, "Who would have thought, master, that we would ever have had to drink such water as that?" It was, indeed, literally drinking the blood of our enemies, for the clearest of it was suspiciously tinted and flavored. It was now about four o'clock and the battle raged with unabated fury. The lines of blue were unbroken and their fire as vigorous as ever while they surged against the solid walls of gray, standing immovable in their front. It was on that ridge earlier in the day Jackson won the name of Stonewall.

But now the most extraordinary spectacle I have ever witnessed took place. I had been gazing at the numerous well-formed lines as they moved forward to the attack, some fifteen or twenty thousand strong in full view, and for some reason had turned my head in another direction for a moment, when some one exclaimed, pointing to the battlefield, "Look! Look!" I looked, and what a change had taken place in an instant. Where those "well dressed," well-defined lines, with clear spaces between, had been steadily pressing forward, the whole field was a confused swarm of men, like bees, running away as fast as their legs could carry them, with all order and organization abandoned. In a moment more the whole valley was filled with them as far as the eye could reach. They plunged through Bull Run wherever they came to it regardless of fords or bridges, and there many were drowned. Muskets, cartridge boxes, belts, knapsacks, haversacks and blankets were thrown away in their mad race, that nothing might impede their flight. In the reckless haste the artillery drove over every one who did not get out of their way. Ambulance and wagon drivers cut the traces and dashed off on the mules. In crossing Cub Run a shell exploded in a team and blocked the way and twenty-eight pieces of artillery fell into our hands.

By stepping or jumping from one thing to another of what had been thrown away in the stampede, I could have gone long distances without ever letting my foot touch the ground, and this over a belt forty or fifty yards wide on each side of the road. Numbers of gay members of Congress had come out from Washington to witness the battle from the adjacent hills, provided with baskets of champagne and lunches. So there was a regular chariot race when the rout began, with the chariots well in the lead, as was most graphically described by the prisoners I captured and by citizens afterwards. We found, occasionally, along the road, parasols and dainty shawls lost in their flight by the frail, fair ones who had seats in most of the carriages of this excursion. Some of their troops, north of Bull Run, did not participate in the panic, and some did not throw away their arms, but the greater part must have done so, from the quantities we found.

Stuart was uncertain whether this was a general or a partial rout, at the moment, and told me to go as fast as I could to either General Johnston or General Beauregard, report what had happened and ask if he must pursue. He, like every one else at that period of the war, did not feel the confidence in himself that we did a little later. I gave Comet the rein and struck a bee line to where he said I would probably find the Generals, taking fences, ditches, and worse than all some fearful gullies as they came.

I found General Beauregard, who of course knew what had happened before I got there, for by that time all musketry firing had ceased, though the batteries were still pounding away at long range at the disappearing fugitives. The General was sitting on his horse, his handsome face beaming with pleasure as staff officers came dashing up from every direction with reports and asking for orders. It was the first time I had seen General Beauregard and I looked at him with much interest. He was then looked upon as the "coming man" but his fame never rose higher than it stood after that battle. He was rather a small man and had a good deal of the manner and appearance of a Frenchman. His friends say that Jeff Davis became jealous of him after this battle and never gave him a chance afterwards, which is quite probable: he certainly behaved with great gallantry that day. He returned my salute very politely and told me to tell Colonel Stuart to pursue at once with all speed. I retraced my steps as fast as I had come and though it was not over half a mile, Stuart was gone before I got in sight of our hill. Knowing well enough which direction he would take, I dashed after him and overtook the command before it reached Bull Run and regained my place at its head before it had risen the hill on the other side, though they were moving at a rapid trot. As soon as we appeared on the crest of the hill one of our batteries, mistaking us for the enemy, opened on us. I felt rather queer. It was bad enough to be killed by the enemy, but that could not be helped; but to be bowled over by our own people, and hit in the back at that, was disgusting. There was no way in the world of stopping them in time; so Stuart, with great presence of mind, gave the order "gallop — march" and away we scurried. Our fellows at the battery, seeing this, redoubled the rapidity of their fire and were getting our range closer and closer, and but for the fact that we had not far to go, would in a moment more have torn us pretty badly. One shot passed between Colonel Stuart's head and mine as we rode together at the head of the column, and burst just beyond.

After crossing the crest of the hill we were safe and resumed the trot. Just then an amusing incident occurred to me. We saw a man run across the road in front of us and take down a little bridle path for dear life. Stuart told me to catch him and find out what made him run so. I went after him; and finding he would not stop by calling and not caring to race Comet who was still panting heavily, I sent a pistol ball over his head which had the desired effect instantly. As I rode up to him, I found a little man in a semi-military blue dress, scared almost to death. His teeth chattered so that it was a long time, impatient to get off as I was, before he could tell me he was chaplain of some Yankee regiment. I had never taken a prisoner before and I felt him rather an elephant on my hands, small as he was. So I asked him if he was armed. lie hurriedly produced a broken-handled pocket knife which I pitched into the bushes, and I then pointed to the road we had come and told him to double quick down it and give himself up to the first of our men he came across, that I would stand there and watch, and if he stopped or looked back I would shoot him dead. When he had gone a little way I turned, and keeping on the grass so he could not hear me, galloped on after the command.

Stuart had taken a road parallel to the line of retreat and about half a mile therefrom, and was pushing along to overtake and strike them in flank. We had gone four or five miles when there appeared, on a hill near the road they were on, some horsemen waving a white flag. Stuart told me to take a dozen men and go over and see what they wanted, and then he rode on. By the time we had nearly reached the flag, we struck a broad stream of stragglers, extending forty or fifty yards on each side of the road. The main body had just passed and the stream I now struck was the wake. We struck it crossing a meadow and my men went wild. They were like a pack of hounds when they see a fox, and I turned them loose. There were at least a hundred foxes in sight and a most exciting chase began. They were running to get over a very large staked and ridered worm fence on the boundary of the meadow, and over it many escaped. All of these men were fully armed infantry, the disorganized fugitives having all passed by. After the chase began I stopped to watch the scene, but just then saw three Zouaves start to run across the meadow, my men being so much engaged they did not observe them; so I drew my pistol and gave chase, overtaking them as they reached the fence. One, a little in advance, had gotten over, but the other two faced about with their backs to the fence and cocked their muskets. I began to feel a little sheepish, but saw instantly that they were uncertain what to do, and that the only chance was to be prompt and peremptory and at the same time let them see I was cool and would not hurt them if they surrendered. I reined up within ten feet of them and fixing my eye on one of them said, in a quiet but commanding tone, "Throw down your musket, sir." He dropped it like a hot potato. When I turned to the other, he did likewise, to my great relief. In the meantime the fellow over the fence was running as fast as he could, but halted and returned when I threatened to shoot him if he did not. I then found that each one of them, after the fashion of the volunteer foot-soldier of the period, was encumbered with a multiplicity of blood-thirsty weapons, a musket and bayonet, a Colt's five-shooting revolver, and a bowie knife a foot long. I took the pistols, threw the knives away, and stuck the bayonets, with muskets attached, in the ground so our ordnance people could see them, and so they would be saved from rust in the meantime. I wore one of these pistols as a trophy throughout the war and have it still, and gave my own of the same kind to a man in my company.

These men belonged to the same regiment we charged that day. Their uniforms were very handsome and showy. During the evening I had a good deal of chat with them and they were very intelligent men. My men now began returning with their captures, in a great hurry to turn them over to me and be off after more. I kept a couple of them as a guard; the rest dashed off, and I proceeded on my mission and found they were some surgeons who wanted a guard for a hospital they had established for their wounded at a house near by. I told them we had at the time no men to spare for a guard, but just then a Lieutenant of our regiment rode up who had been sent with a detail to pick up prisoners; he begged me to relieve him of some twenty-five or thirty he had captured, and as I was already encumbered with about the same number I consented. What it was my duty to do in this unexpected situation was a matter of serious consideration. My orders to investigate the flag and return had been given with no expectation of such an event as had occurred. We were five miles from the battlefield; it would never do to turn the prisoners loose, and it would be out of the question to attempt to take them on after the command with the great uncertainty about finding it before dark.

I thought our army would certainly follow up the victory and that I had better take the prisoners back until I met the infantry and turn them over to them. Acting on this, I started back by the road their army had just passed over, but soon found to my dismay that only the guard of two men were with us: the rest were still in pursuit of more captives. I waited awhile, hoping some, at least, would return, but the evening was far advanced, it was nearly sundown, and I could wait no longer. The road was strewn with all sorts of arms and ammunition, and nothing would have been easier than for our captives, after they had time to find out how matters stood, to pick up some of the muskets and take us as prisoners on to Washington — and a most humiliating and disgusting ending this would have been to the day's adventures. To guard against this danger, I separated the men from the officers, of which latter there were about half a dozen, and then concluded it would be wise to double quick out of them any spirit they might have left. After half a mile of this treatment, through dust ankle deep, with the thermometer in the eighties, they were as gentle as lambs. I took my place at the rear of the column so as to see all in front, keeping my pistol in hand ready for immediate use. One man was placed at the head of the column with orders to capture all single stragglers and to report to me any large number we might come in sight of, the other man was kept with me in the rear.

Presently the man in front halted and beckoned to me. On approaching a bend in the road, he had gone forward to look ahead, and he said that the yard of a house we were approaching was full of Yankee soldiers. I rode forward with him to look around the bend of the road and there, sure enough, were some twenty-five or thirty men reclining under the trees, all armed and evidently an organized body, as several officers were resting, detached from the rest, near the gate. The yard was surrounded by a whitewashed paling fence and was several feet higher than the road, so that those in the yard would have to look through the fence to see those below, passing along the road.

The prisoners were so covered with dust that it was difficult to tell the color of their uniforms, and their number, now increased to about sixty, made quite an imposing array, so I determined to charge down the road with the prisoners at double quick, and capture the occupants of the yard if possible, before they had time to discover the ruse. I told my front man to halt the head of the column just before he got opposite the yard gate, so that if we succeeded, the new prisoners could march out without passing their comrades and discovering who they were. I then rode back and gave the order to double quick, and after getting them well closed up, took my rear man with me to the front, telling him to keep close to my side all the time, and telling the other man to watch the prisoners in the road as soon as we halted, and to shoot down instantly any one who did not keep in ranks or showed signs to those in the yard. The column came up to the yard in fine style, at double quick, wrapped in a cloud of dust, while the canteens of the prisoners produced quite a martial sound as an accompaniment to the tramp of their marching.

Just as they discovered us and sprang to their feet with their muskets cocked, I dashed up to the fence and presented my pistol to the nearest officer with a peremptory order to throw down his arms, which he did; the other officers and the men in turn did likewise except two at the far side of the yard, who jumped the fence and made their escape. I then ordered the privates to march out in the road at the head of the column, which was immediately moved forward, the officers falling in at the rear with the other officers as they passed. It then occurred to me that to prevent conversation and unsafe revelations, some more double quicking would be desirable; so as much was administered as they could stand. We found an ordnance wagon and four superb mules, abandoned by the driver on our approach, and these I brought along for our headquarters team, and found it very useful in transporting such of the men as gave out from the heat and the pace at which they marched.

After this capture a few more stragglers were taken, the last remnant of the flying army, and then the road became lonely in the extreme. There were all the evidences of the flight of large bodies of men and not a soul in sight: the road and a space of considerable width on each side trodden into liquid dust several inches deep, the trees, bushes, and fences covered with it, and in every direction abandoned articles, from a broken wagon to a canteen.

The sun was setting and we were still four miles from the battlefield and ten from Manassas, where I now saw we would have to go. Before it got dark I made a list of the prisoners' names and the commands they belonged to, and found there were eighty-seven in all, and nine among them captains and lieutenants. As I was still absolutely in their power, had they only known it, I adopted a ruse to make them think they were near our troops. After a private understanding with my front man, I called to him in a loud voice from the rear, so they could all hear me, to ride over to General Beauregard's headquarters and ask him what I must do with the prisoners. He galloped off through the woods and in a few moments came back and called to me that General Beauregard said I must taken them on to Manassas and turn them over to the provost marshal there. After this I became satisfied there was no further danger of their attempting to escape, or of taking us prisoners, which they could easily have done, and I relaxed the discipline, letting them stop occasionally to rest.

I also entered freely into conversation with them. The Captain commanding the company in the yard, introducing the subject himself, was loud in his admiration of the way he was taken. "Well, Lieutenant," he said, "you did play the damnedest trick on us I ever heard tell of. Captured us with our own men!" and then they all laughed from one end of the line to the other. The officers being at the rear I talked a good deal with them about the battle and the effect it would have, and there were various opinions expressed. Most of them thought the war was over and the Confederacy established. They told me of the carriage-loads of people who had come out from Washington to see the fight, and laughed a great deal at the way they went back. Both men and officers were all intelligent, members of city volunteer companies mostly. There were four or five Zouaves, and they expressed great admiration for our cavalry and their charge that day on their regiment, and were pleased to find that I had been in it; they said that they "had no cavalry that was worth a damn."

It was after dark when we reached the Bull Run, and as the prisoners were terribly used up and footsore, I halted for nearly an hour to let them drink, cool off, bathe their feet, and rest, for which they were very grateful. While there, many of them brought me delicacies they had in their haversacks, which were very acceptable, for though I had plenty of ordinary rations, I had nothing so nice as what they had. Eight or ten of the prisoners were so badly used up that they had to ride in the wagon, but the rest were now able to move on. Our march now led right through the battlefield, and they begged me to let them stop and minister to the wants of their wounded comrades. Fontaine Beaty of my company joined us here and informed me that our troops had been withdrawn back to their camps, around Manassas, and we were still six miles outside of our lines. But I believed I could trust these prisoners in their fatigued and demoralized condition, so with their promise not to try to escape, and to return in half an hour promptly, I halted for half an hour. I told them they were now in the midst of our army and that if they were caught wandering away they would run great risk of getting shot. Nearly all then dispersed over the field to find their friends, fill their canteens, fix their blankets and receive last messages from those who were mortally wounded.

It was a dismal place, there in the night, listening to the mournful sounds which reached the ear from every direction — groans, sighs, prayers and curses, particularly the latter, with an occasional scream of pain from some poor fellow. Most of them were the wounded of the enemy for ours had been removed. Occasionally a skulking figure could be seen passing noiselessly about the field, the vampires who infest all such places, men in search of plunder, to whom friend and foe are alike, and to whom murder, in the accomplishment of their purpose, is a ready resort.

As we waited here, a party of half a dozen soldiers, bearing a wounded Colonel in a blanket, came by — the first of our troops I had seen, except Beaty of my company who had joined us at Bull Run. I explained my situation to the Colonel and proposed that he should get in the wagon and let his men help me guard the prisoners to Manassas, a proposition he agreed to most thankfully, and I was relieved of all remaining anxiety about their escape. All my men reported promptly on time and very grateful for the opportunity afforded them for seeing their friends.[1]

It was midnight when we reached Manassas and yet the place was more crowded and in greater commotion than when we saw it the day before. The railroad trains were coming in with supplies and being hastily unloaded and sent back with the wounded. Trains of commissary wagons were awaiting or starting out with food for the troops. Ambulances, horsemen, footmen, herds of cattle, trains of captured artillery, long lines of prisoners, and all making a noise — locomotives screaming, drivers cursing, cattle bellowing, and mules braying. Every tent and board shanty was still lighted and the occupants busy attending to business or discussing the events of the day. I reported at headquarters and was ordered to turn the prisoners over to the provost marshal. There I found a space of an acre or so surrounded by a close line of sentinels, and inside were the prisoners. I marched my lot into the ring. They all came forward to tell me good-bye, and many thanked me for my treatment of them and begged me, whenever I came North, to let them know. The list of their names and addresses, much to my regret, was lost by the fire which consumed my office in Lynchburg, when I was Chief Engineer of the Lynchburg and Danville R. R. in 1867. I then went to the tent of the surgeon of our regiment, Dr. Ed. Campbell from Abingdon. He received me most hospitabl3T, and I was furnished with what I needed most of all — food for my noble horse, Comet, who had not eaten a mouthful, except the crackers I got from captured haversacks, since daylight. After seeing him well cared for, I went into the Doctor's tent, where I found Capt. Welby Carter, a good deal bruised by the fall he got when his horse was killed in the charge, but not seriously hurt. They all listened with much interest to my account of all that had happened to me, and it was long after

---

1 Many years have passed since then. Many who were with me that night are no doubt dead; but if these pages should meet the eyes of survivors I hope they will let me hear from them. — Wm. W. B.

midnight when sleep, for a few hours, came to restore strength after the exhaustion of this, the longest and most eventful day I had then ever experienced.

The noise of the camp, which never ceased during the night, was mingled, as I awoke the next morning, with the patter of rain on the tent, rendering the place if possible more wretchedly uncomfortable than before. After a hasty breakfast with Dr. Campbell, I started out to look for Colonel Stuart, knowing that he would be "at the front" under all circumstances, but nothing could I hear as to exact position. My road lay again through the battlefield, and I availed myself of the opportunity to examine it. A battlefield immediately after a battle is always an interesting and instructive study for a soldier. There is to be seen, by the results, the relative strength of positions, and the effect of fire; and nothing cultivates the judgment of topography, in relation to the strategic strength of position, so well as to ride over the ground while the dead and wounded still remain as they fell. You see exactly where the best effects were produced, and what arm of the service produced them, for there lies the harvest they have reaped, each sheaf distinctly labeled with the name of the reaper in the wound received. Artillery tears its sheaves out by the roots and scatters the fragments, while infantry mows them down in well heaped windrows. I made it a point throughout the war, whenever practicable, to ride over the battlefields immediately after the firing ceased, and acquired much valuable information in this way.

On this occasion I saw the field about nine o'clock and all of our wounded had been removed; so I could not study the subject on both sides. But the dead of both sides and the wounded of the enemy were still there, which gave me a pretty fair idea of the action; and to me, then unused to such incidents of war, it was a dismal sight. While I rode among the wounded of the enemy, some begged so piteously for water that I collected their canteens and filled them for them. Several, who were expecting death, asked me to write for them to their friends, but this I had not the time to do, nor can I say that I felt much inclination. I recognized the claims of humanity and was willing to minister to the sufferings of a wounded soldier, but writing to friends they had left to come as invaders of our soil was going a little too far. I drew the line at letters.

I had always felt a horror at taking anything from the dead, not that I thought it was wrong, but I disliked touching them. That morning, however, as I rode through a little grove of pines there lay, with his head covered by an oilcloth, the body of a handsomely dressed Federal officer, and buckled to his neat boots were an elegant pair of gilt spurs. Oh, how I did want those spurs! Then I could get them without touching the body, for there was only one buckle to undo at the instep. Mine were good, strong cavalry spurs, but how coarse they looked after seeing these. I looked all around — no one in sight — it must be done — I could not leave such spurs as those to fall into the hands of the infantry burial party who would be along to bury him. So down I sprang from my horse and began taking them off. "What are you doing there?" said the officer in a weak voice, pulling the oilcloth from his face. I felt the hot blood rush to my cheeks and turning my face quickly aside, so he could not recognize me again, jumped on my horse and galloped away. I ought to have offered to do something for him but I felt so ashamed at having been caught, I could not.

Two of my brothers, Charles and Eugene, were with the army; Charles, a Captain of cavalry in the 2nd Virginia Regiment, and Eugene, a Captain of infantry in the 5th Alabama Regiment. I had not heard from either. Informed that some wounded from an Alabama regiment were at a field hospital near by, I rode over to it. It was a large, old-fashioned, brick house with a porch in front and back, the floor of the porches being about as high as my horse. I rode into the yard of what had once been a handsome residence, but abandoned by its owners and pillaged by the troops, its appearance was forlorn. It was still raining, and not wishing to get my saddle wet by dismounting, rode up to the front door and called. There were many wounded in the house and everybody was busy and I could get no answer, so I rode round to the back door. As I rode up to the porch, Comet snorted and sprang back at seeing what looked like a nice, fat leg of mutton on the floor of the porch behind a pillar of the same. I am fond of good mutton, and not having had fresh meat for some time, my mouth watered for a steak. I concluded to get it and then ride out in the woods and broil it, for it looked uncommonly white and nice. I thought the surgeons were very, careless to let their hospital supplies lie about in that manner, but if they placed such a temptation in the way they could not blame a hungry soldier for helping himself. I opened my knife, and with much patting and coaxing got Comet close enough and leaned over to cut my steak; but what was my horror to discover on the other end of my joint, previously concealed by the post, a, sock! a dirty cotton sock, with holes in the heel and toe. It was a man's leg cut off half way above the knee. I was bitterly disappointed as well as shocked, but could not help laughing.

I could find out nothing about Eugene and had to push on. It was almost night before I found Colonel Stuart. He was much interested and pleased at my report of operations, particularly with the ruse of charging with the prisoners; when I got to that, he rolled over and shouted with laughter, for he was stretched out on his blanket under a porch of a country house where he had his headquarters at the time. He said I did the right thing in going back with the prisoners. I showed him the list and he counted them and laughed again. After I left the command, nothing of importance had occurred; they had taken some prisoners, but not near so many as I had.

We now daily expected a general advance upon Washington. An advance was made as far as Fairfax C. H. by the infantry, and Stuart occupied Falls Church and Munson's hill with a strong outpost of a mixed command, but nothing more was attempted. Our victory had been complete, but among our over-sanguine politicians from the far South, it seemed only a pretext for a relaxation of preparations for war. Encouraged by our overconfidence as well as stung by the reverse, the North redoubled its preparations. The cry among the controlling element from the Cotton states was, "Cotton is King. England can't afford to do without cotton. She will make war on our side to get it," and all sorts of foolish ideas of this kind. At that time the Government could have bought any quantity of cotton for Confederate money or bonds; this cotton could then have been sent to England to furnish the means for supplying all our wants. Instead of that, the "King Cotton" men said cotton must remain on the plantations to starve England into coming to our assistance. That men who claimed to be leaders, and who had gone so far in getting the country into the trouble, should make such a mistake is unpardonable: they will go down to history as shallow politicians with scarcely a statesman among them. There was over one hundred million dollars' worth of cotton in the South in the fall of 1861, one half of which in England would have given us success, for cotton soon rose to four or five times the usual price.

I am glad now we did not succeed in establishing the Confederacy, but I shall always think it was the absence of wisdom on the part of our rulers which prevented it. In my judgment a great mistake was made in not advancing upon and taking Washington, as we could have done, after the battle of Manassas. Our wooden-headed rulers, however, thought a strictly defensive policy was the true one and the fruits of our victory were never gathered. From Munson's hill we could see Washington, and Stuart slept for weeks on that hill, expecting every day the order would come for the advance, but it never came.

While we were at Fairfax C. H. before going down to Munson's, we, that is Colonel Stuart and myself, took our meals at a house in town where General Longstreet boarded. He impressed me then as a man of limited capacity who acquired reputation for wisdom by never saying anything — the old story of the owl. I do not remember ever hearing him say half a dozen words, beyond 'yes' and 'no,' in a consecutive sentence, though often in company with his old companions of the old army. About this time I saw General Fitz. Lee for the first time, on visits he made to Colonel Stuart's headquarters. He was then a captain on Elzey's staff, I believe.

My wife paid me a visit not long after the battle and we both looked forward to the war soon being over, a hope, alas, not to be fulfilled for long years after.

Stuart was soon promoted to a colonelcy and as Adjutant of his splendid regiment I found a great change for the better in the comfort of my life. I got as a servant Gilbert, the son of "Aunt Charlotte," my wife's "Mammy," and a more faithful attendant never was. He remained with me until the end of the war, and was with me in both campaigns north of the Potomac where he could, at any time he chose, have secured his freedom by leaving me. But he not only never showed any disposition to do so but on several occasions, while out foraging for our mess, ran the risk of his life in escaping from foraging parties of the enemy. I now found that one horse was not enough, and hearing one day that a Union man, just outside of our lines, had a number of horses, and among them one which was represented as a very fine animal, I got leave from the Colonel to make a cavalry detail of a dozen men to capture them.

The enemy occupied one side of the farm and the horses were out in a field near their lines. I kept my party concealed, and sent one man, without arms, with his coat off to look like a countryman, to drive them up, telling him to keep his horse at a walk to keep up appearances. He drove the horses out without attracting attention and I then sent some men on back with them at a gallop, bringing up the rear with the main body to prevent recapture. There was no pursuit, however, and I brought in five, turned four over to the quartermaster and kept the fine one I had heard so much about. She turned out to be a large draught horse, very heavy, and entirely unsuited to cavalry; so I swapped her for a dun horse in a battery which had been captured at the battle, and I named him Manassas. He was a dappled, yellow dun with white mane and tail, both of which he carried well up and presented a showy appearance, while his action was good. If I had not had Comet I should have thought him a fine horse, but alongside of Comet all horses seemed inferior. Manassas had none of Comet's engaging ways, in short he was not a gentleman by either birth or education. Still he did very well to relieve Comet and for Gilbert to ride on marches. Colonel Stuart drilled the regiment now regularly, and the camp routine of drills in the morning and dress parade in the evening with picket duty on the outposts occupied our time. Stuart then organized the horse artillery which under Pelham made such a splendid record. As Adjutant, I met all the officers of our army frequently, either when they were visiting Stuart, or when I accompanied him on visits to them.

Then began the impression, which has ripened into conviction since, that the average West Point officer who had reached the age of forty in the discharge of the duties of the army officer, in time of peace, is worthless in war. Of course there are brilliant exceptions in both the Northern and Southern armies, but they are *exceptions*. They are brought up to think that after graduating at West Point there is nothing left for them, in this world, to learn; and twenty years' garrison life in the West, in contact with inferiors, and with nothing to stimulate to exertion, leaves them selfish, narrow-minded, and bigoted. To look at the numbers in our army, and then to count those who were even moderately successful as soldiers, one is astonished at the smallness of the proportion; and still more is this astonishment increased when we count how many were absolutely disastrous failures. The same number of graduates from our best colleges, who had never opened a military book at equal ages with the West Pointers, and taken from the successful businessmen of the country and placed in the same positions at the beginning of the war would, in my opinion, have done better on the average. The young men from West Point, who had to win their way and had not been fossilized by garrison or bureau life, as a rule did splendidly, those of thirty and under, say. The "old soldiers" are so intensely jealous of each other; they look at everything through green glasses! The country or their cause is nothing to them when opposed to their feelings, and it is so deeply seated that they really are not aware of its existence, I verily believe, in many cases. Then, when high in rank, some of them are so afraid of losing their reputation that they won't take the risks necessary in war, and avoid a battle they are not certain of winning, when the chances are still in their favor. We had some brilliant exceptions to this of course, but they were still *exceptions*. As long as we have Indians, we will have to keep an army, and after that a few to take care of the ordnance, but then, I should say, keep West Point up to its full capacity and return the graduates to civil life, or perhaps give them a year or two of employment in going round to see the forts. They would make far better soldiers when called upon in war.

But changes took place in the autumn which again made a great change in my life and put an end for a time to the gay life I led as Stuart's Adjutant, and though my promotion was the cause I felt some regrets. Stuart was made a Brigadier General, Wm. E. Jones, the Captain of my company, was appointed Colonel, and I became Captain of the company. It was a fine company, and I felt great pride in it. My commission dated Oct. 3, 1861. Fitz Lee was appointed Lieutenant Colonel and at once became very popular in the regiment, but Jones was not at all so. Colonel Lee was a fine drill officer and drilled us all the time, and I learned more about it than I had ever done before. We were then picketing at Fairfax C. H., with camp four or five miles back. The Natchez troop from Mississippi, Captain Martin, joined the regiment about that time, and a fine company it was, I remember, though we were all amazed at their bringing two wagonloads of trunks, and this after having left the most of their baggage behind in Richmond. They were the best mounted company I ever saw, even better than mine. General Stuart's headquarters were not far off, and I often visited there. Stuart had now organized the band of stringed instruments and singers which afterwards became so well known and so associated with him. Sweeny, a brother of the celebrated Joe Sweeny, the banjo player who had brought the banjo into European notice by his skill upon it, was one of the band; he played the banjo and sang. Bob, the General's mulatto servant, worked the bones, and then there was a violin player and a guitar player and quite a number of singers among the staff and couriers.

The cavalry command was extended over a long front, sometimes as much as thirty or forty miles in each direction, and to convey dispatches and orders it was necessary to keep at headquarters a considerable number of men detailed from the regiments of cavalry. In making these details, Stuart would have an eye not only to the reliability of the man and horse, but sometimes to the man's accomplishments in the line of enlivening a march, or beguiling the time around a campfire. Whenever he would hear of a man who had any amusing specialty and was willing to come, he would have him detailed as courier at headquarters. For such duty, of course, the wishes of the man were consulted. In this way he collected around him a number of experts, not only in music, but in theatricals and tricks of various kinds, and they added much to the pleasure of camp life. Sweeny and his banjo and his negro melodies were the favorites; and Sweeny always carried his instrument slung at his back on marches, and often in long night marches the life of the men was restored by its tinkle.

I have mentioned before that Jones disliked General Stuart and an opportunity was soon found, now that he was a Colonel, for showing it. Colonel Jones was not popular with his regiment, and the contrast between our ugly, surly Colonel and our handsome, dashing Lieutenant Colonel Lee made him appear in a still more unfavorable light. It was expected that our woodenheaded demagogues in Congress would have a reorganization of the army by having an election of company and regimental officers. Just at that time, not six months after most of the raw recruits had entered the army, some of the officers who had exerted themselves most to establish discipline had become unpopular with their men, for there had not been time enough for the advantage of good discipline to become understood by them. Jones knew that he would stand no chance of election, so he canvassed the men of my company with a view of having it as a nucleus to fall back upon. His assigned plan was to take my company out to southwest Virginia, raise a new regiment and officer it from the men of the company, and this, of course, was hailed with delight by them. I was opposed to leaving Stuart and the grand army for the wretched sort of service in out-of-the-way places, to fight obscure, nameless, little battles. I always felt that if I was to be killed I wanted to fall in a great battle and to have my name connected with the history of the war.

To accomplish his purpose, Jones found it would be necessary for him to break down my influence in the company, for at that time I was very popular with the men, and he soon found an opportunity not only of doing this, but of wounding General Stuart by making me a sufferer from one of his general orders, as he knew that Stuart was very fond of me.

As cold weather approached, General Stuart issued a general order prohibiting fires on the picket line. A case had occurred of a sentinel being shot while standing in the light of a fire, and hence the order. It referred, of course, to the vidette posts and not to the post of the reserve, some hundreds of yards in the rear, out of sight and range of the enemy. Our camp was six miles south of Fairfax C. H. and the regiment picketed at the courthouse, and for two miles on each side. The enemy was at Falls Church, five or six miles north of the courthouse, the space between being neutral ground. A company went down to relieve the guard every morning. Company headquarters were in the village and the outposts half a mile beyond. Each outpost consisted of from four to six men under command of a non-commissioned officer, and each of these kept a vidette, always mounted, one or two hundred yards in advance; the men on the post could dismount, but kept their reins in their hands. These posts were relieved every four hours from company headquarters in the village. At the reserve in the village a sentinel was kept on duty to listen for firing on the line of outposts. In case the enemy appeared, the vidette fired, the men on his post galloped to his rescue and began skirmishing, the sentinel at headquarters gave the alarm and the reserve then mounted their horses ready for action.

One day, a week or two after the frosty weather began in the fall, I took my company down in its turn for picket duty. Accompanied by the Captain of the company I relieved, I rode along the line of outposts, putting my men in place of his, and he rode back to camp. On the Falls Church road, where the post was at some period in the past, a pit for a cannon had been dug about four feet deep, and in this pit, to shelter them from the wind, the men of the post were stationed, and there, entirely out of sight and a couple of hundred yards back of the vidette, the men had kept up a fire ever since it got cold at night. After I had been relieved and had returned to camp, Colonel Jones went down to inspect the picket line and found the fire with the men of the other company around it, not one of mine being within six miles of the place.

This was the chance he had no doubt been waiting for, slim as it was, of hitting me and by good luck, he thought, at the same time hitting General Stuart by making me suffer by violating his order. So he passed by the officer under whose command he found the fire, and in whose command it had been burning several hours, and, making no attempt to find out who started the fire originally, preferred charges of disobedience of orders against me and placed me in close arrest; that is, in confinement to the walls of my tent. Colonel Fitz was going out on a scout with the regiment and I was getting ready to start when Jones sent his Adjutant with the written order, putting me under close arrest for violation of General Order No. 16 (I think it was). Knowing exactly what it all meant, I felt like doing a little murder. It would have been most grateful to me to have run him through with my sabre, but under such circumstances a duel was of course impossible. The next day he sent his Adjutant to me to say that if I would apply for extension of limit he would grant an extension to the limits of the camp. I told his Adjutant to present my compliments to Colonel Jones and to say to him "that I would see him in Hell before I would make any such application." So, afraid to keep me in close arrest, he issued an order extending my limits.

Courts-martial at that time had to be made by detail of officers, and there was much delay in getting one convened. I was under arrest five or six weeks. Jones, in the meantime, would take the company down on picket himself, assigning as a reason that the lieutenants were inexperienced men, and he soon disorganized and demoralized it to such an extent that my influence was undermined and destroyed. After resuming command any attempt at restoring discipline was resented as a tyrannical assumption of power, and the men would go over to pay the Colonel a visit and receive his condolences. They were received and entertained in his tent, he using every means in his power to ingratiate himself with them.

General Stuart called to see me several times and showed plainly enough in his manner his sympathy, though of course the subject of my arrest was not mentioned. The court at last met and, after hearing the evidence, unanimously granted me an honorable acquittal, and then came in a body and dined with me by my invitation. John S. Mosby, who was a private soldier in my company, acted as my counsel. But Jones had accomplished all he desired and expected. I found, on resuming command, a complete change in the men; my influence was gone. On every exercise of discipline I could see them slipping over to the Colonel's tent for consultation, and for the short time I remained with them after this, all pleasure in the service was lost.

General Stuart's headquarters was always a pleasant place to visit and there a cordial welcome ever awaited me, and I spent a good many evenings there.

We went into winter quarters near the battlefield of Manassas and took much pains to build log cabins, thinking they would be more comfortable than tents, a mistake I never made again in the other winters of the war. The tent with a fireplace and chimney at the same end as the entrance is far more comfortable in every way. The fireplace and entrance should never be at opposite ends.

In December, Stuart took a force composed mainly of infantry to Dranesville and there had a severe skirmish with a foraging party of the enemy, but my command was not called out on that occasion.

The battlefield of Manassas lay about a mile from our camp on the road to Manassas Junction and I had often to pass that way, and sometimes at night, my path leading across the spot where we made the charge on the Zouaves. Their graves were shallow, and the rains had washed the earth away in many places, leaving the bones exposed. Just at the point, as nearly as I could judge, the most to the right of any, where I had passed through their line, lay a skeleton with head, shoulders and feet exposed, draped in stained and moldering fragments of a gaudy Zouave uniform. These were in all likelihood the remains of the man I sent into eternity. But such is war! I must confess it made me feel a little queer to see that skull grinning at me through the darkness as I rode alone through the dreary place — and yet his bullet might have placed me in a similar position.

III — 1862

The fields were so muddy that it was impossible to drill, and our picket duty was light; so after attending to the routine of camp duty, time hung heavily. First Lieut. Reese Edmundson and myself occupied a cabin and I amused myself mostly by reading. I had my stable close by and had the floor laid with flattened logs, and Comet used to annoy me sometimes by his pawing to keep warm.

But we were not to be allowed to occupy our huts until the cold weather was entirely over, for events were in progress in the camp of the enemy indicating an early opening of the campaign from another direction. McClellan, who now commanded the Federal army, proposed to attack from the direction of Fort Monroe and in March began transferring his army thither by water, making a demonstration in force towards our position at Manassas, which the cavalry was called upon to meet and delay.

At Manassas, with the usual bad management of our people, vast accumulations of supplies had been made, and great quantities of baggage belonging to the droops, containing clothing which was very valuable to them, had been stored. When the demonstration was made, General Johnston had everything burned and evacuated the place. This may have been the right thing to do, but I have always doubted it. It seems to me he might have met their force, saved his supplies and still have reached the Peninsula in time. But he was always great on retreats. I am sure General Lee would never have sacrificed all that property without striking a blow. As the enemy approached, the cavalry set fire to all the corn cribs. I mean our cavalry. I burned with my own hands a great many, while falling back before their advance. My brother Charles's regiment was operating next to ours, and he rode over one day to dine with me, but that day our rations were short and I could offer him nothing but parched corn. Here, right within our lines and close to the camps, quantities of grain were stored on the farms and we, all the winter, were drawing from Richmond and the interior; and it had all to be burned to keep it out of the hands of the enemy. This may have been West Point science, but to ordinary mortals it looked not wise. At Manassas there were huge piles of bacon burned, as high as a house. The flames did have a curious look, a sort of yellow and blue mixed, and the smell of fried bacon was wafted for twenty miles. The loss of clothing to the men was a very serious one, for many had enough stored there to have lasted them through the war. They advanced as far as Bealton and then withdrew to join the troops going to the Peninsula.

It was here Mosby first attracted attention. He had been cut off from the ford, and we thought captured, but he went off in the woods to one side and then, during the night, found out that they were withdrawing and came across early the next day with the information, and Stuart immediately followed them. Mosby was then Adjutant of our regiment, the 1st Virginia, Warren Hopkins having been promoted to a colonelcy of some regiment in the West.

Johnston now moved down with his army to the Peninsula near Yorktown, where Magruder had a small force holding McClellan in check. During the time we were engaged in meeting this advance demonstration on Manassas, the weather was very bad — snow and sleet and rain — and we had to bivouac in it all. One night in particular I remember as the severest I passed during the war. We had been skirmishing all day in the sleet, and the ground was covered with snow. Long after dark we went into bivouac in a pine wood, expecting to be protected from the cold wind by its shelter, and did not notice that the tops of the tall slender trees were so heavily laden with sleet that they bent way over, sometimes almost to the ground. We halted along the line of a worm fence whose rails afforded plenty of fuel, and we had plenty of corn for the horses, taken from the cribs we had been burning all day, and plenty of rations, largely composed of the poultry and eggs which, from purely patriotic motives, we had removed from the temptation to the enemy.

The cheerful fires soon illumined the sparkling forest around us. Coffee pots and frying pans diffused a delicious odor. Chickens were broiling over the coals, eggs popping in the ashes, while the men resumed their cheerfulness as they warmed and dried their weary limbs and contemplated the feast approaching. But a disaster was hanging over us, literally. When the heat rose through the heavy masses of sleet suspended in the treetops, its icy bonds were loosed and all of a sudden down it came like an avalanche, upsetting the coffee pots and frying pans and extinguishing every spark of fire in camp. Again and again they were rekindled until, absolutely worn out, we had to eat our food as it was, half cooked, and get what sleep we could stretched on the cold snow. Once during this time, when we had built brush shelters for the night and had roaring fires burning in front and I was eating my supper, General Stuart rode by and, finding out whose quarters they were, dismounted and spent the night with me. I was delighted to have him and contrived to make him quite comfortable. We had plenty of leaves to lie on, the brush shelter kept off the wind and the fire kept us warm. He and I combined our blankets and slept together.

On the march to the Peninsula we passed Dewberry and Edgewood in Hanover county and I called to see my kinspeople at those places. Great numbers of people assembled on the streets of Richmond to see Stuart and his now famous cavalry pass through. We went in along Franklin Street to the capitol square and then out along Broad Street. The windows, doors and sidewalks were crowded with ladies waving their handkerchiefs. I met Mr. Robertson and shook hands with him just as we left Franklin Street; we had not met since I left home and I was very glad to see him. My wife was in town, and after reaching camp I came in to see her but had to go on the next day with the command.

After reaching the lines at Yorktown, the long expected reorganization of the army took place. To have disorganized the army in presence of the enemy in that way was a fearful risk to run, and a more enterprising man than McClellan would not have let it pass. All discipline was suspended and every company became the theatre for the arts of the demagogue. I remember passing a company in camp one morning when the roll was being called; not a man turned out, but answered to their names from their beds, the orderly-sergeant walking up and down the tents to awake those still sleeping. One telling point in favor of a candidate was that he would not "expose his men," as they called it; namely, would not make them fight.

There may have been inefficient officers in the army, and doubtless there were, but they could have been gotten rid of in other ways. To introduce the element of democracy into an army, and to strike down numbers of the best men in it, was an injury to the morale of the troops which they never got over. If one set of officers had become unpopular by establishing discipline and had been turned out by a reorganization, why might not another set be served the same way in the future? The lesson was taught: *Keep in with your men, whatever the consequences, if you don't want to be turned out some day.* The officer felt that he owed his place to certain of the men who voted for him, and these men felt they had made him an officer. Could anything have been more destructive to discipline?

In my company they had found out that Jones's scheme was impracticable, and the orderly-sergeant, Connaly Litchfield, who was running for the office of Captain, formed a new platform, equally impracticable, of course, but it served its turn about as most party platforms do; and as this was a miniature party election, they must have a platform, though it was never to be heard of afterwards. So the platform upon which the orderly-sergeant stood was to get the company converted into an artillery company, to accomplish which he claimed influence, and to get it out from under Stuart's command, against whom Jones had diffused his dislike among the men. I could hear him canvassing from my tent. It was not that he wanted the captaincy on his own account — oh, no! but he did want to be transferred to the Artillery and the men knew that I would not agree to this, for I was a Stuart man, etc., etc.

To solicit votes among the private soldiers was a thing I could not bring myself to do, and I made no effort in that direction, and Connaly Litchfield, the orderly-sergeant, was elected.

I returned to Richmond and was at once commissioned Captain of Engineers, and reported for duty to Colonel (afterwards General) Stevens, Chief Engineer Officer of the army, or rather reported to General Gilmer, who was Chief Engineer Officer of the army, and by him was ordered to report to Colonel

Stevens, Chief Engineer Officer of Johnston's army. My commission dated May 26, 1862. Capt. Alfred Rives was in charge of the Engineer Bureau in Richmond, but how wretchedly tame the routine of an office up in the fourth story looked after the stirring scenes in which I had participated, and I was glad to get away to the army again, which had now come to Richmond. General Stevens' headquarters were five miles from town, near General Johnston's.

Going into army headquarters one day, I found General Stevens and a number of general officers, mostly old army officers, sitting in one of the rooms of the country house they occupied, talking about the danger we were in of McClellan's suddenly throwing a force across the James River below Drewry's Bluff and marching up to Richmond, while our men would have to go all the way up to Richmond to cross on the bridges there, and then come down to meet him, for we had no means of crossing the river nearer than that place, and they were all lamenting that we could not build a bridge near Drewry's Bluff.

I listened for some time and felt some diffidence in expressing an opinion in such company, for I then still thought West Point men knew all about war. But as they talked, and as I began to see the importance of the thing, I reflected upon what might be done. At last I said to Colonel Stevens that I thought a pontoon bridge might be built just where they wanted it, above Drewry's Bluff, by using the schooners and canal boats in the docks in Richmond, of which there were many. He asked me where I could get timber to connect them. I told him I thought there could be found enough, of a suitable kind, in the lumber yards and where they were building some large mills in the city. Then he asked me a great many questions about how I could get anchors and how to make a draw for boats to pass through. After thinking a little, he told me to wait there a while; and he went into the next room, and in the course of half an hour came out and handed me a paper. It was an order to proceed to build a bridge above Drewry's Bluff, about one mile, at the most suitable place, without delay. I was thunderstruck, but I was in for it and must do the best I could. I was to have *carte-blanche* to take anything I wanted except men from the army, and those I could not take. I then asked for and was furnished orders to the provost marshal in Richmond to impress any number of men, not in the army, I might call on him for, and also any canal boats, steamboats or vessels, and any material.

By the time the papers were ready, it was midday and I started for Richmond, a little nervous about the responsibility I had brought upon myself, though I felt quite sure I could succeed. I saw at once that organization was the first thing to see to in so large a force of laborers as would be required; that I must find men who had been accustomed to managing large bodies of laborers in the kind of work required, and moreover men who knew the resources of Richmond in skilled labor and material. As I rode up to town I classified in my mind the sorts of work that would be needed. There would be carpentry, of course, and there would be a good deal of handling of boats and cordage, so men in these lines must be found. On reaching Richmond, I called on some of the leading businessmen, stated my orders, explained the pressing emergency, and gave my views of what was wanting in skilled men as managers in the two departments before mentioned.

They all said at once there were two men who would meet these requirements preeminently, one, a contractor for building houses, and a carpenter by trade; the other, a shipbuilder who had a shipyard across the river; both men of large experience and great energy and skill.

These men were sent for, and I explained the situation to them and told them I would pay them well for their labor; they agreed to serve, but would not accept anything more than a moderate and usual price. We then discussed details. They said all their skilled men were enlisted in the army, but these, I told them, we could not get. They then said there were some skilled men in town over military age, and these I told them to get without delay and at any price necessary to secure them. The carpenter said there was plenty of suitable lumber in town and he knew where to find it. We then made a list of all the steamboats in port and all the drays in town. The shipbuilder said there would be a deficiency of anchors, for it would require two to each boat or vessel, one up and the other down stream to provide for ebb and flow of tide, and as canal boats had no anchors there would be a large deficiency. I then told him we must get blocks of stone as a substitute, and on examination we found suitable stones at the stonecutters' yards about the city. I assigned to the shipbuilder the duty of getting all the schooners and canal boats out of the docks and basin into the river below Rocketts and of loading each canal boat with the blocks of stone required for its two anchors, and to the carpenter the duty of getting the lumber loaded upon each schooner and canal boat that would be required to build the span between it and the next boat to it in the bridge, so that there would be no confusion of transfer of lumber after all was afloat.

By this time it was late in the afternoon. I then went to the provost marshal, showed him his orders, and told him I wanted five hundred able-bodied men placed in confinement that night ready for work the next morning, and he said he would place them in a warehouse on the dock under guard until I was ready for them, and furnish a guard to go down with them on the fleet, and a guard to keep them at work while in the city. He then sent out a guard and swept the town, beginning above and landing the haul at the warehouse at Rocketts a little after dark: considerably over five hundred men, white and black, but mostly black. There was quite a commotion among the fashionables at their dining-room servants' absence at tea time that evening. I also gave the provost marshal the list of the drays and steamboats to impress and have ready for duty on the dock at sunrise next day. I then went to the commissary's and ordered him to have three days' rations for five hundred men on the dock at the same time.

I then went to Mr. Robertson's house on Franklin Street, where my wife was, and was on the dock long before daybreak the next morning, where my two excellent assistants, the carpenter and shipbuilder, soon joined me. I have forgotten the names of these two men after so long a time, but must try to get them and record them, for they did valuable service on this occasion. I had their names among the papers destroyed in Lynchburg.

By three o'clock that evening the boats and schooners were all loaded and on the river, the men and rations on board, and five steamers, with steam up, ready. The fleet of schooners and canal boats was then divided between four of the steamers to tow down to the site of the bridge, while I reserved the largest steamer for my headquarters, from whose elevated upper deck I could see everything. After getting everything started, I went on down to the site of the proposed bridge as fast as the boat could go, to select an anchorage two or three hundred yards above; and here was temporarily anchored the flotilla with plenty of space for a steamer to pass among them in selecting those to use during the progress of the work. I then kept two steamers and discharged the rest. One steamer was to be held in reserve to run up to Richmond for anything that might be wanted, and the other, the one I had for headquarters, was to select and bring the vessels or boats to the bridge as they were wanted.

I began at each bank and built towards the middle, where the draw was to be for the passage of boats to and from the fortifications at Drewry's Bluff. The canal boats were put next the banks and the schooners in the middle of the river. I gave the shipbuilder charge of one end and the carpenter the other, and I selected and brought to them the boats as they needed them. Each boat was loaded with all the lumber required for its span and each had some men on board, so all I had to do was to tow the boat or vessel to a point twenty yards above the place it was to occupy; the men on board then heaved overboard the large stone anchor and let her down to the line of the structure by paying out the cable. She was then pulled sideways to the last boat put in, the floor joists were then fastened to the last boat and the new boat pushed back to its place and the joists secured to her. The planking was then spiked down and that span was finished. As we were to work all night, I made them keep a bright fire burning on every deck of the fleet, so the whole river was as light as day. I also detailed plenty of cooks whose duty it was to keep an abundance of cooked food and plenty of strong *coffee* for the men to help themselves to at pleasure. In this way I kept them in good heart and they worked like beavers.

I stood on the hurricane deck of my boat the whole time, excepting a nap between times stretched out on the deck, passing boats first to one side and then to the other, getting up a rivalry between the two ends, and when one kept me waiting I would blow the whistle until they were ready to receive their boat and this would set the other end to cheering. The weather was fortunately fine.

The draw was built as follows: The largest schooner was selected for the draw in the center. Flaps were hinged to the vessels on each side of her; when these were let down the bridge was continuous; when raised, and the vessel floated out, an opening was left for traffic on the river.

Soon after breakfast I found that we were making such rapid progress that the bridge would be finished before night; so to enable me to say in my report that it had actually been tried, I sent off and got a four-mule wagon and had it waiting. I also had a courier on horseback waiting and my report to General Johnston ready written. When the last plank was laid, I mounted the wagon and drove across at four o'clock in the afternoon, and off galloped the courier with the report.

General Johnston wrote me an answer with his own hand, congratulating me on my success in the achievement. This letter, I am sorry to say, was burned after the war, together with so many other papers about the war, when my office was burned in Lynchburg.

I spent a couple of days longer there with a portion of the force, strengthening and improving the structure, and then returned to Engineer headquarters, turning the bridge over to the Engineer Bureau in Richmond, of which Capt. A. L. Rives was the chief.[2]

About a week after this, there came a great flood in James River and I received an order stating that the bridge had been washed away and directing me to rebuild it at once. I went at once to secure the two foremen, two steamboats, and a force of laborers, and went to the spot. The canal boats and schooners were still near by but torn from their anchorage and twisted and tangled in a fearful manner, many swept entirely out of the channel, out upon the sheet of water covering the low grounds. The first thing to do was to tow these last out into deep water before the fall of water left them high and dry. This was done, and after three days the bridge was in place again.

On my return I was ordered over to Petersburg to relieve Capt. Chas. H. Dimmock of the command of the construction of the fortifications around that place. This was my old friend Charley Dimmock, with whom I had served as an engineer on the Virginia & Tennessee Railroad. It seems that he and the commanding officer of the troops, ordered there to occupy his fortifications, had quarrelled about the construction of the works, and I had been sent in consequence. I found he was in the right, and I not only did not want to supersede him, but I had no desire to be put on construction of fortifications instead of active service in the field with the army; so I represented the facts and asked to be relieved.

As soon as General Stuart had heard of my appointment in the Engineer Corps, he had applied to have me assigned to duty on his staff, but these other matters had turned up which had delayed it. It was owing to this that I missed being with him in his first raid around McClellan's army, greatly to my disgust. I heard of it all while in Petersburg and longed to be again with Stuart. Immediately after my return from Petersburg, I received orders to report to General Stuart, and did so just before the beginning of the Seven Days' Battle around Richmond.

As I was passing Mr. Price's house in Richmond one day, I saw Mrs. Stuart standing in the doorway talking to an officer just taking leave of her, and on going up to speak to her was introduced to Lieut. Heros von Borcke, whom I then met for the first time. He had only been in this country a week or two and spoke the language with difficulty, though he afterwards acquired it with wonderful quickness. Von Borcke at that time weighed about two hundred and fifty pounds, was six feet two inches high, but so light and graceful in his movements that his great size was not noticed. He was a thoroughly educated cavalry officer, a gentleman by birth and breeding, and of extremely frank and polished manners. His father was a man of high rank in Prussia, holding a position corresponding to that of a member of the House of Lords in England.

---

2   This account of the building of the pontoon bridge across the James River at Drewy's Bluff was written at a time when no publications of records of the war had appeared, and I had to trust to my memory entirely. I remembered that there was a three-day period somewhere and I thought it was the period occupied in the completion of the whole work. Since then, in making my revision of the manuscript, I find that three days were occupied in preparing, collecting and shipping the material, and that two days were consumed in building the bridge — making five days in all. — Wm. W. B., Lynchaven, Virginia, September 17, 1902.

Von Borcke had been a Lieutenant in the Cuirassiers of the Guard in Berlin, one of the household regiments officered by men of high rank, and being an extravagant fellow, he and his father had quarrelled about money matters; von Borcke told him if he could not support him in that regiment like a gentleman he would resign and come to America, and this he did. Meeting Mr. Mason, I believe it was, in Paris, he concluded to join the Southern side and procured letters of introduction for this purpose, running the blockade at Charleston. Having been boarded by a Federal cruiser in the West Indies, he destroyed his letters and landed in Richmond with only a letter to Mr. Randolph, the Secretary of War, from the German consul in Charleston, who had no previous acquaintance with him, but believed his account of himself to be true. When Mr. Randolph saw him he made such a favorable impression that he sent him to General Stuart with a letter, on trial as it were, where he arrived just before the Chickahominy raid, and on that expedition pleased General Stuart so much that he got him a commission and had him assigned to duty on his staff. Von Borcke and myself became great friends, and though fully appreciating the defects of his character, I could not help liking him, for where it was his interests to be so, he could make himself as agreeable as any man I ever met. I also learned a great many valuable little matters about cavalry service from him, the application of one of which, strange to say, was the means I used to get him off the battlefield when he received the wound which terminated his military career two years after.

The Chickahominy raid, some weeks before, was made to ascertain the position of McClellan's army, more particularly as to whether he had fortified the Totopotomoy Creek upon which his right rested. And finding that he had not, Jackson, fresh from his brilliant valley campaign, was to attack him there. Since Johnston's wound received at Seven Pines, Gen. R. E. Lee had been in command of the army and a far bolder course was to follow in consequence. With great celerity, Jack-son moved down from the valley, his troops full of enthusiasm and confidence in themselves and their now world-renowned leader. Stuart and a portion of the force around Richmond were to co-operate with Jackson, who thus had with him, when he opened the attack upon McClellan's right flank, about thirty thousand men.[3]

I joined General Stuart in Richmond and rode with him to Ashland, where we met Jackson on the 26th of June riding at the head of troops all covered with dust. It was a thrilling sight to see the spirit of these men, evinced in their every movement, and the lightness with which they stepped, in spite of the tremendous march they had made. It was the first time I had met General Jackson since the interview I had with him on the battlefield of the First Manassas; then he was an unknown Brigadier General, now a man whose fame was known to the civilized world.

He was delighted to see General Stuart and rode out to one side of the road with him to have a consultation. Stuart's fame had spread, and Jackson's men cheered wildly as they passed, for they knew well enough what was brewing when those two men conferred in that way. Jackson was then thirty-eight years of age, a little over medium height, of compact muscular build, with dark hair, and eyes that lit up on occasions with great expression, though he did not often indulge in conversation. Until after the battles around Richmond, General Jackson was careless about his dress and equipments, and though always clean, his clothes looked as if they formed no part of his thoughts. After this period, however, there was a change; he dressed well and rode good horses, his men cheering with delight at every new addition to his outfit.

When we met him at Ashland, he was mounted upon a dun cob of rather sorry appearance, though substantial in build, and was dressed in a threadbare, faded, semi-military suit, with a disreputable old Virginia Military Institute cap drawn down over his eyes, presenting a strong contrast to the dashing appearance and splendid mount of Stuart and his staff, all in full Confederate gray uniforms, cocked felt hats with long black plumes, and high cavalry boots.

Stuart with his cavalry was to cover Jackson's left flank while he bore down upon the right flank of the enemy. The dispositions were made with Jackson's usual promptness and the advance upon Mechanicsville begun. By ten o'clock that night the enemy was in full retreat and we slept on the field.

---

3   Jackson had only eight thousand men and Stuart about three thousand with him. — Wm. W. B.

The cavalry had not been engaged, except with light scouting parties of the enemy, but we kept the roads all thoroughly picketed so as to make any flank surprise impossible.

On the 27th of June the advance upon Cold Harbor was begun, to which the enemy had withdrawn during the night and where they were about sixty thousand strong. This was four or five miles farther on down the Chickahominy. The cavalry led the advance and encountered the cavalry of the enemy at several points, but swept them away by the first charge in every case. Indeed, at that period it was a constant regret to us that they would not stand long enough for us to capture their horses and arms, the latter particularly, as our men needed pistols and good carbines.

It was during this advance that we met for the first and last time the Lancers, a Pennsylvania regiment which we had heard a great deal about; it had been gotten up regardless of expense, and was called in the Northern papers "the finest body of troops in the world" — and so they were, as far as their tailors could make them, and they were certainly well mounted, for even Comet could not overtake them in the mile or two race I gave them, though they had only a hundred yards the start.

I must confess I felt a little creeping of the flesh when I saw this splendid looking body of men, about seven hundred strong, drawn up in line of battle in a large open field two or three hundred yards off, armed with long poles with glittering steel points. To think of one of these being run through a fellow was not at all pleasant. The appearance they presented was certainly very fine, with a tall forest of lances held erect and at the end of each, just below the head, a red pennant fluttering in the breeze.

Stuart quickly threw a regiment into line and ordered the charge. I joined in, and down upon them we swept with a yell, at full speed. They lowered their lances to a level and started in fine style to meet us midway, but long before we reached them the gay lancers' hearts failed them and they turned to fly. For miles the exciting chase was kept up, the road was strewn with lances thrown away in their flight, and nothing but the fleetness of their horses saved them all from capture.

The infantry got well to work by two o'clock, and from that time the action was very severe. We were in reserve, but Stuart, with his usual enterprise, was riding everywhere, looking for chances to put in his cavalry, and with Pelham's guns he did some good service on the flanks of the enemy. He and his staff were much exposed to artillery fire but none of us was hit. Seeing some Alabama troops going into action, I found that the 5th Alabama was there and rode along the line to find my brother Eugene, who at that time commanded a company in that regiment. We were delighted to see each other and I rode with him until they got under fire and then bowed myself out. An infantry line in action is not a wholesome place for visitors, by any manner of means. As I galloped back to the General, when very near him I saw a thing that I never saw before nor have ever seen since; it was a clear view of a fragment of shell in the air just after the shell exploded. It burst close to my ear, coming from my right and almost deafening me. Turning my head in the direction the fragment flew, I saw distinctly for a considerable distance a fragment in its flight. General Stuart happened to be looking towards me at the time, and as I rode up to him he asked if I was hit, and said he was glad to hear I was not, for he was sure I had been.

While we were all sitting on our horses in a conspicuous part of the field, a battery noticed us by a round. One of the shots passed screaming a few inches over our heads. We were not so well accustomed to artillery then as we became afterwards, and most of us involuntarily ducked our heads. Capt. John Esten Cooke, while so doing, bowed a little too low, lost his balance, and fell sprawling on the ground. We were all a good deal shocked, for we did not doubt for a moment that his head had been carried off. Stuart leaned down from his saddle and in a most sympathizing voice said, "Hallo, Cooke! Are you hit?" But Cooke jumped up looking very sheepish as he dusted himself and said, "Oh, no, General; I only dodged a little too far." The reaction of feeling from the uneasiness we had felt for him, and his ludicrous appearance as he scrambled back into his saddle, still covered with dust, was perfectly irresistible, and we laughed until we could scarcely keep our seats in our saddles. For months after, almost every time Cooke appeared at the breakfast table, the General would call to him, "Hello, Cooke! Are you hit?" or "No, General; I only dodged too far." He loved a joke, and would ring the changes on one until a better one turned up.

The battle closed with complete victory on our side and the enemy was again in full retreat, with the cavalry hanging on its rear and capturing great numbers of prisoners. We encamped on the battlefield, surrounded on all sides by the dead and wounded, but they were mostly those of the enemy at that spot. The fact that the sufferers are of the enemy makes a great difference in the horrors of a battlefield. There is, of course, something soothing in seeing a good harvest by the dread reaper when they are not of our own side. Still, to hear even enemies groaning and praying all around you all night is not agreeable. From the result of the action of the 27th it was apparent that McClellan's army was beaten and that retreat was his only recourse. General Jackson came to see General Stuart where we were bivouacked that night, and it was determined that the next morning Stuart was to march upon the "White House" on the Pamunkey River, where McClellan had his headquarters, and if possible to capture the place.

Bright and early on the morning of the 28th of June the cavalry was on the march to the "White House," fifteen or sixteen miles distant. We encountered several scouting parties of the enemy but brushed them aside without much delay and reached the "White House" that evening, finding the place strongly guarded by infantry, with gunboats in the river. Not being able to take it, the next best thing was to make them destroy the vast depot of supplies at the place; and to this end Stuart dismounted some of his men and marched them about in sight of their lines to make them think we had infantry, and then he made Pelham fire quantities of ammunition at long range into the place, changing the position of the guns from time to time to make them think we had a great number. The ruse succeeded and soon after nightfall great columns of smoke and a bright illumination announced that they were setting fire to the great town of canvas and board houses that had sprung up at the place since its occupation by the Northern army. The enemy had evidently "thrown up the sponge" and was destroying his vast accumulation of munitions of war to prevent them from falling into our hands. This information General Stuart sent at once to General Jackson.

All night long the conflagration continued and the country for miles around was as light as day, while vast clouds of smoke rose hundreds of feet in air, and explosions of shells and other ammunition were of frequent occurrence, sounding sometimes like a battle. The next morning only one gunboat remained, and this, after exchanging a few shots, steamed away.

Escorted only by Col. W. H. F. Lee's regiment, General Stuart and staff went in to take possession. The destruction had been great, but yet vast quantities of things remained which had either been overlooked in the hurry of the evacuation or had failed to burn. It was a curious thing to see the evidences of the luxury in which the Federal army indulged at that period of the war. Their sutler's shops were on the most elaborate scale — quantities of barrels of sugar, lemons by the millions, cases of wine, beer and other liquors of every description, confectionery, canned meats, and fruits and vegetables, and great quantities of ice, all still in excellent condition. The eggs were packed in barrels of salt, and where they had been exposed to fire, the salt was fused into a solid cake with the eggs, deliciously roasted, distributed throughout the mass; it was only necessary to split off a block and then pick out the eggs, like the meat of a nut.

There was a place where embalming was done and several bodies were under treatment, presenting a ghastly spectacle. These were no doubt officers killed in recent engagements, but there was no record of who they were. Before he was aware there was liquor within reach, some of Colonel Lee's men began to get drunk and many of them had bottles stowed away in their clothes; so Colonel Lee caused a report to be started that the enemy had poisoned all the liquor, leaving it there for us as a trap, and that one man had just died in great agony from the effects. As the report extended along the column, bottles of champagne and beer and whiskey went sailing through the air, exploding as they fell like little bomb-shells; while the expression of agony on the tipsy faces of those who had indulged too freely, as they held their hands to their stomachs, was ludicrous in the extreme.

For several days since the fighting began, we had been living on salt meat and crackers and were well prepared to appreciate the luxuries before us as we spread the delicacies we had collected for a lunch out upon the grass under the trees near the river. Great buckets of iced lemonade to begin with to quench our thirst, for the day was intensely hot; pickled oysters, eggs roasted in blocks of salt, canned beef and ham, French rolls, cakes and confectionery of all sorts, and last but not least, boxes of delicious Havana cigars, and coffee. No one but a soldier can appreciate the pleasures of such a repast. If they had such a dinner as this every day, it was no wonder that McClellan's men had rather run away than get killed. It does seem to be a fact that the better troops are fed and clothed, after their necessary wants are supplied, the worse they fight. When they have a hard time of it, it seems as if they had just as soon die as live, provided they can have the pleasure of sending plenty of the enemy across the dark valley before them.

When the news of their reverses first reached the North, an attempt was made to conceal the truth and prepare the public mind by publishing that from motives of profound strategy McClellan contemplated "a change of base" from the York to the James River. After this conflagration, when these newspapers reached us, and knowing as we did the cause which produced the change of base, the idea of its having been done voluntarily was greeted in our army with shouts of derision. "Changing his base" became a catchword among our fun-loving troops, to signify discomfiture or defeat: If two dogs fought and one ran, the men cheered and shouted, "Look at him changing his base"; if a man fell in the mud, his comrades would laugh and ask him what he was changing his base for; or if the rain flooded the place where they were sleeping they would say, "Come, fellows, let's change our base."

We captured at the "White House" a pontoon train, which was afterwards of great value to us, and numbers of new cars and locomotives that had been brought from the North to run on the railroad between the "White House" and Richmond. Being so accessible to their gunboats and not knowing but that the enemy might attempt to come for what had been left behind, General Stuart was in doubt whether to destroy the locomotives and cars or not. I knew that such things would be valuable to us; so at my suggestion he gave me orders to damage them to such an extent as to make it necessary to send them to a shop, and at the same time not to injure the costly parts. On reflection I concluded the best thing to do would be to put a cannon ball through their boilers, across through the middle. This would break some tubes and puncture the sides, and though rendering the machine absolutely useless for a time, the cost of repair would be moderate. A rifled gun was ordered up and at a distance of fifty yards a shot through the boiler of each locomotive placed it effectually "hors de combat."

During the 30th the work of placing the capture property in safety and guarding it from recapture continued without the occurrence of any event of importance.

Leaving a regiment at the "White House," General Stuart moved back towards the Chickahominy with the remainder of the cavalry and camped at Forge Bridge that night.

The next morning we received orders to move eight miles higher up the Chickahominy and to cross over and attack the enemy in flank, but on reaching the crossing place the orders were countermanded and we returned, the enemy having passed the place on his retreat. On reaching the Forge Mills we found the enemy in occupation of the opposite bank, and we attacked and drove him off, crossing and pursuing him some miles. The rapid marches and the combat, combined with the intense heat, now made it absolutely necessary to rest the horses of the command and we halted for this purpose. Wishing to keep General Jackson informed of his movements, General Stuart now sent me with a small escort of picked men and a guide, for the country was full of scouting parties of the enemy, to inform him of his whereabouts. He told me to feel my way carefully and to strike for a place called Malvern, on James River, in the vicinity of which I would probably be able to hear where General Jackson was. I was also furnished with guides who knew the country thoroughly. It was some ten miles distant, the weather fearfully hot, and in those low stretches of level wood not a breath of air stirred the dismal pine forests. I had, besides, been in the saddle since daylight and it was then four o'clock in the afternoon.

I had not gone far before I heard the boom of artillery in front of me, but this had been of such frequent occurrence for the last seven days that it attracted little attention. As I advanced, the sound increased and in course of time the rattle of musketry became a continuous roar and it was evident that a first-class battle was in progress. The battle of Malvern Hill it was, the last and, to us, the most bloody of the famous seven days' series.

It was dark before I reached the battlefield, though the hoarse roar of artillery and the angry growl of the musketry still broke at lengthening intervals the stillness of the night. My approach lay through a forest, and the horrors of the rear during an action were, if possible, increased by the glare of the torches and lanterns around the amputating tables of the surgeons on either side of the road. Illuminated in this way, the forest looked like a vast hall into whose corridors poured lines of ambulances and stretchers borne on the shoulders of men, all loaded with mutilated humanity, while limping along in great numbers came those whose wounds were less serious. It was a repetition on a far greater scale of that scene, previously described, at the First Battle of Manassas.

To find General Jackson in the darkness and confusion was no easy matter and it was some time before I succeeded, for he was moving about in every direction over the field. Meeting a wounded soldier hobbling along, I asked him if he knew where I would find him; leaning upon his gun and looking up at me with a twinkle in his eye he said, "Yes, I know." Vexed at getting so indirect an answer, I answered sharply, "Well, where is he?" He replied, "Do you hear that 'ar firing?" "Yes," said I, "of course I hear it." "Well," said the fellow with a chuckle, "that's just where you will always find old Jack." "Old Jack" was the name his men delighted to call him, and the admiration and affection they bore their great commander was boundless. Jackson's utter disregard of danger was one great attraction with the troops. No matter how hot the fire, Jackson was always at the front. He and Stuart were the only two men I ever knew whom I thought unconscious of the feeling of fear. There were many as brave, but these two never seemed to feel that danger existed. The men cheered Jackson whenever he passed near them, either on the march or in camp, and one of his many peculiarities was that he always started to gallop by as quickly as possible, though recognizing the compliment by lifting his hat. This modesty made them cheer him the more. When a rabbit jumped up and the men gave chase, great cheering would arise, and we used to say when we heard cheering that it was either Jackson or a rabbit.

I found General Jackson giving final orders for the night and gave him General Stuart's message that he would be with him during the night, also a brief outline of what had been done at the "White House." "That's good! That's good!" said he. "Changing his base, is he? Ha, ha. Now, Captain," said he, "I shall be through here in a few moments and then you must stay with me tonight," an invitation I accepted most gladly, for I was much fatigued by sixteen hours in the saddle in the fearful heat. He seemed in good spirits and asked me many questions about the affair at the "White House" as we rode together to his headquarters. He had attacked the rear of their army in its retreat in a strong position that evening where their gunboats were close at hand in case of disaster, and they had made an obstinate defense. They had concentrated a large number of guns in one place and our loss had been very severe.

The next morning before daylight General Jackson was out again and I offered my services to serve on his staff until I could join General Stuart. There was a heavy fog, and a drizzling rain falling, which made the scenes on the battlefield, if possible, more ghastly.

Large details of men were put to work collecting and placing our dead in rows at convenient spots and covering them with blankets and oilcloths, and Jackson gave the operation a degree of personal attention which surprised me. I have never seen a battlefield where there was such frightful mutilation of bodies as there was at Malvern Hill, owing ta so much artillery having been used by the enemy. Many were cut entirely in two. Some were headless, while fragments of bodies and limbs were strewn about in every direction.

There was another peculiarity about this field which I have never seen to so great an extent elsewhere, that greatly added to its horrors. It is a fact well-known among medical men, as I have since learned, that under certain circumstances the condition of the system is such that when death comes suddenly from a wound the muscles become, instantly, perfectly rigid and so remain. Owing probably to the extreme fatigue and excitement Jackson's troops had been through previous to this battle, many of the bodies presented instances of this phenomenon, their bodies and faces remaining exactly, in every muscle, as they were at the instant death struck them.

One man lay on his back with his legs raised in the air, one hand clutching a handful of grass on the ground, the other holding aloft at arm's length, right over his head, a bunch of turf torn up by the roots, at which he was glaring with his eyes wide open. The lips were drawn back, exposing the clenched teeth, and the whole expression and attitude was so lifelike that I could scarcely bring myself to believe by close inspection that the man was really dead. Another was sitting with his back to a tree, his arms resting on his knees, and his chin on his breast in a perfectly natural attitude, but a cannonball had passed through the tree and taken off the top of the head to the roots of the hair. Quite a number held their muskets with one or both hands, and one poor fellow died in the act of loading, one hand grasping the gun, the other the ramrod, but the body had fallen to the ground.

It took several hours to collect all our slain, and I was more and more surprised that General Jackson should give so much of his personal attention to such a matter at such a time. He had the bodies laid side by side in rows, numbering from a dozen to forty or fifty, according to convenience to the places they occupied, and he then had their blankets and oilcloths spread over the rows, concealing their faces and figures completely. After this was done he had their muskets and accoutrements collected and laid in piles in gullies so as to be out of sight; then, not satisfied with this, he made the men pick up every scrap of clothing and caps, and every piece of human flesh scattered around, such as legs and arms, etc., etc.

I had heard that "Old Stonewall" was eccentric, and indeed at that time some who disliked him said he was unsound in his mind; and I thought this, to me absurd, attention to cleaning up the battlefield was an evidence of it. Still he evidently had a motive and to him an urgent one. There was nothing idle or objectless in the way he acted, but on the contrary the intense vigor and sharpness of his commands, as he trotted incessantly about in every direction among the working parties, so hurried them that the men omitted even to rifle the pockets of the slain, venting their feelings at this loss of opportunity in suppressed curses, "not loud but deep," when their General's back was turned.

My curiosity was aroused, and I determined to watch an opportunity and ask him his reasons. Stonewall Jackson was very pleasant and agreeable when he chose to be so and when his mind was at ease, but he was not the man to talk to when he was busy, by any manner of means. I exerted myself to the utmost in assisting him, for which he thanked me very graciously, and after a while even he could find nothing more to pick up, and the field certainly did look very differently; the dark bloodstains, soaking the ground, alone marked the numbers who had fallen. The number of the dead now appeared very much less. There did not appear to be one in ten since they were collected together. Jackson had swept his dust into piles, like a good housewife, and the floor looked clean though the piles were still there.

When at last he became quiet and disposed to talk, I asked him why he was having the field cleaned in that way. "Why," said he, "I am going to attack here presently, as soon as the fog rises, and it won't do to march the troops over their own dead, you know; that's what I am doing it for." Then, I thought to myself, if you are crazy there is surely "method in your madness," for it would have been a most demoralizing preparation for battle for men to have marched over the field as I first saw it that morning.

After sitting on our horses, talking a while, General Jackson became restless and would ride off suddenly and wander about in different directions in an abstracted manner, and I noticed that the fog was clearing away a little. I have since thought that he was then engaged in prayer, preparatory to opening the battle. General Stuart now joined us and Jackson told him what he contemplated doing. The fog having become much thinner, General Stuart told me to ride out and see what was in our front, which meant, in the then condition of the atmosphere, in all probability, to ride until I drew fire at close range, for objects could be seen distinctly only at a distance of forty or fifty yards.

On nearing the crest of the hill I observed figures moving but could not make them out, as a glass was of no use in the fog. It was, of course, necessary to be absolutely certain, and the only resource was to put Comet to a gallop and approach by zigzags so they would have to take a cross shot if it was the enemy. On getting quite near, they proved to be some of our men who had wandered out on a private scout of their own.

The position had been evacuated during the night and I galloped back to report the fact. General Stuart then told me to take an escort and push on after them and report their position as soon as possible. Taking about a dozen picked men, all well mounted, I pushed on down the road which seemed most travelled. I had already found that for obtaining information a small party is the best for many reasons, and ultimately I never took but three unless it was necessary to send back reports before I returned, and then I took only as many more as would be required for this purpose. With three, besides myself, I would ride as near as possible to the enemy without attracting attention, and if the view could not then be commanded I would dismount and take two dismounted men with me, leaving the other man to hold all the horses. We would then advance, availing ourselves of all cover and inequalities of the ground, until a good view of the enemy could be had from some commanding point. While I examined them with my glasses, the men watched to see that we were not flanked and to call my attention to anything they saw in front. The men delighted in this sort of service and I soon selected such as suited best and had them always detailed to go with me, for I had a great deal of this sort of duty to do and it was necessary to have men on whose judgment and courage I could rely. A reconnaissance in force was, of course, another thing, for then we drove in the pickets to see what they had, but on many occasions I saved the necessity for the loss of life by my examination. It was exciting work and we had many thrilling adventures and hairbreadth escapes. I was always mounted on horses that I knew no fence or ditch could turn, and no horse in their army could match in speed, so unless they could hit on the wing, I was safe enough.

After going a few miles, we began to overtake stragglers, from whom we learned that their main body moved off early in the night. We captured nearly a hundred. I had neither men nor time to spare for securing them, but I adopted the plan followed with the little chaplain I captured at Manassas. I disarmed them, throwing their arms away, and ordered them to double-quick to the rear, telling them if they halted or looked back they should instantly be shot, and then I proceeded on my way with my little party.

The road led to Westover and Harrison's Landing, some five or six miles below, where the "Young Napoleon" had established his "new base." When I reached the edge of the high ground surrounding the valley, in which the two plantations of West-over and Berkely are situated, a magnificent panorama of the encampment of what was left of "the finest army the world ever saw" burst upon my view. Stationing videttes around to give me timely warning of any approach of the enemy from the rear, I divested myself of my coat and boots, and with the assistance of pushes from long poles from my men, and with my field glasses and sketch-book slung to my neck, I climbed to the top of a tall tree growing on the edge of the basin.

The valley was formed between the highlands and the river and was two or three miles long and a mile or two wide. Their whole army had marched in and encamped, and that was all — not a sentinel nor an outpost had they put out. I could have ridden right on into their camp without being halted, and would have done so if there had been any information to get beyond what I could get from the tree. With my glasses I could see everything except the portion immediately on the river, which was too low to be seen from where I was. I could see the chimneys and in some cases the upper decks of the gunboats and steam transports on the river, of which there were a great number. The nearest part of their camp was not over three hundred yards distant and I could hear their voices distinctly. I sketched a map of the position and then came down and wrote a report, sending them off at once to General Stuart.

General Stuart came down with the cavalry, and Longstreet lost his way as he was coming and nothing of consequence was done. Stuart shelled them a while with the horse artillery and opened on them with a Congreve rocket battery, the first and the last time the latter ever appeared in action with us. It had been gotten up by some foreign chap who managed it on this occasion. They were huge rockets, fired from a sort of gun carriage, with a shell at the end which exploded in due time, scattering "liquid damnation," as the men called it. Their course was erratic; they went straight enough in their first flight, but, after striking, the flight might be continued in any other course, even directly back towards where it came from. Great consternation was occasioned among the camps of the enemy as these unearthly serpents went zigzagging about among them, and the demoralization among "Young Napoleon's" mules was complete when the bursting of the rocket sprinkled the "liquid damnation" on their backs. A few tents were fired but the rockets proved to be of little practical value as an agent of destruction; shells were far better.

The country below Richmond was stripped of forage and the cavalry was ordered up to the country around Hanover Courthouse for much-needed rest. I was much gratified one day soon after by General Stuart's showing me his report of the seven days' battles, in which he mentioned my name as follows: "Capt. Wm. W. Blackford of the Engineers, assigned to duty with me the day before the battles, was always in advance, obtaining valuable information of the enemy's strength, movements and position, locating routes and making hurried but accurate topographical sketches. Pie is bold in reconnaissance, fearless in danger, and remarkably cool and correct in judgment. His services are invaluable to the advance guard of the army."

I had purchased from Mr. B. K. Buchanan, some time before this, a young blooded mare to be delivered to me as soon as she was delivered of a most disreputable baby in the shape of a mule colt. When the Salt Works property passed into the hands of its Yankee owners, there were a number of young blooded colts which Mr. Preston had reared, and not appreciating their value all the mares were bred to a Jack, and among them the superb animal of which I became the owner. I found that two horses were not enough to stand the riding I now had on Stuart's staff and I sent for "Magic," who was at last in a condition to come.

Magic was a first cousin of Comet, a dark chestnut without a white hair, sixteen hands high and four years old. She had been ridden very little, and like Comet never had a collar on her neck, and was scarcely bridle wise. Coming fresh from her mountain pastures, she was as wild as a deer upon the mountains from which she came. Unlike Comet she was of an extremely nervous temperament, requiring much attention to make her eat if the least thing was going on that excited her. If there was firing or cheering or marching of troops when she was being fed, no matter how hungry she might be she would toss her head, cock her ears and listen for a moment before she would chew up and swallow what she had in her mouth; then, after taking up another mouthful, she would do the same thing again. If artillery was firing anywhere near and she was picketed or in a stable, she would prance, and paw, and rear, and kick by the hour unless I went to pet and soothe her, but then she would become perfectly quiet. In all my experience in horse flesh I have never seen her match for quickness and fiery spirit. Sometimes when she would be in one of her gales I would, in using my toothpick, make a cluck which she chose to construe as intended for her, and several times she bounded forward so suddenly as to very nearly unhorse me. For a long time on marches she would prance and fret for hours until it required a strong exercise of patience to keep me from blowing her brains out. Her fretfulness lessened as she became older and more used to army life, but her spirit never flagged; no amount of hardship or fatigue could subdue it. The only way to do anything with her was by gentleness. If I spurred her for fretting she would keep it up frantically the rest of the day. She was as fleet as the wind and as active and quick as a cat, and no fence or ditch could stop her with my weight on her back.

It was this wild, skittish, devilish thing which arrived the day after Malvern Hill, and I had now to introduce her to military life as her chaperone. Everything was new to her and infinite pains and patience were requisite to reason her out of her fancies. The first thing I did after getting settled in camp, while still near Malvern, was to try Magic. She had been resting several days and Gilbert led her out looking sleek and fine but with the devil in her eye.

General Stuart and staff assembled to see the start. Out she came, trotting round and round Gilbert, tossing her head and snorting at almost everything. After much coaxing I got her to allow me to come alongside, then to put my foot in the stirrup and hand on her mane, and that was all I needed her consent for. As I lit in the saddle she reared and bolted off and I gave her half a mile or so of a full run and then pulled her gently but firmly down to a moderate gait.

For miles in every direction the country was strewn with carcasses of men and horses, and her terror at sight of them was great. She would come to a halt a long way off, snort and try to wheel, but I kept her head to the object and tried to reason the matter with her by soothing with voice and hand. Putting her nose to the ground she would take a long snuff and then go a little nearer and repeat the process, and so on; after perhaps an hour the first time, she would come up close to it. Each time the fear was less, until finally the unsightly objects scarcely attracted her attention. It is curious how allowing horses to put their noses to the ground satisfies their fears; ignorant horsemen pull the head up and thus check the course nature intended for them — that of smelling the ground and listening with the nose pressed against the soil.

We were now to enjoy six weeks of the bright side of the soldier's life. As in art high lights are produced by contrast with dark shadows, so must our greatest pleasures be developed by hardship and trouble. After remaining below Richmond for a couple of weeks to offer McClellan battle, should he again advance from that direction, we ascertained that he was embarking his army, and greatly to our satisfaction we were ordered to move up above Richmond to recruit and rest in the fresh country near Hanover Courthouse. On the 12th of July cavalry headquarters were established at Mr. Timberlake's near Atlee's Station, and soon after, we had our first brigade review attended by all the ladies in the country round, and we of the staff had the agreeable duty of seeing their carriages well placed and of entertaining them during the intervals of duty. Mrs. Stuart was present and enjoyed the event very much. She must no doubt have felt proud of her gallant husband, who, in one year, had risen from the rank of Lieutenant in the old army to that of Brigadier, commanding all the cavalry of Lee's army.

While at this camp, a young English nobleman, Lord Edward St. Maur,[4] became our guest for a day on his way northward after a visit to the Confederacy. He seemed about twenty years of age and was a gawky youth.

On the 21st of July we moved headquarters to Hanover Courthouse and occupied the courthouse yards for that purpose. Around the village were encamped the cavalry and horse artillery, eight thousand strong. Two days after our arrival the enemy made an advance from Fredericksburg, and General Stuart, with a detachment of two thousand cavalry, went out to meet him; but he withdrew and we returned after going to within ten miles of the town.

On the 29th there was another brigade drill, which came off with good success and was a fine sight. General Stuart had, a day or two before, been promoted Major General, and there were now considerable additions to the cavalry command from North and South Carolina, and an organization into three brigades was made, commanded by Brigadier Generals Hampton, Fitz Lee and Robertson.

Some promotions on the staff followed and General Stuart tried his best to have me advanced a grade, but the authorities would not give high rank in the Engineers at that time. There were a lot of bureau officers who had never seen active service who would, of course, not agree for an officer in the field to be promoted before they were. But a very great addition to my comfort and convenience followed, even though no increase of rank resulted. As Chief Engineer Officer on the Major General's staff, it became necessary for me to have an equipment for making maps, and receptacles for preserving them, and this required transportation. I had therefore a wagon and driver and a pair of powerful horses assigned to my exclusive use, and the comfort this gave me was inexpressible. My outfit now consisted of two servants and five horses. Gilbert was my body' servant and on marches took charge of my two spare saddle horses — Comet, Magic and Manassas were my mounts — riding one and leading the other. In camp the wagon driver became the groom of the five horses, so far as the hard work at the curry comb was concerned, while Gilbert was responsible for the important duty of feeding. Having the wagon to keep forage in when found on the road, and two excellent foragers in my interests, Gilbert and Albert, it was a cold day when my stable was entirely empty of food for my mounts.

With the duties I had to perform in action it was absolutely necessary for me to be well mounted and for my horses to be in good condition, and knowing that my life or liberty might be the forfeit, I took care that they should be so always. Gilbert was a capital servant and remained with me till the close of the war. He was a son of "Aunt Charlotte," my wife's "Mammy." He was with me in both campaigns north of the Potomac, and several times risked his life in escaping from scouting parties of the enemy while he was out foraging for our mess, when his capture would have given him his freedom. I remember, when we first

---

4   Son of the Duke of Somerset. — Wm. W. B.

crossed the Potomac in the Maryland campaign, I told him one day that if I was killed over there I wanted him to see that my body was brought back to Virginia, and he burst into tears as he promised me he would.

General Stuart had a warm heart, and though a member of the church and a consistent, conscientious Christian, he was fond of gay company and of ladies' society and of music and dancing. Superficial observers sometimes made the mistake of considering him frivolous, but this was not so. Stuart was closely attentive to his business and a hard worker. I have often seen him busy arranging for some of his most brilliant cavalry movements, and after all was prepared, come out of his tent, call for Sweeny and the banjo and perhaps for some of the men to dance for him, and then, to our amazement, order everybody to mount and be off after the troops who were already on the march. He could keep a secret absolutely; the gayer he was the more likely it was we were to move soon. But it was in action Stuart showed to the greatest advantage. I have never seen his superior on a battlefield.

His relations with his staff were like those of a brother. Quick and warmhearted in his feelings, he was liable to form sudden fancies for those who courted his good will, and in this way he put on his staff sometimes men who were not at all suitable; but though influenced by feeling, no one was quicker than General Stuart in detecting inefficiency, or want of courage and coolness in danger, or any departure from the course of a thorough gentleman, and no one was quicker in getting rid of the man who did not meet the requirements of his standard. It was the enmity he incurred in this way that originated the ridiculous stories of frivolity which found some listeners in those days. But the main body of his staff was composed of as fine a set of fellows as ever drew a sword. Fie liked his staff to present a handsome, soldierly appearance, and he liked a handsome man as much almost as he did a handsome woman. The members of his staff, the ladies all said, were remarkable for their personal appearance, and with perhaps one or two exceptions this was the case.

There was Pelham, who commanded the horse artillery but who always lived at headquarters as a staff officer, as the General would not agree for him to do otherwise, for he loved him dearly. Only twenty-one or two years old and so innocent looking, so "child-like and bland" in the expression of his sparking blue eyes, but as grand a flirt as ever lived. Three girls put on mourning for him when he was killed. He was tall, slender, beautifully proportioned and very graceful, a superb rider, and as brave as Julius Caesar.

Maj. Norman Fitzhugh was a fine fellow who had seen many years of life among the Indians and told many interesting stories about them. He was taken prisoner.

Von Borcke was a very fine-looking man and of polished manners. Like most soldiers of fortune he was selfish, but kept it concealed under the soldier's frankness of manner pretty effectually. He was a charming companion, however, and was very popular in the army. In his book he makes out a great deal more to his own credit than belonged to him. In repeated cases throughout the book, he coolly speaks of having done things which I did myself and which, though present, he had nothing to do with. Judging by my case he may have appropriated the acts of other members of the staff also. Still, I was very fond of Von Borcke, and saved him from falling into the hands of the enemy when he was shot and disabled permanently.

Captain Farley was a modest, retiring young fellow in disposition and very handsome, and gallant in action. He was killed at Fleetwood by the same shell that took off Colonel (afterwards General) M. C. Butler's leg.

Hardiman Stuart, the General's cousin, was Captain of our Signal Corps and was killed at the second battle of Manassas.

Capt. Redmond Burke was a rough man but one of extraordinary courage and enterprise in action. He was killed while out on a scout.

Maj. Channing Price, who was killed at Chancellorsville, was the best Adjutant General I ever saw, and a charming fellow. His loss was deeply regretted by all of us.

Dr. John Fontaine, our medical director, killed late in the war, was a splendid fellow. Though in the medical department, he was always ready to serve on the field on staff duty, and was very efficient as such.

Capt. John Esten Cooke was ordnance officer; Dr. Talcott Eliason, medical director before Fontaine; Lieut. F. S. Robertson and T. R. Price, assistant Engineer officers, and both very handsome men; Captain Frazier, signal officer; Lieut. Col. St. Leger Grenfell, with us only a short time. Major Terrell was with us a short time and so were the two Major Hairstons, relatives of General Stuart. Maj. Dabney Ball was also with us a while and afterwards became chaplain. He was a very brave man, and though a minister by profession could use his revolver in action with coolness and effect. At the 1st Manassas I saw him sit on his horse ten paces from the line of the New York Zouaves and empty every barrel of his pistol as deliberately as if he was practicing at a target. We all liked and respected him very much.

Lieutenant Goldsborough, aide-de-camp, was taken prisoner at Fleetwood a week or two after he joined the staff, was in prison two years, and was killed in the first action he went into on his return. He was a splendid looking fellow and proved himself to be full of dash the short time he was with us. Lieut. Chiswell Dabney was the Adonis of the staff; he was very young, scarcely of age, I believe, and was remarkably handsome.

Maj. Andrew Venable was a capital officer, bluff in manner but warmhearted and brave. He was captured, but made his escape by jumping from the train as it was entering Philadelphia.

Maj. H. B. McClellan, our last Adjutant General of the Cavalry Corps, was a fine looking man and a capital officer, and a polished and highly educated gentleman.

Maj. Marshall Hanger was our Quartermaster after Fitzhugh was captured. Col. L. T. Brien was on the staff early in the war but was promoted into a regiment in the line. Lieutenant Hullihen, aide-de-camp, was noted for his courage; though very young, I never saw a braver fellow. Captain White, another very gallant man, was wounded at Fleetwood. It was a sad feeling to feel the loss of so many dear comrades and friends. Capt. Theodore Garnett, aide-de-camp, was a remarkably fine officer and as faithful and brave as could be; he helped to get General Stuart off the field when he fell.

Col. J. S. Mosby was on the staff a short time before he began his brilliant career as a partisan leader. He entered the service as a private in my company from Washington County.

As the cavalry lines often extended over a front of thirty or forty miles, and sometimes even more, it was necessary to keep at headquarters a picked body of thirty or forty men, selected for their reliability and from among the best mounted troopers, to act as bearers of dispatches; these men were called couriers. With the couriers and all the departments connected with the Cavalry Corps headquarters, our encampment was a large one, numbering over one hundred persons and about two hundred animals. We had a large fly, under which our mess table was, and there General Stuart and his military family met in many a pleasant reunion. There was scarcely a day when we were without guests when in camp. Almost all visitors to the army felt their visit incomplete without seeing the headquarters of the Cavalry Corps and its famous chief. General Stuart was very hospitable and always invited parties of distinguished strangers, who came to the army, to spend some of their time with him on the outposts. In this way we had as guests at different times several Englishmen of distinction — Lords, Members of Parliament, and officers of their army — whose society we enjoyed very much. During the day we were either out with the General on some military duty or engaged in any official business that might be on hand, or reading in our tents. After supper the General liked us to assemble around his fire, and then conversation, story-telling, music, singing and what not whiled away the hours until bedtime, unless we all went with him visiting somewhere in the neighborhood, which was often the case.

General Stuart always dressed well and was well mounted, and he liked his staff to do the same. In our gray uniforms, cocked felt hats, long black plumes, top boots and polished accoutrements, mounted on superb horses, the General and his staff certainly presented a dashing appearance.

Having now given a sketch of our military home and its members, I will proceed with the story of our life.

The next few days after our return from the fruitless expedition towards Fredericksburg were passed in charming social intercourse with the refined and hospitable families of the neighborhood, particularly with the family of Dr. Price at their place, "Dundee," a few miles away. His two lovely daughters were then unmarried and their house was the rendezvous of numbers of the officers of the cavalry. We had a splendid review, or rather drill, of the cavalry division, at which all the ladies for many miles around assembled in their carriages or on horseback under the escort of their military friends. We of the staff shone resplendent.

On the 4th of August, General Stuart took a strong detachment on a scout towards Fredericksburg, via Port Royal. I took General Stuart in to introduce him to my wife's cousins, the Bernards, at "Gay Mont." Three of the ladies were at home in sole possession, Mrs. Guest, Mrs. Scott, and Miss Helen, who afterwards married Phil. Robb. It was a lovely old place, all embowered in trees, shrubbery and flowers. The house was a large, rambling structure, built at different times, and furnished with the elegance which the refined taste and ample means of the family supplied. When they saw the Confederate gray of Stuart and staff the trembling ladies were surprised and delighted beyond measure, for it appeared that a party of the enemy had just left the house and the ladies mistook the tramp of our horses for theirs. They told us that a party of fifteen or twenty had just been there and had gone all through the house, but in the main had behaved well, that they had carried off nothing of consequence and had only made them prepare a meal for their refreshment. They had, however, robbed the old carriage driver, Cye, of his watch.

General Stuart told me to take a party and catch them, as they could not have gone far, and I could get back in time for dinner, to which we had been invited by the ladies. I took one of the ladies aside and asked her privately if these men had in any way treated them with disrespect, but they assured me they had not. Pushing on towards Fredericksburg with a party of twenty men at a rapid trot, keeping a vidette well in front so as to make sure of not getting in their view until quite near, we got sight of them in a couple of miles. I then waited until they turned a bend in the road and went after them at full gallop, getting within a hundred yards before they saw us, and we captured the whole party.

I then asked them if they saw all those slender pine saplings standing around us, for we were in a pine wood. "Well," said I, "those ladies back yonder tell me you men treated them with respect when you were there; if you had done otherwise, I would now have bent those saplings over and have hung every one of you to them by our halter straps. Now, one of you stole a watch from an old negro back there; hand it to me." There was a pause of evident surprise on the part of most of them and then one fellow came forward, looking sheepish, and handed me a huge old silver timepiece of the last generation. Leaving the prisoners to follow, I then galloped back to Gay Mont, and delighted old Cye beyond measure by handing back his lost and valued watch. After a charming dinner we resumed our hot and dusty march towards Fredericksburg, encamping for the night at Round Oak Church, twelve miles distant from the town.

Our scouts informed us that an expedition under Generals Hatch and Gibbon was starting out of Fredericksburg, and Stuart determined to attack them by cutting in on their flank near Massaponax Church. Their object was to destroy the Central Railroad. Their main body had passed, and their wagon-train was still behind. When we struck the Fredericksburg road, Stuart instantly charged down the road after them with the main body, holding some in reserve, the horse artillery under Pelham charging through the fields on either side, and one regiment was sent in the opposite direction to capture the train. They were thrown into the wildest confusion by this wholly unexpected attack so near their starting place. It was like giving a snake a tap on his tail when he was gliding unconsciously along through the grass, making him throw himself into a coil and offer battle, and there remain in a coil as long as danger threatens. It was no part of Stuart's plan to give them serious battle, for they outnumbered us five to one; so after engaging them long enough to secure the captured wagons and about two hundred prisoners, we withdrew towards the Bowling Green and they gave up the expedition and returned to Fredericksburg. The enemy used on this occasion exploding musket balls which made a crack like a pistol when they struck a tree, and must have been very uncomfortable things to be hit with. I believe this was the first and the last time I ever saw them used during the war.

The next day we returned to headquarters and I found, to my delight, that my dear wife, whom I was expecting the very day we started, had arrived during my absence and was a guest at Dr. Price's, at which place Mrs. Stuart was also staying. The next ten days was a period of absolute rest and enjoyment. After spending a few hours in the middle of the day at headquarters, I would ride over to Dr. Price's hospitable mansion to enjoy the rest of my time in my wife's society and that of their charming family. But events were in progress that were soon to put an end to our enjoyment.

McClellan's failure to take Richmond had encouraged his rivals in Washington to try to supersede him. McClellan was a specimen of a *manufactured* soldier, labelled with the best brand of the West Point factory, like so many that both the Northern and Southern armies were encumbered with. But he lacked what nature alone can give: the nerve, the moral courage, decision — call it what you will — which, when the supreme moment in the life of the soldier comes, when the die is to be cast, when the dogs of war are to be loosed, when the troops are to be launched into the great trial of battle, will enable him to. take the final step and leave the rest to the arbitrament of the sword. McClellan had been so puffed by the Northern press, had been so often called the "Young Napoleon," and his army had been so lauded, that we were surprised at the ease with which he had been overthrown.

General Pope had been put forward by the party opposed to McClellan, in the hope that he could secure sufficient success to warrant the supersedure of McClellan. By some successes in the West and by loud boasting, Pope had impressed the authorities in Washington with the belief that he was worthy of the high command which his inordinate vanity prompted him to seek. By a series of undignified and ridiculous orders dated "Headquarters in the saddle," etc., he had provoked much ridicule in our army, and we looked forward with keen delight to see this inflated gas bag punctured by the keen rapier of our great commander, and that such an event would follow we never doubted a moment. Pope had been concentrating a large force around Culpeper Courthouse and had made himself a terror to the women and children, left in the country through which he had passed, by brutal and stringent regulations about citizens.

So much had been said about changing base that Pope announced that "in future his army was to have no base," that "the rear was to take care of itself," and that "in the West he had been in the habit of seeing only the backs of the foe." But it took only two weeks for General Lee to send this braggart into a retirement from which he appeared not again during the war.

Jackson was sent to check his advance until General Lee could move to his support. The day after our return, General Stuart was summoned by a telegram to meet Jackson at Gordonsville, where he went alone by rail; he remained with Jackson some days, not returning until the 15th, and during that time took a distinguished part in the battle of Cedar Mountain, fought by Jackson with Pope's advance guard, but none of the staff were with Stuart.

I now took leave of my wife, who returned to her father's country house near Abingdon, for on the 16th we started for the front. The General and staff went up by rail, sending the camp and horses on by common road. Owing to some delay my horses did not reach Orange Courthouse promptly, and I was a guest at Gen. R. E. Lee's headquarters for two days. General Stuart's horses and those of the rest of the staff were on hand, and they went on to Verdiersville to meet General Fitz Lee's brigade, where the whole party was nearly captured by the enemy. I joined them a half an hour after and found the General bareheaded, his hat and haversack, containing his maps, having been captured. Poor Fitzhugh, who had been sent down the road to meet Fitz Lee, had been captured, and witnessed with dismay, as he told us afterwards, the narrow escape of Stuart and staff. Expecting Fitz Lee's command by that road, the approach of the enemy's troops was supposed to be Lee's command, and had attracted no special attention until they fired and charged on the party sent with Fitzhugh. They were at the gate of the yard in which Stuart had slept, before he and his staff could mount and jump the back fence. There was a great laugh through the army at Stuart's loss, but he got even a few days afterwards by capturing General Pope's coat and hat at Catlett's Station, as we shall see.[5]

Having brought up the main body of his army from Richmond on the 20th, General Lee began his advance from Orange Courthouse. The cavalry of the enemy was in large force around Culpeper Courthouse, and Stuart was ordered to attack them. They fell back to the plains around Brandy Station and offered battle. Stuart's attack was so fierce, however, that they were soon put to rout, and we scored the first victory on the spot where so many cavalry actions were fought afterwards. At that time their cavalry could not stand before us at all, and it was not until the great battle on this same ground on the 9th of June, 1863, "Fleetwood Fight," that they offered us any determined resistance. From that time the difficulty of getting remounts acted disastrously upon the strength of our cavalry arm, not only in diminishing the numbers but in impairing the spirit of the men. Many of the men knew that when their horses were disabled they could not get others, and this injured their dash; they were willing to risk being shot themselves but not willing to risk being sent into the infantry service if their horses were killed.

Lee's army now occupied the line of the Rappahannock, and Pope the opposite bank. The morning after our cavalry affair, General Lee's camp being near us, he invited us to breakfast with him, which, as our servants with our supplies had not arrived, we did with great satisfaction. I have noticed in many of the war narratives mention is made of General Lee's frugal repasts, rye coffee, etc., etc., all of which is stuff. General Lee never lived luxuriously, but all his appointments were soldierly and complete. His table, whenever I sat down to it, which I frequently during the war had the pleasure of doing, was supplied with a sufficiency of good wholesome food and often with delicacies sent to him from friends, near whose house he happened to be. In books written since the war it seems to be considered the thing to represent the Confederate soldier as in a chronic state of starvation and nakedness. During the last year of the war this was partially true, but previous to that time it was not any more than falls to the lot of all soldiers in an active campaign. Thriftless men would get barefooted and ragged and waste their rations to some extent anywhere, and thriftlessness is found in armies as well as at home. When the men came to houses, the tale of starvation, often told, was the surest way to succeed in foraging.

During the action on the flank where the cavalry now took its position and where we were annoying Pope's right, I saw a curious thing. One of our men was struck in the side, just above the hips, by a cannonball. The upper part of the body was cut clean off and hurled some distance, while the man's horse galloped off the field with the remainder of the body seated in the saddle with the feet still in the stirrups. In going from one part of the field to another with orders, I had to cross a road down which the batteries of the enemy had concentrated a terrific fire. On reaching the place I did not see at first how I could cross, but found there were slight intervals of a second or so between the discharges, which tore up everything, and between them I spurred over.

We were this day to start on our celebrated Catlett's Station raid to attack Pope's reserve trains some ten or twelve miles in his rear. Crossing at Waterloo Bridge with two thousand cavalry, General Stuart reached Warrenton early in the afternoon and was received by the inhabitants with great demonstrations of joy, as he and his staff at the head of his splendid cavalry rode down the street. Ladies came out to meet us with tears of joy streaming from their eyes, and our gallant commander halted to exchange greetings with them and to get the information about the movements of the enemy, which they always managed to procure for him.

Upon hearing that we were going to attack Catlett's Station that night, a very pretty young girl, a Miss Lucas, clapped her hands with delight and exclaimed, "Oh! General Stuart, if you will only capture Captain (I do not remember his name) of Pope's quartermaster department he will win his bet with me,

---

5   The hat which Stuart lost on that occasion was won from General Crawford of the Federal army. I was in charge of the flag of truce for burying the dead at Cedar Mountain. Stuart came out and met Crawford and Bayard, two cavalry Generals of the U. S. army and his classmates at West Point. Stuart bet Crawford a hat, in my presence, that the papers would claim Cedar Mountain as a victory to the Federal army. A few days afterwards a hat came over, under a flag of truce, with a copy of the *N. Y. Herald* for Stuart. — C. M. B. [Maj. Charles M. Blackford, a brother of the author of these memoirs.]

and then if you will bring him by here I will pay him. Won't that be too funny for anything?" Our curiosity was excited and she proceeded to explain.

During the occupation of the place, her family had taken, as a boarder and protector, a quartermaster who proved himself a gentlemanly fellow and was very kind to them. In their discussions about the war, she had maintained that Pope would be beaten as soon as he met General Lee, and he, that they would succeed in going into Richmond. The result was a playful bet, offered by him and accepted by the lady, of a bottle of wine that he would be in Richmond in thirty days. So now, if he went there even as a prisoner, she would lose the wine. We all laughed heartily and, turning to me, Stuart said, "Take his name, Blackford, and look out for him" — which I did.

Reaching the vicinity of Catlett's Station a little before dark, Stuart halted the command and sent me out to reconnoitre the position. Throwing an oilcloth over my uniform, I rode all around the outskirts of their encampment, and found a vast assemblage of wagons and a city of tents, laid out in regular order and occupied by the luxuriously equipped quartermasters and commissaries, and countless hangers-on and stragglers of the army, but no appearance of any large organized body of troops; and with the exception of a small camp guard at a crossroads, a few hundred yards from the camp, they had no pickets whatever posted.

I reported the facts, and as soon as it was dark we quietly captured the camp guard at the crossroads, putting an equal number of our own at the place, and with them captured the numerous marauders who came straggling in from their foraging expeditions among the country people around. By cross-questioning these, General Stuart had no difficulty in not only finding out what was in the camp, but where each part lay. To his delight, he found that General Pope's headquarters train was there with all of his official papers, the army treasure chest, and all the personal baggage of the General and his staff; here was a chance for revenge for the loss of the hat and haversack at Verdiersville. As good luck would have it, a guide now presented himself. Through the darkness we heard approaching a voice singing, "Oh, carry me back to old Virginia," and a rattling accompaniment on a tin bucket. The terror of this darky, as he proved to be, when he found himself in our midst, deprived him of speech for a time, but he then made a clean breast of it; he was a "contraband" in the service of an officer of Pope's staff, and readily undertook to guide us to the spot on the terms we offered: kind treatment if faithful, and instant extermination if traitorous.

We also found that there was only one regiment at the place, the Bucktails, so called from each man's wearing a deer's tail as a plume. This was an infantry regiment from Pennsylvania and they occupied the depot building.

The darky was mounted behind a trooper with a guard on each side to insure his fidelity, and assigned as a guide to the regiment which was to have Pope's headquarters as its objective point. Another regiment was to attack the depot and overcome the force there, and was the leading regiment in the attack.

Holding a part in reserve, the rest of the column was to charge all together when the bugle sounded, but each regiment, with a different destination, was to branch off when it came to the proper point, thus spreading out like a fan. The leading regiment was for the depot; the next was to go for Pope's headquarters under guide of the negro, and the remainder were to scatter among the tents and wagons, burn them and collect prisoners and horses and mules. The Federal quartermasters and commissaries in the early part of the war lived in great luxury, and this camp was a collection of elegantly furnished tents, lighted by handsome lamps, in which the dandily dressed occupants were just taking their grog before sitting down to the capital suppers smoking on the tables. Around innumerable fires outside were grouped cooks, orderlies, and teamsters, while the whole atmosphere was pervaded by delicious odors of steaming coffee and savory viands. The camp was as light as day, while sounds resembling the hum from a populous town arose from it; all as merry as crickets and little dreaming of the thunderbolt about to burst upon them. In truth, the rear was "taking care of itself" most comfortably.

Having made all his dispositions, and having ridden up and down the column several times to see that everything was thoroughly understood, and having enjoined upon the men to give their wildest "Rebel yell" when the charge sounded, General Stuart moved the column up so that its head was just outside of the camp light; and then, riding out of the road a little way so as to have a good look at them as they passed, he nodded to the Chief Bugler, Freed, who with bugle in hand was eagerly watching him, and said, "*Sound the charge, Freed.*" Instantly the bugles rang out, on the still night air, half a note of the stirring call — the rest was drowned by a roar like Niagara. From two thousand throats came the dreaded yell, and at full gallop two thousand horsemen came thundering on. A member of the staff was assigned to each attacking column with orders to see that everything was done to secure the general object in view and to report progress frequently to the General at the reserve.

I went in with the leading regiment, and the consternation among the quartermasters and commissaries as we charged down the main street, scattering out pistol balls promiscuously right and left among them, made the men laugh until they could scarcely keep their saddles. Supper tables were kicked over and tents broken down in the rush to get out, the tents catching them sometimes in their fall like fish in a net, within whose folds we could trace the struggling outlines of the frantic men within.

One of the line officers captured, an old friend of Stuart's in the U. S. Army, who was there for the night, told us the next day that he and some friends had made some toddy, and were sitting around a table sipping it when one of the party said, "Now this is something like comfort. I hope Jeb Stuart won't disturb us tonight." Just then our yell broke upon their ears, and the speaker, striking the table with his fist, exclaimed, "There he is, by God!" and they never finished their glasses.

At the first alarm the Bucktails sprang to arms and awaited us in the wide doorways and on the platform of the depot. Receiving one withering volley, our men dashed among them with their sabres, leaping their horses upon the low platform and crashing right into the freight room. In less time than it has taken to tell the tale, all was over, and no further resistance was afforded to our work of destruction so far as the enemy was concerned. The tents and wagons were fired and burned merrily, and each moment the light increased as busy hands spread the conflagration, making it the easier to collect the thousands of mules and horses into droves, for there were too many to lead, and to gather in the multitude of prisoners around us.

Just as we completed the capture of the depot, I heard the slow and labored puffing of an engine, and hastening around the building saw a train just starting for Washington. I rode up alongside of the locomotive and ordered the engineer to shut off steam but he would not, and leaning over in my saddle I fired my pistol into him and threw my leg over the pommel of the saddle preparatory to jumping on the engine to stop her. By this time she was moving fast enough to keep Comet at a trot, and just as I was going to jump aboard, Comet came to a borrow pit, or depression of some sort, into which he plunged, pitching me over his head; and before I could get myself together again the locomotive was out of reach and the train escaped but with the throttle wide open and no engineer to stop her.

I now got a detail of men and had the telegraph wires cut in several places, taking out lengths so as to delay repairs as much as possible, and then exerted myself in keeping the men at work burning, and collecting the mules and prisoners. With the rich booty before them there was great temptation to continue plundering too long on their private account. The way they went through the trunks in the tents was amusing; the blow of an ax answered the place of a key and a kick from the foot spread the contents out for inspection. I felt very uneasy for fear some of the men would get drunk, for there was plenty of liquor in every tent, but the importance of restraint was appreciated, and none took more than they could carry. Numbers of fine saddle horses were eagerly appropriated and led by their halters, and did not escape as so many of the mules did in the latter part of the night from the droves they were formed into. Though so busy superintending what was going on, I captured several dozen prisoners myself as I would come across them singly, or in groups hidden away in a wagon or tent, or making a run to escape; sometimes I would find a man squatting down under a small bush or pine sapling, not higher than his head, for concealment.

All was going on as well as we could wish, when a violent clap of thunder and a furious wind announced the coming of a storm; then came a deluge of rain; it seemed to come not in drops but in streams, as if it were poured from buckets, and it was driven almost horizontally with such stinging force that it was impossible to keep a horse's head to the blast. Whole regiments of horses would rear and wheel around to get their backs to the storm. Every fire was extinguished and we were left in utter darkness, save where the vivid flashes of lightning came, which served only to make the darkness blacker. It was impossible to light another fire. The rain had beaten through the canvas wagon tops to such an extent that their contents were thoroughly wet. I myself used up a whole box of matches trying to kindle the baled hay with which some of them were loaded, without success. Panic-stricken by the flashes of lightning and crashes of thunder, the mules stampeded and scattered everywhere. The prisoners slipped through the line of the guard under the horses' bodies and sometimes under their necks, unobserved in the inky blackness of the dark. One flash showed the road full of them, but when another came there would be the empty road.

An important object of the expedition was the destruction of a railroad bridge near Catlett's. General Stuart detailed Colonel Wickham's regiment, the 4th Virginia, to destroy it, and sent me along with the Colonel to direct the operations for this purpose as Engineer officer. The regiment was standing in columns of fours in a road nearby when Colonel Wickham and myself received the order, and started together, approaching the column from the rear. On reaching the head of the Color Company, Wickham rode back to the rear to give some order, asking me to await his return. The Captain of the company and myself entered into conversation and talked and talked, and wondered what had detained the Colonel. Presently a flash of lightning came and showed us the road in our front entirely empty. Colonel Wickham had passed me in the darkness, and on reaching the head of the column began the march, thinking that I would join him as soon as I found the regiment moving. The men had all followed except our company, and under the circumstances its Captain had not observed the movement of those in front. There we were, feeling very foolish, one-half of the regiment gone with the Colonel and the guide on an important expedition and the other half with the Engineer officer left behind in the road. I could have cried for vexation, for I knew the importance of destroying the bridge before Pope sent troops to protect it. After waiting a few moments in hope that the Colonel would send for us, and it being impossible to follow without the guides he had with him, I returned to General Stuart. After hearing my doleful tale, to my surprise Stuart burst into shouts of laughter, for there at my side stood Colonel Wickham, who had just told his tale of woe, saying also that he had sent back several of his men to look for us, and in the multiplicity of roads around the camps they had not been able to find the lost rear of his command. I guided the Colonel back and we again started towards the bridge.

It was now near midnight; the escaped prisoners and many who had not been captured, encouraged by the darkness, had assembled in the thickets around about and had begun to annoy us by their fire. Our road lay at one place along the edge of a dense thicket, opposite which there was a clear open field. In this thicket a large number had assembled, and when our column got opposite them and at a distance of less than ten paces there flashed a blaze of light from one end of the wood to the other. A flash so vivid and so close caused the horses to wheel and dash off a few yards into the field before their riders could stop them. Our loss was surprisingly small considering how close they were, but it was useless to attack them in such a place even if we had time to spare; so the Colonel moved on towards the bridge, keeping out flankers and an advance guard to avoid any more ambuscades. We had gone but a short distance before the advance guard reported a force of infantry drawn up to protect the approach to the bridge. On going forward to examine them, they could be dimly seen drawn up in an open field in relief against the lighter ground, not twenty yards from the road, waiting for us to get opposite to pour in their fire. With such a force to dispute it we could do nothing towards burning the bridge, so any further effort was reluctantly abandoned.

I had been so busy all the early part of the night that I had not secured a single souvenir of the trip from among the rich booty scattered around; but now on passing a handsomely furnished tent in which there was a lamp still burning, I rode to the door, pulled up the flap and looked in. The tent had been undisturbed; there set a neat camp table with a lamp, a book or two, and a portable writing desk. The floor was of plank and on one side there stood a camp bedstead with neat mattress and red blankets of fine quality and a magnificent buffalo robe, upon one corner of which where it had fallen on the floor, lay a large Newfoundland dog. Here was my chance for a souvenir. I was wet to the skin and cold and this robe would be comfortable, so down I got from my horse to get it. No sooner however had I opened the tent than the dog, a magnificent animal, sprang up and offered battle. The robe was not in reach of the door without entering. I tried to pull it towards me with my sabre but the dog seized the blade and prevented it. I wanted the robe very much but it was evident I could not get it without killing the noble animal, and that I could not do. So after trying many expedients, and being very nearly bitten several times, I reluctantly remounted my horse and left the robe in the dog's brave keeping.

The capture of Pope's headquarters had given us possession of all his papers and among them the morning reports of his army up to the day before, by which we learned as much about his force as he knew himself, for there was the report of the "present for duty" of every command he had. We also secured his army treasure chest which I afterwards heard contained $500,000 in greenbacks and $20,000 in gold. From Pope's private baggage a full dress uniform coat and hat was taken to General Stuart as a trophy, in compensation for his loss at Verdiersville. The General sent them to a friend in Richmond, who placed them on exhibition in the window of a bookstore on the Main Street with a card labeled "Headquarters in the saddle" and "the rear taking care of itself." It attracted much attention from the crowds of amused spectators, as an evidence of the puncture of the inflated and brutal man who had given so much uneasiness to noncombatants, and who now was so easily circumvented when brought in contact with their defenders. The booty secured by the men was of great value. Officers secured many field glasses, for in those days no quartermaster or commissary in their army seemed to consider himself equipped without a splendid pair slung round his neck and a cavalry revolver in his belt. The men, and indeed some of the officers too, got quantities of excellent underclothing from the trunks, and no end of watches and handsome jewelry, and a great many pistols, and of delicacies for their haversacks and canteens there was of course an abundant supply.

After my failure with the buffalo robe I made no other attempt to plunder, and came away without a thing. Though perfectly right and proper to plunder the enemy I always felt reluctant about actually committing the deed, and generally got one of the men to get for me what I wanted.

Of the thousands of prisoners we had captured we only brought *off* about four hundred and some four or five hundred horses and mules. Among the prisoners there was a woman dressed in a man's uniform, and she wanted General Stuart to release her; but he told her if she was man enough to enlist she ought to be man enough to go to prison. So she went on in a state of great indignation.

As daylight approached we withdrew and after marching a few miles halted for breakfast. I now bethought me of our pretty friend's quartermaster, and without much hope that we had actually caught him, I thought I would see. After referring to his name, which I had taken down, I sought out the prisoners, who were assembled under guard in a field and looked very disconsolate. Riding up to them I asked if Capt.

Q. M. D. was in the party. A much surprised and genteel looking young man came forward, who after hearing the story laughed very heartily, in which he was joined by his comrades with keen relish. It seemed to restore them all to good spirits, and they resumed the march talking all the way about the won *wager*.

General Stuart was delighted when I told him *we* had Miss Lucas' quartermaster, and told me to ride on to Warrenton and let her know so she could be ready with the bottle of wine as we passed. Stuart halted the prisoners in front of the house and the Captain stepped forward to receive the bottle of wine from the pretty hands of the lovely girl, amid the enthusiastic cheers of his comrades, and then without further incident, we rejoined the army.

Longstreet's corps having come up from Richmond, Jackson's troops had for some days past been quietly withdrawn from the front and now crossed the Rappahannock, on a march no one knew whither. About midnight I was sent by Stuart to communicate to General Jackson some details of the route that he expected to take with the cavalry, but found when I reached Salem that Old Stonewall had started an hour or more before and, hoping to overtake him in a short time, I followed. But I little knew then the rapidity with which Jackson marched, nor the difficulties of following. While engaging Pope's attention in front, General Lee had sent Jackson around in his rear to destroy his great depot of supplies at Manassas Junction, and he was now engaged in this enterprise, and this movement culminated in the second Battle of Manassas.

This day's ride, following after our great General, along narrow roads choked with troops, was the most fatiguing and exasperating I ever made. Instead of overtaking him in a few hours, as I expected, it took me nearly twelve. It gave me an insight, however, into the way Jackson managed to move his men with such wonderful swiftness for such great distances.

Feeling secure from sudden surprise or attack by the curtain of cavalry Stuart interposed by his parallel marching column, Jackson made no attempt to keep his column closely closed up. The men were given plenty of room to march rapidly and regularly at the paces which suited them best, without wearing them out by the fatiguing and vexatious alternations of halts and double-quicks usually so frequent on marches. It was like each man was walking the distance alone, stopping to rest a moment or drink, within certain wide limits. The pace, kept up for twelve hours, averaged about three miles per hour. The spirit of the men, their unbounded confidence in their leader, and their perfect faith in the success of the expedition, whatever that might be, was abundantly evinced by their talk on the march. The feeling seemed to be a dread with each one that he would give out and not be there to see the fun. Towards the latter part of the day the troops began to show the effects of the severe labor, and of the heat to which they were exposed. Many fainted, and great numbers became footsore, and some, taking off their shoes, limped along barefooted carrying them in their hands. The rear guards exercised a good deal of discretion and allowed the disabled to lag behind, enjoining upon them to make up for it after night, which they promised to do, and no doubt did. Still the bulk of the command reached its destination in time to accomplish the purpose Jackson desired.

It is almost impossible to pass infantry on the march when going in the same direction, as any horseman who has tried it knows to his sorrow. To pass a column meeting you is easy enough, for the men see you and get out of the way; but going in the same direction, you come up behind the men who with their muskets on their shoulders in every position completely block the road, and as they are all laughing and talking it is necessary to be continually shouting to them to clear the road; and if an officer loses his patience and they find he is angry they pretend not to hear and keep their muskets crossed from one to another so as completely to bar the way. If, after extracting some strong language from the horseman, they suddenly open for him with profuse apologies and he rides by, he finds the very next files are doing the same thing to the unbounded amusement of all behind. Our troops seemed to make it the study of their lives to get up jokes of a practical nature, particularly on marches, and the author of a particularly good one became famous among his comrades.

Upon ordinary marches frequent halts are made, during which the troops lie down to rest on each side, leaving the road clear, but halts on such marches as this were few and far between, and I soon found I must take my way through the fields on each side. Of course a fence at every field had to be crossed, and no end of ditches and creeks, and occasional swamps and thickets. To leap a horse so often and on such a march was of course out of the question and the fences had to be pulled down, and the water-courses frequently made it necessary to return to the road.

For twelve mortal hours did this race for the head of the column continue. I could not stop a moment lest somewhat of that which had been gained would be lost, and in spite of all I could do my progress was but little greater than that of the column. After rapid trotting over rough fields, scrambling through brier patches and letting down fences, I would sometimes find when I went back to the road that the very same regiment was there which I had left an hour before.

Jackson's objective point was Bristoe Station on the Orange and Alexandria, now the Virginia Midland R. R., some few miles south of Manassas Junction, where he wished to break up the railroad and then proceed to the Junction. I overtook Old Stonewall about four or five o'clock in the afternoon just as he halted the head of the column half a mile from the station to allow the rear time to close up, throwing a curtain of cavalry across his front to conceal his presence, for up to this time the enemy had no conception that the dread of their lives had his fangs in their vitals ready to tear them to pieces.

I delivered my message, which of course was by this time useless, explaining to the General at the same time how it happened I was so long in reaching him. I would have turned back early in the day if I had known where to rejoin Stuart, but as he was on the march also this was impossible. I knew the quickest and surest way to reach him was to go to General Jackson's headquarters. I found him (Jackson) in the front room of a little farmhouse seated in a cane-bottomed armchair tilted back against the wall, and already asleep, his staff stretched out on the floor, and Sandy Pendleton, his Adjutant, lying in the passage at the front door ready to receive dispatches or staff officers, and he too asleep. I stretched myself out on the parlor floor and had just begun to doze when a staff officer rode to the door and gave some communication to Pendleton who came in with it to the General. It seems that a few miles back at a fork of the road, to avoid mistakes, General Jackson had placed a guard from the leading brigade with orders to remain there until their brigade had passed, then to give directions to the commander of the next brigade to relieve them, and to follow their command and so on all down the column. Jackson was very rigid with his officers and never overlooked disobedience of orders in them, and what now occurred showed how he acted in such cases.

Upon entering the room, Major Pendleton laid his hand on the General's shoulder to awaken him and said, "General Jackson, General —— failed to put a picket at the crossroads and the following brigade took the wrong road." Old Stonewall opened his eyes as soon as Pendleton aroused him, and without altering his position in the chair had listened attentively to what he said, and then replied, "Put him under arrest and prefer charges," and in a moment was gently snoring again.

About sundown Jackson ordered a brigade to deploy and advance on Bristoe Station, for it was about the time the evening trains from Pope's army had been in the habit of passing, as we ascertained from citizens. Up to this time Jackson did not know what force was at the Station; so everything was in readiness to support the attack with his whole corps if necessary. There were only two or three companies of infantry at the place, however, and these after one volley surrendered. General Stuart now joined us and arrangements were made to meet the force we all expected Pope would send up to protect his rear, not thinking it possible that he should still be in ignorance of the fact that Jackson was in possession of his communications. But this was the fact. Up to this time Pope was in absolute ignorance of the dangerous position he was in. Just after we captured the place, from some blunder about turning the switch a train from Pope's army got by, much to our vexation, as this might put the forces at Manassas Junction and Alexandria on their guard; but in the darkness it seems they did not realize what force we had.

To make all sure for the block of trains expected every moment, the switch beyond the depot was changed so the train could come to the depot without obstruction, but after leaving it would plunge down an embankment near which the switch was situated. All along in front of the depot about fifty yards distant was our brigade of infantry, whose orders were to open fire as soon as the troops in the expected train began to disembark. By this time it was pitch dark. Generals Jackson and Stuart and their staffs were on a small hill on the flank of the brigade, just opposite the open switch. Presently we heard a train coming and soon her headlight appeared coming round a curve. Just then Stuart turned to General Jackson and asked him if he was *sure* the switch was turned this time. He said yes, he supposed so, as he had sent his Engineer officer to have it done. But to make sure Stuart turned to me and said, "Blackford, gallop down there and see if it is all right." I dashed off but on getting to the railroad found the switch was up on the bank and that it was so dark I could not see anything about it from horseback, so I jumped down, leaving Comet unhitched, and ran up the bank. Finding the switch properly arranged for throwing the train off, I started back to my horse.

By some misunderstanding of orders, or by getting overexcited, the men in the brigade did not wait for the train to stop to see if it had troops on board; but as soon as it came opposite their flank they opened fire and the whole brigade followed as the train rolled by. The engineer, thinking probably they were only "bushwhackers," as they called our scouting parties of cavalry, opened his throttle valve and came thundering on past the depot at the rate of about fifty miles an hour. When I started to return I found the train was within a short distance of me and if I got on the side of the bank next the troops I would, in another moment, be in front of the fire directed upon the approaching train and would have but a slim chance of escape at so short a range. I barely had time to get back, crossing the track only a few feet in front of the engine, and to run down the bank on the opposite side when the train came rushing on to its doom, the air above the embankment becoming at once filled with the screaming bullets as they tore through and through the sides of the empty box-cars. Down the embankment rushed the engine, screaming and hissing, and down upon it rushed the cars, piling up one upon another until the pile reached higher than the embankment, checking further additions to its confused heap, and arresting the rear half of the train upon the track. The train was a long one, composed mostly of empty cars among which a few sick and wounded were distributed. As soon as the firing ceased, I crawled under the cars on the track and went to where I had left Comet, with no expectation, however, of finding him alive, my only hope being that he had become alarmed at the approach of the train and had left before the fire reached that place. Not finding him, I walked on to the place I had left Stuart. I was greeted most cordially by some of Jackson's staff who were still there; they told me that when my horse galloped back to them when the firing began they all thought I had been hit, and that General Stuart had sent some couriers with my horse to look for me, and that he had been obliged to push on to Manassas. I then went back to the place, but could find no traces of the men or of my horse. It seems that they had called and looked for me but being unable to find me in the noise made by the steam escaping from the prostrate engines, and in the darkness and confusion, they had concluded I was killed and had so reported to General Stuart, who had directed that Comet should be taken along with them to Manassas. I then went back and joined the officers of Jackson's staff and watched with deep interest further developments.

On the rear of the captured train were two red lights indicating, according to railway signal laws, another train behind; and these were at once smashed. In a few moments the headlight of another train came in sight around the curve and, seeing no red lights, advanced, entirely unconscious of the presence of either the wrecked train or of our troops.

When it was opposite the flank of our brigade, fire was opened as before, and as before the engineer attempted to run by. Seeing no red lights to warn him, on he came at full speed and into the rear of the wrecked train he went. The locomotive ploughed under the first three box-cars, setting them crossways on its back and on the back of the tender. The impetus having been communicated to the cars, they telescoped each other or got each other crossways on the track, while the jar caused some of the cars in the moving train to leave the track. Many cars were forced out upon the pile over the locomotive, and the general effect was extremely destructive. This train also had some sick and wounded aboard, but for the most part was composed of empty cars. There were red lights on this train also, which were at once extinguished by a blow from the back of a sabre in my hands, and we awaited placidly the coming of the train which they indicated was yet to come.

Presently the light appeared but soon stopped, and then, with a loud, long, protracted scream which lasted until lost in the distance, the train went back, the bearer of the first intelligence General Pope had of our presence. Men from the first trains had doubtless escaped and given this train warning of the fate which awaited it.

After removing such sick and wounded as had survived the collisions, the whole confused mass was fired, and the track torn up so as to cut off any trains Pope may have had still with him.

As it would have been impossible to find General Stuart that night, and as I was very tired from my long march, I spent the night at General Jackson's headquarters and the next morning borrowed a horse and rejoined Stuart at Manassas. The General, in his warmhearted way, put his arms around me and gave me a hug when I met him, and my comrades of the staff gave me a welcome as one risen from the dead; among whom the report of the men sent to look for me had left them no doubt that I was. They were, they said, about to send an ambulance back for my remains.

Manassas Junction had been taken so completely by surprise that not a thing among the vast accumulation of supplies there had been destroyed. The force guarding the place was small and made little or no resistance, but the next morning, after I arrived, there was a demonstration made from towards Alexandria to retake it, but as soon as they found we had infantry they withdrew. The cavalry and the infantry Stuart had with him in taking the place got all the clothing they wanted, and so did Jackson's corps when they came up, and still there were great quantities burned upon the approach of Pope for want of transportation to bring it off. The display of luxuries among the sutlers' stores was even more extensive than at the "White House," for none had been destroyed before we got possession. I exchanged my somewhat worn saddle for a capital new one of the McClellan pattern, and secured some fine blankets. I also got a capital overcoat for Gilbert, with which he was highly delighted when he joined us again, for I had left him with the headquarters train, as I always did during very active campaigning.

Finding out at last that Jackson was in his rear, Pope hastily began his retrograde movement towards Alexandria so as to reopen his communications, to get supplies from which he was entirely cut off. Upon his approach, Jackson burned everything left at Manassas and took up a strong position at Groveton, near the battlefield of the 21st of July of the year before, and here he awaited the coming of General Lee with Longstreet's corps. The position was a wonderfully strong one along the line of an old railroad where there were successive cuts and fills of from eight to fifteen feet, making most formidable breastworks for infantry both in the cuts and behind the banks, while the elevated ground in rear gave position for artillery to fire over their heads.

The left flank was covered by Bull Run and the right rested on the crest of a ridge which could be crowned with batteries to enfilade the whole front. The high ground was wooded, and in these woods Jackson massed his corps, hiding them completely, while Stuart surrounded them by a curtain of cavalry to keep off their scouting parties who were in search of Jackson's dreaded men.

General Stuart sent me to General Jackson with some reports of the movements of the enemy on the morning of the 28th, with orders to remain as usual at Jackson's headquarters until I could get back to him, and as he was on the move all the time, skirmishing and reconnoitering with the advancing columns of the enemy, I remained all day, and thus had the honor of opening the great battle by drawing the first fire and taking the first prisoners, as I will now relate. Jackson's troops had ample supplies of cooked rations, so orders were issued that no fires were to be kindled, the better to conceal our position. The men were packed like herring in a barrel in the woods behind the old railroad: there was scarce room enough to ride between the long rows of stacked arms, with the men stretched out on the ground between them, laughing and playing cards in all the careless merriment of troops confident in themselves, their cause, and their leader. No music or shouting was allowed but the men had no restrictions as to laughing and talking in an ordinary voice, and the woods sounded like the hum of a beehive in the warm sunshine of the August day. After their hard marches this perfect rest seemed to be all they desired, though under other circumstances the close packing would have been irksome.

On the elevated ridge upon which his right rested, Jackson and many of his officers spent most of the day anxiously awaiting news from General Lee, and receiving reports of the advance of the columns of the enemy. This position was off to the west of the line of Pope's retreat, and the bulk of his army was moving in a direction which would pass us several miles. On this hill I spent the day also, meeting with many of my old friends. Here I met my old friend, relation, and schoolmate, Col. Lawson Botts, who, alas, fell in the action that evening. Our position was a critical one unless Longstreet effected the junction before Pope's army fell upon us, for though impregnable in front, and on the flank covered by Bull Run, the position could easily be turned on the right along the ridge we were upon.

General Jackson has been often criticized for waiting so long at this place, for there is no doubt that if Pope had been a commander of talent and enterprise he could have fallen upon Jackson before Lee with Longstreet's corps joined him. But in war the knowledge of the character of your opponent is a perfectly legitimate warrant for action. Jackson knew his man thoroughly and acted accordingly. If Pope had by any chance displayed intelligence, still Jackson could have retreated towards some of the gaps in Bull Run

Mountain, behind which Lee was approaching, and no serious disaster could have occurred, for he was unencumbered by wagon trains. Lee has also been criticized for not crossing to Jackson the day before he did. But the same answer may be given in this case. Lee knew Pope, and what is more he knew Jackson, and he probably thought that if he effected the junction, Pope would continue his retreat to Alexandria without giving battle.

We all felt, however, that we would like to hear that Long-street was in supporting distance, for otherwise we would be tremendously outnumbered. Stuart's cavalry was fighting all around us. We could hear his artillery first in one direction and then in another, beating back their scouting parties and advanced guards, but the sounds approached nearer and nearer. Pope had not the slightest idea of where Jackson was, as his own reports show, thanks to the precautions taken to conceal our position. All he knew *was* that Jackson was in his rear.

General Jackson rode about all day in a restless way, mostly alone. When he was uneasy he was as cross as a bear, and neither his Generals nor his staff liked to come near him if they could help it. The expression of his face was one of suppressed energy that reminded you of an explosive missile, an unlucky spark applied to which would blow you sky high. Our attention was directed particularly to sounds from the direction of Thoroughfare Gap, through which Longstreet was expected, and which we knew was in possession of the enemy; but not a gun had been heard from that quarter nor a message or dispatch.

Towards evening a courier on a jaded horse appeared in view, spurring towards us, and as he joined the group of horsemen on the hill he asked anxiously for General Jackson, saying he had a dispatch from General Lee. General Jackson had a short time before ridden off down the line, and the man's horse was so much jaded that Dr. Eliason of our staff, who was on the hill, took it to him at full speed. Old Stonewall's face beamed with pleasure. It was a dispatch saying that Lee was at the Gap and would cross in the morning. "Where is the man who brought this dispatch?" said Jackson. "I must shake hands with him," and when he and the doctor rode up on the hill he did so. Several other messengers had been sent with this dispatch, or rather duplicates of it, but none had gotten through but this one; they had probably been captured.

While we were all talking over this good news a cavalryman told me there was some buttermilk to be had at a farmhouse half a mile off, and one or two of us went to get some. After drinking all I could, I filled my canteen and returned, and finding General Jackson there gave him some which he enjoyed very much, he said, and thanked me most cordially, for he was now in the best of humor since receiving the dispatch from General Lee. Old Stonewall had taken a long, deep draught and there was not much left, but this I handed round to the other officers present. Just as the last drop was drained General Ewell rode up and asked me what I had, and when I told him buttermilk, with sparkling eyes he said, "For God's sake, give me some." I shook the canteen and told him I was very sorry it was all gone, but if he would send his orderly with me I would show him where he could get some more and fill his canteen for him, a proposal he joyfully accepted. As I started with the orderly, three or four others joined the party and off we trotted. Upon coming in sight of the farmhouse, I discovered five horses hitched in front, which I found by a glance through my field glasses belonged to the enemy, as shown by their equipments. The riders were evidently after buttermilk too, and in the house. Telling two of my party to move to the back door to cut off retreat, I charged with the rest, getting between the horses and the house before the men could reach them. Five men ran out, four of whom surrendered at once, but the other jumped the yard fence and ran for it as hard as he could through the corn field. As soon as we began firing on him, a sharp volley was returned from a little hill across the corn field, about a hundred yards off, and we then found that this spot was occupied by the infantry of the enemy in some force. Hastily filling our canteens in the house from pitchers setting on the table for a dinner just prepared for our captives, and sweeping the hot corn cakes, butter, eggs and fried ham into our haversacks, we moved off with our four prisoners and five horses to rejoin our friends, under a rattling fire from the infantry advance guard on the hill beyond the corn. But when they saw that I made the prisoners walk behind to get the benefit of their fire, they soon stopped it.

64

This was the opening of the Second Battle of Manassas at Groveton. General Ewell enjoyed the hot corn cakes and buttermilk immensely and had a hearty laugh at my report of the capture. "Trust a cavalryman for foraging," said he. Half an hour after this he lost his leg on almost the very spot we were then standing upon. The horses, like most of their cavalry horses in that day, were not worth my attention, so the infantry officers took them.

The party from which we had received the volley was the advanced guard of King's division marching along the Warenton Pike, apparently unconscious of the proximity of the terrible Stonewall Jackson's corps packed in the woods. The Pike passed within a quarter of a mile of our troops in the woods, who had now been resting quite long enough to refresh them after their labors of the march, and were burning with enthusiasm. The sound of the firing had informed our Generals that something was up before I reached them, and General Jackson received my report of the approach of the enemy with his usual calmness. Knowing, as he now did, that Longstreet's corps was at Thoroughfare Gap ten miles off, he felt no longer uneasy, particularly as it was now late in the evening.

Soon after reporting to General Jackson my capture of prisoners and the presence of infantry in large force, which information I had gotten from the prisoners, the head of their column appeared coming down the turnpike, with a heavy line of flankers out and everything in compact order. Jackson rode out to examine the approaching foe, trotting backwards and forwards along the line of the handsome parade marching by, and in easy musket range of their skirmish line, but they did not seem to think that a single horseman was worthy of their attention — how little they thought that this single, plainly dressed horseman was the great Stonewall himself, who was then deliberating in his own mind the question of hurling his eager troops upon their devoted heads.

Many of our Generals and Colonels, as I have said, were on the ridge across which the enemy were now crossing, and these were watching Jackson's every movement with intense interest, for we could almost tell his thoughts by his movements. Sometimes he would halt, then trot on rapidly, halt again, wheel his horse and pass again along the front of the marching column, or rather along its flank. About a quarter of a mile off, troops were now opposite us. All felt sure Jackson could never resist the temptation, and that the order to attack would come soon, even if Longstreet was beyond the mountain.

Presently General Jackson pulled up suddenly, wheeled and galloped towards us. "Here he comes, by God," said several, and Jackson rode up to the assembled group as calm as a May morning and, touching his hat in military salute, said in as soft a voice as if he had been talking to a friend in ordinary conversation, "Bring out your men, gentlemen!" Every officer whirled round and scurried back to the woods at full gallop. The men had been watching their officers with as much interest as they had been watching Jackson, and when they wheeled and dashed towards them they knew what it meant, and from the woods arose a hoarse roar like that from cages of wild beasts at the scent of blood.

As the officers entered the woods, sharp, quick orders to fall in rang from rank to rank, followed by the din of clashing arms and accoutrements as the troops rapidly got under arms, and in an incredibly short time long columns of glittering brigades, like huge serpents, glided out upon the open field, to be as quickly deployed into lines of battle. Then all advanced in as perfect order as if they had been on parade, their bayonets sparkling in the light of the setting sun and their red battle flags dancing gayly in the breeze. Then came trotting out the rumbling artillery to positions on the flanks, where they quickly unlimbered and prepared for action. It made one's blood tingle with pride to see these troops going into action — as light-hearted and gay as if they were going to a dancing party, not with the senseless fun of a recruit who knew not what he had to expect, but with the confidence of veterans who had won every battle they ever fought.

As soon as the enemy saw what was coming they halted, came to a front face, advanced to meet our troops half way, and the battle opened. In a moment everything on the field was wrapped in smoke. The musketry became a roar, the individual shots merging into one continuous sound, broken upon by the rapid booming of the artillery accompaniment. In a few moments wounded men made their appearance, limping back as best they could, some still bearing their arms but some scarcely able to drag their bodies along. The stream of wounded became greater and greater, and then an officer of rank, slung in a blanket and borne by men, would be brought out, all seeking the place the surgeons had selected for their field hospital where immediate assistance could be rendered to enable the patient to reach the regularly established hospitals further removed from the dangers of the field.

There being no way for me to render any particular service, I assumed a point of observation from which I could see to the best advantage, and watched the conflict with intense interest. It was clear it could be an affair with no very decided results either way as it was too late in the evening for either party to follow up a success on either side. For an hour the combat raged with great fierceness and then darkness put an end to the fight by the withdrawal of the enemy under its cover. The artillery on our side continued to illuminate the night by firing where they supposed the enemy to be, but this soon died out and all was still again. I rode out over the field to examine it. The positions of the two lines of battle were about seventy yards apart and had not been changed during the action. The lines were well marked by the dark rows of bodies stretched out on the broomsedge field, lying just where they had fallen, with their heels on a well defined line. Our wounded were being removed on stretchers by details from their commands, the troops having all marched back to their former position in the woods.

A fresh battlefield is a painfully interesting sight, though a terrible one, and darkness by stimulating the imagination increases inexpressibly its gloomy grandeur. Human nature confronted with death and stripped of all disguise is here presented in the noble calmness of the hero or the abject grovelling of the coward. While regular details for the duty were engaged in removing the wounded, many friends of the wounded and dead were wandering about the field looking up their friends, ministering to their wants, or taking last messages sent by those who were expecting to die. As I wandered about from one part of the field to the other, many touching scenes came under my notice.

In one place I heard through the darkness the shrill voice of a boy apparently not over fifteen or sixteen years old sobbing bitterly. I started towards the place to render him some assistance but as I reached the place his father, who it seems was the captain of his company, came up and said, "Hello, Charley, my boy, is that you?" "Oh, yes," said the boy, "Father, my leg is broken but I don't want you to think that is what I am crying for; I fell in a yellow-jackets' nest and they have been stinging me ever since. That is what makes me cry — please pull me out." The stings and the wound proved too much for the plucky boy and he died in his father's arms soon after.

General Stuart and most of his staff I now ascertained were bivouacked a short distance off where I joined them and we sat around the campfire until late telling of the events of the day and speculating upon the great battle which it was now evident must take place on the morrow.

The preliminary duties of the cavalry had been performed and the issue now rested with the infantry and artillery. Pope had massed his forces, in plain view, a mile distant, upon the ground of the battlefield of the year before, while Jackson occupied the line of the old railroad, all further concealment being unnecessary; the action of the 28th having made it plain enough that he was there in full force. General Stuart spent the greater part of the early morning on the hill where I had been all the day before, and I availed myself of the opportunity to ride over the scene of the action close by with some of our staff officers. The positions of the lines of battle were still more singularly distinct by daylight than they had appeared the night before. The bodies lay in so straight a line that they looked like troops lying down to rest. On each front the edge was sharply defined, while towards the rear of each it was less so. Showing how men had staggered backward after receiving their death blow. All of our wounded had been removed, the dead alone, except occasionally a man not yet dead, too badly hurt to remove, being left on the ground. The wounded of the enemy however were all there and had received no attention whatever. With their usual neglect, no effort had been made by their people to minister to their wants. To send a flag of truce to minister to the wounded or to bury the dead was a humiliation they could not undergo. The great Pope who a few weeks before published in general orders that, "he never saw anything but the backs of his foe," could never do this. What difference did it make to him if there in plain view lay hundreds of his men helpless and perishing for want of attention? There, ready hitched, were long trains of ambulances and every conceivable appliance of art for the purpose, but how would it look in the Northern papers to see that after the first battle he, the great conquering hero, had sent to get his wounded under a flag of truce? Oh, no! that would never, never do — let them all die of gangrene first. Seeing General Jackson crossing the field I galloped over to him and reported the condition of these men, and he told me to tell his medical director to attend to them as soon as the wants of all of ours were supplied, and this I did. I then returned and told the poor fellows what General Jackson had said, for which they expressed much gratitude; and then we filled the canteens of some with water for the want of which they were nearly dead.

General Stuart now looked with anxious eyes for the approach of Longstreet's corps, for the enemy were moving up to Jackson's front in heavy bodies and the battle would begin soon. General Jackson finally told General Stuart to open communication with Longstreet, and taking a regiment of cavalry he started to do so. The exact time of day when we started, in connection with establishing the hour of the arrival of Longstreet, became, twenty years after, a matter of interest in the celebrated Fitz-John Porter trial, in which I was a witness in the session of the court held on Governor's Island, N. Y. In my testimony in the case I could not say positively what time it was by the clock but remembered distinctly it was early in the day. I remember that the trees still cast shadows off to one side and that the bushes still held dew as they brushed by us on the march. It was probably about nine o'clock when we started. We rode rapidly, keeping scouting parties out on front and flank, as at any moment we might encounter the enemy's cavalry, but none appeared. McClellan is in error in stating in his *Campaigns of Stuart's Cavalry* that Stuart met the force which got in our rear that morning, while on this trip. Two or three miles from the battlefield we came in sight of Longstreet's dust. The weather had been very dry and the roads were very dusty and the march of large bodies of troops raised a cloud that could be seen for miles as it rose above the tops of the trees. At this welcome sight Stuart, accompanied by his staff only, galloped ahead to meet the long expected column.

To keep his dust from annoying the troops General Lee and staff were riding a hundred yards in advance of the column, and here General Stuart joined him. Generals Lee, Longstreet and Stuart then rode on still further in advance, so as to confer freely, and General Stuart explained all that had happened and the position Jackson then held. When within about half a mile of the battlefield General Lee and General Stuart rode off to one side of the road, dismounted and sat down on the grass. General Stuart, taking out his map of the country, spread it out and proceeded to explain the position of affairs more fully for about a quarter of an hour. Longstreet's corps in the meantime were marching past at a swinging step, covered with dust so thick that all looked as if they had been painted one color, but full of life and unbounded enthusiasm, which found vent in wild cheering as they recognized the two men bending over the map on the grass. Nearly a division had passed before the conference between the two Generals had come to an end and before General Stuart started across to the right to join his cavalry two or three miles off in that direction. The head of Longstreet's column had undoubtedly reached the field on Jackson's right before we left the pike, a point, that, as will hereafter appear, was of great importance in the history of this battle, so far as Fitz-John Porter was concerned.

We galloped over to the cavalry in high spirits, all uneasiness having been removed by General Lee's arrival. Before reaching the position occupied by our cavalry along the hills bordering Dorkins Branch a scout reported the enemy advancing, and General Stuart sent me out to ascertain whether it was infantry or cavalry, and their approximate numbers.

They were marching along a road grown up on the one side with high bushes and trees, and this together with the dust, made it very difficult to ascertain what they were. But by means of the powerful field glasses I had, I ascertained by the color of the trimmings on their uniforms that the flankers and skirmishers on foot which they threw out were infantry and not dismounted cavalry, and that there was quite a large body of them, a division or more. This was the division of Fitz-John Porter, and this the movement about which he was afterwards court-martialed and dismissed from the service, to save Pope from a like fate, for the loss of the battle.

Their plan was for Porter to turn Jackson's right flank while Pope engaged him in front with partial attacks, but the arrival of Longstreet made the plan, of course, impracticable.

The trial of Porter took place soon after the battle and the case turned upon the time of Longstreet's arrival, the prosecution charging treachery and disobedience of orders, and that there was nothing to prevent Porter from attacking, and Porter claiming that Longstreet had arrived. Positive proof of the time of Longstreet's arrival was wanting at that time and Porter was condemned. After the war, when Confederate evidence was available, a re-hearing was granted and the court recommended him for reinstatement. Congress passed a bill reinstating him which President Arthur vetoed from political motives.

After twenty years had passed there was great discrepancy in the testimony of the Confederate officers in their recollections of the time of day at which Longstreet arrived, as might naturally be expected. But in the evidence I gave at Governor's Island when a witness in the trial the connection between the two events was not from memory of hours, for I could not remember the time of day, but from the sequence of events. I left the pike with General Stuart after the junction between Longstreet and Jackson had been effected, and before any report of the approach of Porter had reached us, then went three miles to Dorkins Branch and there saw the approach of Porter half a mile beyond.

I reported the result of my reconnaissance to General Stuart and he at once informed General Lee, who sent some infantry over to confront Porter. While awaiting this reinforcement, General Stuart, with that fertility of resource which characterized him in emergencies, caused his cavalry to get branches of pine trees and, after tying them to their halter straps, to gallop backwards and forwards, dragging them on a dusty road which led through some old fields grown up in bushes, where the clouds of dust rose up in sight of the enemy. Seeing this long, heavy cloud of dust rising above the trees, Porter naturally thought it was heavy bodies of troops and was no doubt influenced by it in advancing no further than Dorkins Branch, though he had found out through the report of his cavalry previously that Longstreet was near at hand.

Porter remained at Dorkins Branch the rest of the day, withdrawing that night to take a conspicuous part in the decisive action of the next day, the 30th.

The responsibility of the cavalry at this point ceased after the arrival of Longstreet's infantry in Porter's front, and I then turned my attention to other parts of the field. As Engineer officer my duty, on the approach of a battle, was to reconnoitre the positions of the enemy and ascertain and report his movements. For this purpose I had three picked men who remained with me to assist in getting suitable posts for observation and to carry my written reports of anything I might discover to General Stuart.

Longstreet formed his line on Jackson's right, extending nearly to Dorkins Branch, and kept it retired out of sight behind the crest of the ridge, covering a front of something over two miles. Jackson occupied the line of the old railroad, covering a front of about two miles, with his left resting on Bull Run, the two wings making an angle at their junction concave to the enemy and offering in the aggregate a front to the enemy of something over four miles in length, with a force of about seventy thousand men.

Besides the flanking column of Porter the enemy was massed in large force on the battlefield of the year before near Stone Bridge, a mile in Jackson's front, and the country in that direction being open and rolling, the display they made was both formidable and magnificent. Pope's whole force was about equal ours, but from ours being completely concealed, and his exposed to full view it appeared overwhelmingly greater. By the most remarkable stupidity Pope was in utter ignorance of Longstreet's arrival with thirty-five thousand men and was still expecting Fitz John Porter to appear on Jackson's flank, and pending this event he occupied the day of the 29th in continued partial, though fierce attacks on his front. The presence of Porter on his right probably prevented General Lee from pressing matters that day, but being fully aware of the strength of his position he was quite willing to await the result, so long as there was a hope of Pope's final attack, the fear being that he might retreat during the night.

About dark General Stuart and staff went into bivouac on the field near the pike to get some repose after the toilsome day to be fresh for the great battle which might be expected on the morrow; unless Pope should conclude to make an exception in our favor and see something other than "the backs of his enemy," as he had so often proclaimed.

We had just unsaddled and opened our haversacks for an evening meal when down the pike in our front half a mile off there broke out a furious musketry fire accompanied by rapid discharges of artillery, which lasted ten or fifteen minutes and then ceased as suddenly as it had begun. After waiting a little while and all still remaining quiet, General Stuart told me to ride down and find out what it was all about, for this having occurred on the infantry front, no report would be brought to him. Pope had, it seemed, taken up the impression that Jack-son was retreating and had sent a brigade up the pike in pursuit which ran head foremost into Wilcox's division which was deployed in line of battle across the pike near Groveton. Being on the paved pike their approach was heard in the dark and Wilcox, after allowing them to come quite close, poured in a murderous fire which routed them instantly but not until they suffered heavy loss before getting out of range.

As I approached our line of battle and when fifty yards distant, a crash of a dozen or two shots broke the stillness of the night and I heard the clatter of horses' hoofs galloping towards me and like a flash, a horseman darted past so close that he brushed my stirrup and close enough for me to see that he was a Federal officer. A few yards beyond, as I turned to follow him, I saw his horse rear and then drop dead. As he extricated himself and stood up I demanded his surrender, accompanied by a presentation of the business end of a revolver. He was a Major in the force which had been repulsed, he informed me, and turning him over to the infantry, I rode on to find some officer who could explain what had happened. This officer had gotten lost and had ridden up to our line thinking he was going towards his own army. The fire he drew killed his horse, which before he fell rushed by them, as I had seen. This little incident was the occasion of my being arrested a moment later by our own men. I had not gone more than a few steps, carefully picking my way through the dead bodies of some of our men who had fallen in the skirmish, when I was ordered to halt by half a dozen men, one seizing my bridle and the others presenting their bayonets to my belt, demanding my surrender. It was no use telling them I was a Confederate officer; they insisted that I was not, for it was too dark now for them to distinguish my uniform. I at last thought of letting them feel the lace on my sleeve, which satisfied them and with many apologies they allowed me to proceed, directing me to an officer who gave me the information I wanted as to what had happened. I then returned to headquarters fully prepared to enjoy a sound sleep in the balmy night air on the soft, thick carpet of broomsedge grass, which so aboundeth in old Virginia, to the satisfaction, at least, of those who have to sleep out of doors.

The morning light of this eventful day revealed great masses of the enemy covering the whole face of the earth in front of us as far as the eye could reach, and as they occupied the open rolling ground in full view and our troops the wooded land behind the ridge or in the cuts or behind the fills of the old railroad, their numbers appeared far greater than ours though in reality they were about equal.

The first half of the day was occupied by them in moving masses of troops towards Jackson's front, and as the time approached the death-like stillness became oppressive, like the sultry calm before a storm. It was apparent that Pope was preparing a heavy column to penetrate our line a little to the left of the centre opposite the village of Groveton.

Our cavalry was placed on the two wings of the army, General Fitz Lee's brigade on the left near Sudley Springs and the rest under Stuart's immediate command on the right near Dorkins Branch. General Stuart sent me to get the best possible post of observation of the approaching action with orders to keep him informed, by frequent written reports, of everything that occurred, as it was important for him to have prompt information for the regulation of the movements of the cavalry. Getting between Longstreet's front and the enemy I found a hill near Groveton where, with precautions to avoid the skirmish fire of the enemy, I succeeded in finding a place from which a magnificent view of the whole field could be had. All along the old railroad an occasional head peeping out, or the glitter of a bayonet was all that could be seen of our left wing excepting batteries on the heights beyond, and mounted officers, and orderlies bearing orders galloping about from one part of the line to another. Upon the high ground on Jackson's right, and so placed as to be on the flank of the column of attack the enemy were preparing, were planted twenty-two guns under the command of Stephen D. Lee, and these guns were destined to play an important part in the engagement.

About three o'clock the storm broke upon us. From Groveton something over half a mile distant across the clear open fields leading up to the old railroad, with a front of nearly a mile, and in three lines of battle, the mighty column moved forward with intervals between the well formed lines of from fifty to one hundred yards.

The period which elapsed during the passage of this mighty mass of men across the intervening space seemed an age. There seemed to be nothing to oppose them, for the Confederate infantry lay low for protection from the storm of shells now rained upon them. The advance began in magnificent style, lines as straight as an arrow, all fringed with glittering bayonets and fluttering with flags. Between the lines officers in gay uniforms galloped back and forth with drawn swords waving on their men. But the march had scarce begun when little puffs of smoke appeared, dotting the field in rapid succession just over the heads of the men, and as the lines moved on, where each little puff had been, lay a pile of bodies, and half a dozen or more staggering figures standing around leaning on their muskets and then slowly limping back to the rear. These were the puffs of smoke from the explosion of the shells from a hundred cannon firing at the rate of about twice a minute. Two hundred shells a minute carefully aimed at lines in the open field at close range must have produced considerable effect on their strength and courage long before a musket was fired.

The clear spaces between the moving lines became thickly dotted by prostrate bodies and by numbers slowly moving to the rear, but still the march continued with thinned but unshaken ranks until within pistol-shot of our lines. Then all along the crest of the cuts and fills of the railroad a dark, low line arose, of men showing less than half their bodies; there was an instant's pause as their bright musket barrels were leveled, and then through a bursting cloud of light blue smoke gleamed a deadly flash of flame. The first line of the attacking column looked as if it had been struck by a blast from a tempest, and had been blown away. Back they rushed pell-mell, carrying the second line back with them, and in some cases the third to a distance of a hundred and fifty or two hundred yards to a place where a depression in the ground gave them shelter from the rain of bullets pouring upon them. Here assembled a dense mass of disorganized men, among whom, seizing the colors, the officers rode, waving the flags over their heads and calling upon the men to re-form, while upon them our artillery still poured their projectiles, mowing them down with greater effect than ever.

Presently the efforts of their officers began to tell, and shooting out like forming crystals, lines could be distinguished in the confused crowd, which soon absorbed the whole mass, and they again advanced to be again and again hurled back.

Along so long a line these movements were not of course all at the same time nor alike. Sometimes a stand would be made and the first and even the second line would close in a hand-to-hand bayonet fight on the railroad where the conflict was deadly, but in no single instance that evening, I believe, did they penetrate our lines. The sides of the cuts and fills were covered with rounded stones as big as one's two fists, and these the Confederates collected in great numbers as reserved ammunition, particularly on the embankments. Breechloaders were not then in use among the infantry and when one of these determined charges was made there was no time to load after delivering fire; but the interval between their last shot and the time when they would come close enough for the bayonet was utilized by Jackson's men in showering down these stones on the heads of those climbing up the bank to them; and one such stone was as good as a cannonball so far as the man it hit on the head was concerned. After the battle little piles of these stones were left all along the top of the banks where each man had made his collection, and as the supply ran short after each repulse the men ran forward down the bank to recover those they had already used.

This contest went on about two hours, the intervals between the repulses becoming longer and longer and the tendency being to concentrate their attacks upon one spot at a time. Over broad spaces in our front the ground appeared, from where I stood, so thickly covered with the fallen that it looked like one vast blue carpet. I do not mean that the ground was really entirely covered, but at a distance, one body obstructing the vision of several yards of ground beyond, the effect was that described. All the fighting had been done by Jackson's corps alone up to this time, Longstreet's half of the army comprising the right wing not having fired a shot, except from the artillery under the command of S. D. Lee before mentioned, which did such splendid service. Longstreet's line was retired behind the hill out of sight and Pope probably did not know of his presence even then.

General Lee sat on his horse on the Warrenton Pike calmly watching the enemy exhausting his strength upon the impregnable position along the old railroad, and awaiting his time to order Longstreet to come down upon them. About five o'clock in the evening the order was given, and with a cheer that rang out for miles our right wing swept forward.

Seeing that the time had come for the cavalry I dashed off to rejoin General Stuart, who had been kept informed through frequent written reports of every event of the evening, sent by couriers detailed from cavalry headquarters to accompany me for this purpose. It was a grand sight to see our lines four miles in length with bayonets glittering in the evening sunlight and flags flying move rapidly forward, and before them in broken masses the enemy withdrawing. Pope had been prudent enough, however, to keep some of his force in reserve, and these Longstreet encountered and sharply engaged three-quarters of a mile from the field. They could not resist, however, the fury of the attack and in half an hour joined their comrades in retreat. This stand had given Pope, however, time to throw his shattered columns into the deep depression made by the Sudley Road at the very spot where the Zouave regiment we charged in the last year's battle had emerged upon the field, and here as the night came on Longstreet's advance terminated.

General Stuart with his cavalry covered Longstreet's right flank during his advance and soon encountered the cavalry of the enemy on the fields near Bull Run. Munford was in the advance and when the enemy first appeared, charged gallantly upon what he supposed to be only a regiment of about equal strength with his own; this he broke, but beyond were heavy reserves which came up at a charge and drove him back in some confusion. Then Stuart arrived with his reserves and swept them in turn, in utter discomfiture, driving them back pell-mell across Bull Run and killing and capturing a large number. This was the first time their cavalry had ever made any show of resistance and the sight of the charges and sabre fighting in the clear, open fields was very fine. Munford made a mistake in beginning his charge too soon and got his ranks opened too much before the shock came, while the enemy advanced at a trot and only took the charge pace when within a hundred yards of the meeting; his ranks were then solid and Munford's opened, strung-out force was dashed aside.

During the night the enemy withdrew and continued their retreat to Centreville, General Lee following the next day, and the cavalry in advance captured two companies of the 2nd Regiment U. S. Cavalry, which we came upon and surprised. Fitz Lee's brigade was in the advance and captured them. It was the very regiment he had belonged to before the war and the officers of course and men all knew him, at least all who had not joined since. We were pushing on towards Fairfax C. H., the enemy moving in a parallel direction along the turnpike in continuation of his retreat. At Fairfax C. H. they made a show of throwing up entrenchments and offering battle, and there they made a sharp attack upon our advanced guard of cavalry and drove it back in some confusion upon the main body, and we encamped for the night near Chantilly.

Comet had cast a shoe the day before and on September 1st it was absolutely necessary to have one of those I always carried in my saddle pockets put on at once. The forges of the infantry's artillery were on the march near us and more convenient than the cavalry forges, which were always overstocked with work; so I got leave of absence and got the blacksmith of one of them after a round fee to promise to do the work at the first halt the column made. I had to follow along the road for this purpose some time. Across to our right a mile or so was the column of the enemy marching parallel to our course, the route being marked by long lines of white-topped wagons all guarded by infantry marching in column with them. Presently there was a halt made and orders came for the wagons to park and the artillery to prepare for action. The wagons belonging to the battery I was with and the battery forge went into park in rear of a small hill upon which the guns of the command were placed. Now was my time, and after submitting to another levy of a fee from the blacksmith on the ground that we were just going to have a fight and that to shoe a horse in action with cannonballs about was worth something extra, he at last lit his fire and put on the shoe. It was with inexpressible joy that I once more felt my noble horse tread freely and without a limp as I mounted to see what was going on and why the halt was made. As I rode into the road by which we had been marching I saw at once the unmistakable evidence of the near approach of the enemy in the appearance of our troops, though no enemy was in view within the limited vista some small open fields afforded. The men were in line of battle along the road, crouching down behind the sheltering bank at its side, with a quiet intensity of expression on their faces that to the experienced eye betokened an approaching storm, which soon cast its preliminary drops in the form of shells whizzing by and bursting beyond.

As I reached the crest of the hill General Lee and his staff, who had been standing on the spot for some time, moved on down the road. As this was a commanding place, I halted to look around. Across the valley a thousand yards distant, on a hill just appearing over the tops of the trees, was the battery from which came the shells. The road was half filled with crouching men availing themselves of the sheltering bank where the road cut through some four feet high at this place. The rain was pouring down in torrents. While sitting on my horse scanning the scene a shell passed through the crest of the bank and exploded right among the men before me. I was covered with the sand and earth it threw up, and was contemplating the destruction it had produced, the largest I have ever seen from one shell, with no little satisfaction at having escaped, for a dozen men lay writhing and jumping about at my feet, when I felt myself slowly sinking and my feet almost touched the ground. Comet had been struck in the neck, and from the wound the blood spouted several feet in a stream as large as my finger. To spring to the ground, unbuckle the girths and strip off the saddle was the work of an instant, for I knew it was very difficult to get a saddle off a dead horse. The cool rain upon his back revived him and he stood up, turning his head and looking me full in the face with his large, beautiful eyes, as plainly beseeching assistance as if he had expressed himself in words. I could not keep the tears from trickling down my cheeks; and from his eyes the tears in large drops fell in the agony he suffered as he gazed wistfully at me. I screwed my handkerchief into the wound and stopped the flow of blood; in a few moments the nervous shock was passed and I had hope of his recovery.

My first thought was one of thankfulness that General Lee and his staff had passed on. The shot had been evidently intended for them and some of the party would inevitably have been struck if they had been there. The poor fellows who had fallen were quickly taken off and the gap in the ranks closed up. Several of the men came around to offer me assistance and showed more sympathy for the horse than they had done for all their fallen comrades. Such is the soldier — for a man to be killed is a matter of course; if not his comrade it might have been himself, and his feeling is that of relief that his turn did not come that time. But to see a beautiful horse bleeding and suffering so calmly was quite another thing, and they wept.

Taking my saddle on my arm, I led Comet down the hill to where the forge and wagons of the battery were, and after the action Captain Carrington, who commanded it, invited me to spend the night with him and kindly lent me a horse to rejoin General Stuart. I could not, of course, see anything more of the action, which was a sharp attack intended to check our pursuit, and in this it was partially successful, enabling Pope to withdraw without serious molestation; he had, moreover, received heavy reinforcements from Alexandria. After an hour or two I found that the handkerchief could be withdrawn from Comet's wound, and during the night I employed the sentinel to watch and give me notice if the bleeding occurred again. His appetite was good and I had hopes of his recovery. It was necessary for his food to be up on a level with his head, for the neck soon swelled up to such an extent that it was impossible for him to reach the ground, and I determined he should have every chance given him for recovery which the circumstances would admit, or that money could buy. I employed a man in the battery to lead Comet and attend to feeding him until I could find some farmer who would undertake to nurse him until we got back from Maryland, where it was evident we were now going.

Captain Carrington had lent me a horse to rejoin Stuart. Going first to General Lee's headquarters to find where to rejoin the staff, I was delighted to see General Stuart ride up. He was really distressed to hear about Comet, for next to having a staff composed of handsome men about him, he liked to see them mounted on fine horses, and Comet's beauty was a source of constant delight to him.

While we were talking about Comet a report was forwarded to headquarters that the body of a Federal General officer had been found on the battlefield, who had one arm. They all said it must be that of General Kearny, and General Stuart went out to see and I went with him. The body, dressed in a plain undress uniform, had been laid in a house and proved to be, as supposed, that of Kearny, and General Lee had it sent back under flag of truce.

Before reaching the Potomac I was fortunate enough to find a farmer who was willing to take Comet and who was particularly well situated for keeping him. He had a meadow next the barn, in which stood stacks of hay from which Comet could eat and an elevated trough from which he could drink without putting his head down, and here I arranged for him to stay. After our return from the Maryland Campaign, while at "The Bower" in the Valley, I came over and got him. The farm was then within the lines of the enemy, but getting an escort of three men I went in at night and took him from the immediate neighborhood of their camps. The farmer said that several times parties of the enemy had examined the horse but thought him not worth taking in his condition. I sent him home and the wound continued to run so as to render him useless for the rest of the war. After the war I had an operation performed and he got well and did me good service for several years.

General Lee now abandoned any idea he may have had of attacking Washington via Alexandria and moved his army up towards Leesburg to cross over into Maryland. Pope, thoroughly beaten, withdrew within his fortifications and was himself retired from public view to some frontier post in the far west, leaving behind him in Virginia a name only formidable to the women and children and non-combatants who were so unfortunate as to be within his lines; for to these, for the short time he flourished, his brutality almost equalled that of Butler in New Orleans.

Public opinion at the North was so much excited over the collapse of this campaign of Pope, about which such magnificent promises had been made, that some one had to be sacrificed. There was strong feeling against McClellan among the Republican Party and in the Cabinet, owing to his popularity at this time and their fear that in him might develop a successful presidential candidate in the future. This jealousy, McClellan's friends claimed, had occasioned his defeat around Richmond by not giving him adequate support, and Pope had been put forward in the hope that the laurels he would win would overshadow the bruised wreaths on McClellan's brow and enable them to retire McClellan. But here General Lee had interposed an unexpected dilemma in thrashing Pope so thoroughly that if the laurels on McClellan's brow were withered and bruised those of Pope were so utterly mashed that even McClellan's looked fresh beside them. But Staunton, the Secretary of War, was master of the situation — for what does he do in conjunction with Pope and McDowell but say that the battle was lost by treachery on the part of Fitz-John Porter in his flank movement on Jackson's right! Porter and McClellan were staunch friends and here was the chance for giving the "Young Napoleon," as McClellan was called, a mortal stab, even if it became necessary to continue him in command of the armies for the present. It was true that Porter had done most of the fighting on the 30th and had behaved with great gallantry, and that weeks had passed without a word against him; public feeling at the loss of the battle demanded a victim or it might turn upon and rend even the Administration itself. Porter was tried for his life and escaped with dismissal from the service, thus saving Pope and McDowell, his senior officers, from a like fate.

McClellan was now busy in reorganizing the army out of the broken fragments that remained of his and Pope's commands, together with large reinforcements hurried on from all the Northern states. For was not Lee advancing to cross the Potomac and to march right upon Philadelphia and New York, as all the Northern papers said, at the head of an enormous army? In reality, Lee's force had been seriously diminished by the casualties of the vigorous campaign he had made and the reinforcements that our government should have had in readiness had not been called out to any adequate amount and those we had were not prepared and came in but slowly.

With unlimited means within our reach in the one hundred millions of dollars' worth of cotton we had in the South and with our ports still open, the past year had been allowed to pass without preparation, in the belief that locking this cotton up would cause England to make war for us to get it. So it came to pass that when one decisive victory north of the Potomac would, in all human probability, have ended the war in our favor, Lee had to enter the enemy's country with less than one-third the force they brought against him; of all this, however, the men in the army knew nothing then. They only knew they had beaten the enemy wherever they had met him and felt confident they could do so again. To cross over from war-wasted Virginia to the fresh rich fields of Maryland, where the people were represented as only awaiting our coming to flock to the Southern standard, was a source of delight to the whole army.

General Stuart with his cavalry, forming the advance guard of the army, crossed the Potomac at White's Ford near Leesburg on the 6th of September and pushed on to Poolesville, where we encountered a force of the cavalry of the enemy which we quickly put to flight, and the next day cavalry headquarters were established at Urbana. Our infantry occupied Frederick, eight miles to the west, with a line extending north and south so as to serve as a cushion against any sudden attack from towards Washington and thus allow the infantry time to prepare for action.

While at Urbana our life at headquarters was a delightful one, an oasis in the war-worn desert of our lives. There was nothing to do but await the advance of the great army preparing around Washington, and though constant vigilance was necessary, General Stuart like a good soldier knew how to improve the passing hour in the enjoyment of the charming society the country round afforded. Our horses stood saddled day and night, and Stuart and his staff slept in the open air in the shady yard of the residence of Mr. Cocky, with clothes, boots, spurs and arms on, ready for instant action, but with these precautions we enjoyed the society of the charming girls around us to the utmost. One hour's acquaintance in war times goes further towards good feeling and acquaintanceship than months in the dull, slow period of peace. This no doubt makes a military people like the French call it "Merry War."

It was the 11th of September before we were disturbed in our enjoyment of these scenes and pleasant associations at Urbana. One bright event occurred of which I must say something as illustrative of the life we led with the dashing and brilliant leader of our cavalry. A rosy light hovers around it still, illuminating the vista of dark and lowering clouds of war overhanging the past. General Stuart was fond of dancing, and in return for the hospitality we had received he determined to give a ball. On the edge of the village stood a large, vacant building which had been in peace times used as a female academy, and the staff was soon busied in having a large room prepared there. The walls were decorated with regimental Confederate flags collected from the regiments around, an army band furnished the music, and lovely moonlight lit the beauty and fashion of the country on their way as they assembled in response to our invitation. The officers came prepared for any emergency, fully armed and equipped, picketing their horses in the yard and hanging their sabres against the walls of the dance hall. As the delightful strains of music floated through the vacant old house, and the dancing began, the strange accompaniments of war added zest to the occasion, and our lovely partners declared that it was perfectly charming. But they were destined to have more of the war accompaniment than was intended by the managers, for just as everything had become well started and the enjoyment of the evening was at its height, there came shivering through the still night air the boom of artillery, followed by the angry rattle of musketry. The lily chased the rose from the cheek of beauty, and every pretty foot was rooted to the floor where music had left it. Then came hasty and tender partings from tearful partners, buckling on of sabres, mounting of impatient steeds, and clattering of hoofs as the gay cavaliers dashed off to the front.

The ladies could not be persuaded to believe that they were not taking a last farewell of those who would sleep that night in bloody graves, but being assured that it was probably only a night attack on the outposts to feel our position, and that we might all return to finish the evening, and being influenced possibly by that curiosity which the dear creatures are said to possess, they at last agreed to await our return.

McClellan's advance guard had struck our outposts, but after a sharp skirmish they withdrew for the night and we hastened back "covered with glory," at least in the ladies' eyes. Dancing was resumed and was at its height again when, alas, it was doomed to a final interruption. Heavy tramping of feet in the passage attracted the attention of the lady who was my partner, standing at the time next the door of the ballroom. Looking out, she clasped her hands and uttered a piercing scream. The scream brought all the dancers trooping out to see what was the matter now, and there on stretchers the wounded were being carried by to the vacant rooms upstairs.

It was no use talking to them of any more dancing that night. There, like a flock of angels in their white dresses assembled around the stretchers, they bent over the wounded men, dressing their wounds and ministering to their wants, with their pretty fingers all stained with blood. One handsome young fellow, as he looked up in their faces with a grateful smile, declared that he would get hit any day to have such surgeons to dress his wounds. All that was left for us now was to escort the "lovely angels" home by the light of the moon and to bid a last, tender farewell to them and to the happy days we had spent among them, for we knew that the morrow would bring again war's stirring scenes around us.

I suppose General Lee never entertained the idea of doing more than make a campaign in the enemy's country of the "offensively defensive" kind, for our force was less than thirty thousand men. When McClellan at the head of three times that number advanced, we retired up the north bank of the Potomac, slowly followed by the mighty host opposed to us. The cavalry covered the rear and engaged in constant and fierce conflicts with the advanced guard of the foe. Their cavalry never, at this time, ventured within our reach without heavy infantry support, so that all we could do was to drive them back a short distance behind their reserves.

In passing through Frederick I called to take leave of my kind friends, the Rosses, at whose house my father lived while studying law in Mr. Ross's office when he was a young man. I had called to see them several times since crossing the Potomac and they entertained a warm feeling of regard for me on my father's account. We had a cavalry engagement in the streets of Frederick, in which Hampton's command was engaged. One of the ladies at Mr. Ross's at the last moment ran out as we were taking leave under a skirmish fire and insisted upon my taking a splendid plum cake she had made for me, and there was nothing to do with it but strap it to my saddle, to be enjoyed around our campfire that night.

Harpers Ferry was occupied by a garrison of eleven thousand men which, strange to say, had not been withdrawn when Lee entered Maryland. To pass up the river with this force on our flank and McClellan's whole army in our rear was out of the question; so Jackson was dispatched in advance to capture them, moving rapidly past them to Sharpsburg and then crossing the Potomac and coming down on the southern side, the side upon which their troops were. Lee's army by this time was opposite the place, cutting off escape northward, and after Jackson's investment they were completely surrounded.

McClellan followed our army with his usual deliberation until an event occurred which, in the hands of a more enterprising General, might have closed the war then by the annihilation of Lee's army. Upon beginning his march from Frederick westward, General Lee issued, as usual, the general order for the regulation of the movement of the various divisions. In this paper the road each division was to take was indicated and the time of arrival and departure from certain points prescribed. Each Division Commander was furnished with a copy of this paper for his information and guidance. Gen. D. H. Hill, in leaving his camp, dropped this order and it fell into the hands of McClellan, giving him as full information of our position and movements as we had ourselves. The march of the army was through a mountainous country where support from one column to another was difficult. Lee's whole force was less than thirty thousand men, one-half of whom were away investing Harpers Ferry. Behind the remainder came McClellan with ninety thousand men and on our flank was the garrison at Harpers Ferry of eleven thousand fresh troops. All this was revealed to our enemy by the loss of this unfortunate paper.

Never had a General such an opportunity of crushing his opponent as McClellan had at this moment and why he did not do so is unaccountable.

Stretching northward from Harpers Ferry is Pleasant Valley, a narrow" depression between Elk Ridge and South Mountain, through which the road to Harpers Ferry northward lay. In this valley Stuart with the bulk of his cavalry was on the evening of the 14th holding the passes of Elk Ridge and supported by infantry. After dark a vigorous attack was made by the enemy upon the passes above, which resulted in his getting possession of the valley road and placed us in a most critical position between them and the garrison, closing the only outlet southward. The morning of the 15th opened with heavy cannonading from the Ferry five miles below us, where Jackson was beginning his bombardment. Up the valley we could see heavy masses of infantry bearing down upon us, their lines of skirmishers extending clear across from mountain to mountain as they came hastening down to the relief of the beleaguered garrison. If they had continued their advance with vigor they would inevitably have succeeded in relieving the place, but they halted and delayed. Ten o'clock found them only just beginning a skirmish fire with our dismounted cavalry, while since daylight the thunder of the guns told that Jackson was vigorously pressing his attack, and so long as this firing continued we knew our retreat in that direction was closed. Stuart was prepared to contest every foot of ground, but the disparity of numbers was fearful.

A little incident occurred just here which I must mention as an evidence of how the soldier snatches pleasure among the most trying scenes. The people occupying the pretty farmhouses around us, expecting a battle, had fled locking their doors but leaving everything behind them. The staff had found their hasty early breakfast rather scant, and as the morning advanced a sharp appetite made itself felt in spite of the gravity of the situation. While reconnoitring the advance of the enemy my attention was attracted to a farmhouse near their lines, from which a good view could be had. It was a lovely cottage, all embowered in trees, with quantities of ripe grapes and peaches around but everything deserted. General Stuart coming up just then, I suggested that something more substantial might be had, and proposed that we should investigate, and to this proposition he eagerly agreed. Finding a lower window unfastened, I entered and found myself in a pantry richly stored with everything that could tempt the appetite. In the safe were cold meats and pies, bread, butter and milk and cheese in the greatest profusion, and handing them out of the window to my hungry comrades we made a glorious meal and stored our haversacks to their utmost capacity. The bullets were singing through the trees above us from the advancing enemy as we galloped back to our lines.

Their skirmishers were within two hundred yards of our lines when the roar of Jackson's guns suddenly ceased. There followed a few moments of painful suspense. The enemy halted, evidently arrested by the significant quiet. Then from away down the valley came rolling nearer and nearer, as the news reached the troops, ringing cheers and we knew the Ferry had surrendered and soon a courier came spurring in hot haste with the official information of the fact. A skirmisher of the enemy, as our cheers rang out in response, sprang up on a stone wall and called over to us, "What the hell are you fellows cheering for?" We shouted back, "Because Harpers Ferry is gone up, G—— d—— you." "I thought that was it," shouted the fellow as he got down off the wall. General Stuart, now at the head of his troops, rapidly withdrew to the south side of the river to march up and recross at Shepherdstown, to rejoin General Lee at Sharpsburg on the Antietam Creek where the battle was to be fought, as it turned out.

The scene as we passed through the little town of Harpers Ferry was a striking one. Eleven thousand men and seventy-three pieces of artillery had fallen into our hands. These troops had not been in active service in the field, and in their luxurious garrison life they looked as if they had come out of a bandbox, with their untarnished uniforms, white shirt collars and polished boots. There had not yet been time to disarm them and there the eleven thousand men stood in crowds along the sidewalks with their arms and accoutrements, scowling savagely at us as we rode by for the rough jokes our merry, weather-beaten, dust-covered, and travel-stained troops showered upon them about their dandy appearance and easy capture.

War develops an infinite amount of wit and humor among soldiers. In every company there were aspirants for the honor of being the "funny man" of the command, whose study it was to get off good jokes; and between the companies of a regiment there was rivalry as to whose man should produce the best and make a regimental reputation. Every conceivable subject on the line of march was made to contribute to this harmless amusement and the officers encouraged it, submitting good-humoredly to being sometimes the victims themselves. The clatter of tongues and merry laughter along a dusty road would make one think they belonged to the weaker sex, bless their dear talkative hearts.

The men of the surrendered garrison, not having been exposed to the weather, were not at all sunburned, and this paleness to us at the time looked peculiar in soldiers, contrasting so strongly with our berry-brown complexions. As we marched along the street one of our troopers sang out to one of the men on the sidewalk, "I say, Yank, what sort of soap do you fellows use? It has washed all the color out of your faces," at which our side cheered. To this the man retorted, "Damn me, if you don't look like you had never used soap of any sort." Shouts of laughter greeted the reply from our men as well as the Yanks, and our man called back as he rode on, "Bully for you, Yank; you got me that time."

Though the place was commanded by the heights around, it did seem strange that so large a force had not made more effort either to hold out or cut through when they knew relief was so near at hand. Colonel Miles, the commanding officer, had been killed and this may have had some effect. To our infinite disgust in the cavalry, we found that a regiment of cavalry eleven hundred strong had escaped from the place during the night by going up the tow path of the canal where, from strange oversight, no guard had been posted. To think of all the fine horses they carried off, the saddles, revolvers, and carbines of the best kind, and the spurs, all of which would have fallen to our share, and the very things we so much needed, was enough to vex a saint. This party not only got off, but pitched into and captured a wagon train from us with which they made good their escape.

The forces engaged in the capture had now to hurry on to the Antietam to extricate General Lee with Longstreet's corps from his perilous position, for though pushing on not with the vigor he should have used under the circumstances, McClellan had still advanced so much faster than was expected of him that there was danger of his crushing Lee before a concentration could be effected. We did not know how to account for this vigor in the movements of the usually deliberate McClellan until later when we saw about the lost order in the Northern papers.

In his advance the action on South Mountain had occurred in which poor Sam Garland fell in command of his brigade. At Harpers Ferry most of the staff got separated from our General, who went off with Robertson's brigade while we were looking for him, and it was late at night before we overtook him at Sharpsburg, and spent the remainder of the night at the house of Dr. G., sleeping as usual on the porches or in the passages with our saddles for a pillow, for during active campaigning Stuart himself never occupied or allowed his staff to occupy a bed.

The position General Lee selected to give the battle his adversary seemed so eager for was along the south bank of Antietam Creek, or rather the southwest bank of it, near the town of Sharpsburg — the battle in the South being usually known by the name of the town, while in the North it bears the name of the creek, which is a better sounding name for it.

For three or four miles before emptying into the Potomac, Antietam Creek flows parallel to the river and then turns suddenly towards it, forming a sort of peninsula. With his right resting on the Potomac, Lee's lines extended two miles and a half up the creek with a good frontage, but his left was "in the air" and could be easily turned, and there the main attack was made. No battle of the war displayed the indomitable pluck of our army more conspicuously than Antietam, and in none were the odds more fearfully against us. As the great masses of the enemy came pouring through the passes of South Mountain and came in contact with our infantry occupying the line of hills along the creek they opened the engagement, gradually moving further and further to our left. General Stuart was actively engaged during the morning of the 16th in a reconnaissance to discover their movements in that direction. Seeing skirmishers enter a field further to the left than they had yet appeared, General Lee ordered Stuart to discover and unmask their intentions and if necessary for this purpose to attack them with his whole cavalry force. What General Lee wanted to know was whether at this particular point they were in force or whether it was only cavalry. The place was very unfavorable for a cavalry attack, and General Stuart, telling me the purport of the order, asked me if I did not think I could find out what was wanted without his having to make a reconnaisance in force. I told him I thought I could. He then told me he would have the column formed for the attack and would await half an hour, and gave me some couriers to bring my reports to him. Taking my little band of three experienced and well-mounted men to accompany me, and placing the others sent for the purpose as a sort of reserve, I galloped off. Mention has been made of a field glass of unusual size and power, which I was fortunate enough to secure from some importations of our ordnance depot in Richmond. It was the only one of the kind I have ever seen and its great utility for purposes of reconnaissance was now to have a conspicuous illustration.

Pushing rapidly and cautiously around on their flank, I discovered a piece of rising ground quite near their lines, from which a full view could be had, but unapproachable on horseback. Dismounting and leaving one of my men to hold the horses and taking the other two with me, we crawled along the ground to the spot and from there could see their whole line of skirmishers a hundred and fifty yards distant, crouching down behind the stumps, bushes and grassy covering of the field. If I could find out what branch of the service they belonged to I would know what their reserve, massed in the wood beyond, was. Our horse artillery was sweeping the field at long range and the men kept so close behind their cover that nothing but the power and clearness of my glasses enabled me to tell what they were from the small portion of their bodies in view. But my glasses brought them close and soon revealed the blue trimmings and bayonet scabbards of the infantry soldier and not the yellow of the cavalry. Having obtained this information I hastened back, meeting General Stuart advancing to the attack. On hearing my report he halted the command and accompanied me back to the place to have a look through the glasses himself, as it was a question of great importance. Thus a loss of a considerable number of men, who must have fallen in the attack, was saved. In making the examination, we had drawn the attention of the enemy, and many shots were fired at us; but with precaution never to stand erect except when in movement, no one was hit.

On our return von Borcke, who had been left in Sharpsburg, joined us and during the evening he and I got separated from the General, who was riding about the field in every direction, sending first one and then another of his staff off on some duty from which it was often difficult to rejoin him. Finding night coming on we concluded to pass it by some haystacks, which furnished both a luxurious bed and welcome food for our weary horses; the remains of the pantry plunder with which we had stored our haversacks in Pleasant Valley afforded us an excellent supper, and a well near by supplied deep draughts of cool water, of which we stood much in need after our hot day's work from early dawn.

It was quite clear from the way the enemy had massed his forces that the 17th would see a general engagement. As soon as it was light enough to see, von Borcke and myself started in search of General Stuart, whom we found occupying the yard of a small farmhouse not a quarter of a mile from our resting place. The cavalry was posted along a line closing the entrance to the peninsula formed by Antietam Creek and the Potomac, with its left resting on the river and its right connecting with our infantry left flank. The horse artillery did good service during the day but otherwise the cavalry was not engaged. Not so, however, General Stuart and his staff, for he was constantly riding over the field watching the progress of the action.

The fighting was very severe. I cannot attempt a detailed account of all its features from memory but to the eye of the soldier engaged, whose field of vision is always limited, they gained no advantage over us. Little incidents impress themselves on the memory, and telling such may interest those who may read these pages more than accounts of what they can see, better told in histories of the war.

Standing on the hill in rear of our infantry lines toward the latter part of the day with General Stuart, a battery came past us at a trot from out of the action, whose ammunition had become exhausted, and I recognized one of its non-commissioned officers, my kinsman, Charles Trueheart, and we exchanged cordial greetings. Behind the battery came hobbling as best they could a string of fearfully mutilated horses which had been turned loose as they had received their wounds, and who had followed their comrades when they left the spot where they had been in action. After they had all passed, I saw a horse galloping after them and dragging something. Thinking it was his rider as he emerged from the clouds of smoke on the field of battle, I moved to intercept and stop the animal, but to my horror discovered that the horse was dragging his own entrails from the gaping wound of a cannonball, and after passing us a few yards the poor brute fell dead with a piercing scream. The wounded horses of a battery will stay around their mates as long as the battery is in action and then try to follow, whatever their condition may be. On many battlefields my pity has been so much touched by the sufferings of wounded horses that I would stop to put them out of their pain by a friendly pistol shot. In one case I remember I came near being seriously hurt by a large horse springing forward as he fell and nearly bearing me and my horse down under him as my ball pierced his brain.

Between our cavalry lines and the enemy stood a handsome country house in which, it seems, all the women and children in the neighborhood had assembled for mutual protection, not thinking that part of the country would be the scene of conflict. Between us and the house was a roughly ploughed field. When the cannonade began, the house happened to be right in the line between Pelham's battery and that of the enemy occupying the opposite hills, the batteries firing clear over the top of the house at each other. When the crossing shells began screaming over the house, its occupants thought their time had come, and like a flock of birds they came streaming out in "Mother Hubbards," and even less, hair streaming in the wind and children of all ages stretched out behind, and tumbling at every step over the clods of the ploughed field. Every time one would fall, the rest thought it was the result of a cannon shot and ran the faster. It was impossible to keep from laughing at this sudden eruption and impossible to persuade them to return. I galloped out to meet them and represented to them that they were safe, probably, where they had been, but it was no use; so swinging up before and behind as many children as my horse could carry, I escorted them to our lines and quieted the fears of the party, assuring them that they were not in danger of immediate death. Seeing what was going on, the batteries on each side ceased firing until the little party was disposed of. Von Borcke and I spent the night at Dr. G.'s in Sharpsburg. The town had been shelled badly and some houses were burned during the day, and the streets and houses were filled with wounded men, presenting a strong contrast to the quiet, prosperous looking little place we found it two days before.

The next day we all expected the action to be renewed and General Stuart accompanied by his staff was early in the saddle, riding about over the field and visiting the headquarters of Generals Lee arid Jackson, and Longstreet. The loss of the enemy had been terrific, and ours heavy, but our men were in splendid spirits and ready for anything their idolized commander might require of them. The idea that the battle was over never entered our minds, or if it did, as the day passed on without a renewal of the attack, it was with the belief that we were the victors. In point of fact we *were* the victors so far as the two armies were concerned. All day long we offered them battle and not a shot was fired. In the late afternoon they sent in a flag of truce and asked permission to bury their dead, which was given.

Towards evening General Stuart came back to where he had left his staff, to go to an interview with General Lee, to which he had been summoned, and told me he wished me to proceed, at once and examine the Potomac River in our rear above the regular ford near Shepherdstown, and find, if possible, a ford by which cavalry could cross, and that I must do this without making inquiries among citizens; that if such a crossing could be found, to place some men at it and station a line of men at intervals of a couple of hundred yards along the route leading to the place so that I could guide a column of cavalry to it in the dark without fail, and that I must report to him by sundown. There was no time to be lost, so taking twenty men I started at a rapid trot to the river and then up the banks of the stream, noticing carefully every indication of shallow water. The only way to prove the fact was to ride in until the water became too deep, and in this way I soon became wet up to my neck, for suddenly sometimes Magic would step off a ledge into swimming water.

At last, however, I found a crossing just below a fish trap where a shallow dam had been built of loose stones over which the water poured. For a distance of ten or fifteen yards below this dam the water was shallow enough for fording and then it became deeper and deeper until it was clear past the saddle. The place was very rough and the water swift, but it was the best that could be had; so after crossing several times to learn the position of some dangerous places, I stationed a picket at the bank with orders to answer my call if I came in the dark, and returned to General Stuart, noticing carefully the unmarked route and leaving men along at intervals to guide from one to the other.

With his habitual caution General Stuart had not told me what this ford was to be used for, nor did I ask him, for I could tell well enough. By this time we had become pretty familiar with strategy and could tell what military movements meant, as by instinct.

As soon as it was dark, fires were lighted all along our lines as usual, but the movement to the rear soon showed that my surmise was correct and that the army was going to cross back into Virginia. First the wagon trains, then the artillery, and then the infantry took up the line of march to and across the river. I was sent to guide Hampton's brigade to the ford I had found, and reached it without trouble, thanks to the precautions taken, for it was very dark and a heavy fog arose from the river, wrapping everything in an impenetrable veil of mist.

The head of the column by my guidance, keeping close to the fish dam, crossed safely, but then there occurred one of those mishaps which will occur in war even after every conceivable precaution apparently has been taken. As before stated, the ford was a narrow one, along just below the fish dam; below this the water was deep and swift, and the distance across the river at this place was considerable. The fog was so thick that only a few horses' lengths in front could be seen, and in the column each horseman followed the one before him. Each horse was pressed to a certain extent downstream, and not having been told they must keep close to the fish dam, they followed their leaders all the time, losing ground by the current as they advanced. The result was that the rear of the column found itself in swimming water and had great difficulty in saving itself. Some men, I believe, were drowned and several horses were lost. The right thing would have been to post men all along the ford on the lower side, but this no one thought of until too late.

The next morning by daylight General Stuart started with two brigades of cavalry and a force of infantry and artillery to execute one of those skillful manoeuvres for which General Lee was so noted. To check a sudden movement to follow us on the part of McClellan, Stuart was to move up the river fifteen miles and attack vigorously an outpost of the enemy at Williamsport and produce the impression that a serious attack upon our enemy's flank was contemplated. We remained at the place two days, driving off the force posted there and posting our cavalry pickets three or four miles from the town and giving out to the citizens that Lee with his whole army was coming on behind. Having accomplished the object of the expedition and having drawn a considerable force of the enemy to the spot, we recrossed the river on the night of the 20th of September. During our stay we had numerous skirmishes with the enemy but could never get their cavalry to meet us away from strong infantry support. While we were at Williamsport, McClellan had thrown a force across the river in Lee's rear, but this had been fallen upon by Jackson and driven back across the river with great loss to them.

General Lee now posted his army between Winchester and Martinsburg, the cavalry occupying the line of the Potomac from Williamsport to Harpers Ferry with cavalry headquarters at Hainesville for a few days; but on the 28th they were established at "The Bower," a more convenient point from a military point of view, and the most charming in its social aspects that it has ever or since been our good fortune to encounter.

The Bower was the residence of the Dandridges, as it had been for many generations, eight miles from Martinsburg and about ten from Charlestown. A large, old-fashioned Virginia mansion, cresting a hill around which wound the silvery waters of the Opequan, and upon whose broad slopes grew noble oaks whose branches shaded the buffalo and deer long before the white man ever rested beneath them. The family consisted of Mr. Stephen Dandridge, his wife, and a house full of daughters and nieces, all grown and all attractive — some very handsome. Our headquarters encampment, consisting of about one hundred persons including staff officers, couriers and servants and about two hundred horses, was pitched in the edge of the beautiful park a few hundred yards from the house. The white tents and gay uniforms seen through the trees presented a most attractive view of this aspect of war — and war, terrible as it is, has its attractive side undoubtedly. The brilliant scene appeared like magic to the retired inmates of this elegant country home. Where the evening before only the squirrel disturbed the solitude of the park, the morning broke upon this camp of war awakened to life at sunrise by the stirring strains of martial music. To the eyes of the lovely girls who peeped through the curtains of their chambers in the light of the early morn, we were heroes of romance fresh from fields of glory — patriots ready and pining to die in the cause of their country. With such prepossessions in our favor it would have been strange indeed if the handsome young men of the staff and the gay and gallant commander of our cavalry had failed to win the friendship of our charming neighbors during the month we spent at the Bower. This was before wounds and death had made serious inroads into our military family. Hardiman Stuart, the General's aide-de-camp and relative, was the only one of us who had fallen up to that time, and little I thought how many of those assembled at the Bower would share his fate.

The month passed at the Bower was the most remarkable combination of romance and real life that it had ever been my fortune to encounter, and with none other than that warmhearted, gay, brave and enterprising soldier, our leader, would it have been possible. Unsurpassed for close attention to duty, General Stuart had the remarkable faculty of preserving his lightness of heart under all circumstances; he was as conspicuous as a leader in a ballroom as he was on a field of battle. Those who saw him only in his hours of recreation could form no true estimate of his character, and from such as these the impression prevailed with some that he was frivolous and indeed, it was even charged, dissipated and licentious. On the contrary, though he dearly loved, as any good soldier should, to kiss a pretty girl, and the pretty girls dearly loved to kiss him, he was as pure as they; and as to dissipation, he never touched wine or spirit of any kind under any circumstances. All this I know to be true, for it would have been impossible for it to have been otherwise and I not to have known it, associated with him as I was so long as a member of his military family, and one with whom he was perhaps more intimate than any other. Then, too, among all the ladies he met, and among their connections, there is not one who does not regard his memory to this day with feelings of respect and affection. From the Bower several bold cavalry movements were made, occupying sometimes several days of absence, when the partings and the greetings from our dear friends there, as we went out and came in from the stirring encounters, were as warmhearted and sincere as they were charming to us.

The host and hostess were fine specimens of Virginia country gentry under the old regime, hospitable, cultivated, and kind-hearted. Every afternoon, after the staff duties of the day were performed, we all assembled at the house for riding, walking or fishing parties, and after tea, to which we had a standing invitation which was generally accepted, came music, singing, dancing and games of every description, mingled with moonlight strolls along the banks of the beautiful Opequan or boating upon its crystal surface. The very elements seemed to conspire to make our stay delightful, for never was there a more beautiful moon or more exquisite weather than during that month we spent there.

Our General was the life of the party but he was ably seconded by von Borcke, Pelham and others of his staff, together with officers of cavalry regiments encamped near by, among whom was Colonel Brien of the 1st Virginia. Von Borcke was a thoroughly accomplished man of the world, and having been an officer of a household regiment in Berlin, in such a position he had acquired great facility in contributing to the pleasure of others in society. Brien was also good at this and these two got up some capital things for the entertainment of the company. Though so large a man, von Borcke was a fine dancer, with a step as light as a feather even in the heavy cavalry boots reaching away above the knee, which we all wore. Private theatricals, tableaux and many games new to us, von Borcke introduced.

One amusing series of scenes these two figured in which I had never seen before. A sheet was stretched across the hall, against which from behind the shadows of the actors were cast. The range of subjects adapted to this style is limited, but within its scope when well executed the effect is capital. A scene in which von Borcke lay stretched on a couch with Mr. Dandridge's capacious nightshirt on, stuffed to enormous size with pillows, was very amusing. The scene opens by roaring groans from this huge sick man, nurse appears and is sent for the doctor. The doctor, Colonel Brien, in an old mashed stovepipe hat, huge spectacles, an old-fashioned swallow-tailed coat of some Dandridge of past generations, and a bottle of physic with a streaming label attached to the neck, appears, or at least his shadow appears, and in a voice perfectly disguised begins his professional jargon with the patient. A deep draught from the bottle is administered to the sick man, and then, on the sly, the doctor takes one too, to the great delight of the audience. Between groans and ludicrous twitches of agony the sufferer communicates to the doctor that he has been to a dinner party and enumerates a long list of articles upon the bill of fare which he had consumed, comprising beef, venison, oysters, cabbage, etc. The doctor pulls up the corners of his huge standing collar, protruding away beyond his chin, lays down the old battered fragment of an umbrella tucked under his arm, and proceeds to feel the pulse and examine the tongue, pressing his hand from time to time upon the mountain of a stomach beside him, at which the patient screams and writhes and says, "Mein Gott! Mein Gott! Doctor!" Having informed the sick man in a ludicrous professional manner what is the matter, the doctor proceeds to relieve the patient by forcing his arm down his throat and, with great effort of muscular power expended in jerks and tugs, pulls out in succession, and holds up for inspection, a pair of deer's horns, some beef's horns, cabbages, stalks and all, quantities of oyster shells, etc., etc., and finally a pair of boots. At each delivery an assistant concealed behind the couch abstracts a pillow from under the nightshirt, and expressions of relief follow from the patient until a complete cure is effected and the reduced man springs up, embraces the doctor and they begin swigging at the bottle of physic with the long label attached, until they become tipsy, and the performance closes in an uproarious dance of doctor and patient. The effect of forcing the arm down the throat was, of course, produced in shadow by running the arm down alongside of the face. The wit and humor displayed in this performance I have rarely seen equalled and its effect on the audience was convulsive. All the negroes on the place were allowed to come in to see it and their intense appreciation of the scene, and their rich, broad peals of laughter added no little to its attractions.

One evening, when there was an invited company and the parlors were all full, von Borcke and Brien gave us another capital performance. They were to appear as Paddy and his sweetheart. Mr. and Mrs. Dandridge were the only two persons in the secret, and von Borcke and Brien were taken upstairs secretly for preparation under their care. Von Borcke was transformed into a blushing maiden weighing two hundred and fifty pounds and six feet two and a half inches tall; a riding skirt of one of the girls, supplemented by numerous dainty underskirts and extended by enormous hoops according to the fashion then in vogue, hung in graceful folds to conceal the huge cavalry boots the huge damsel wore. Her naturally ample bosom palpitated under skillfully arranged pillows, and was gorgeously decorated with the Dandridge family jewelry and ribbons, while "a love of a bonnet," long braids of hair, and quantities of powder and rouge completed her toilet, and in her hand she flirted coquettishly a fan of huge dimensions. Colonel Brien was admirably disguised as an Irishman dressed in holiday clothes, with a flaming red nose, Billycock hat, a short pipe, and a short, thick stick stuck under his arm. The absence of these two had been accounted for on some plausible pretext, so that when they made their appearance in the ballroom the surprise was complete. Both acted their parts to perfection. Paddy entertained the fair girl on his arm with loud and humorous remarks as they sauntered around the room, to which she replied with a simpering affectation that was irresistibly ludicrous. No one had the faintest conception as to who they were, so perfect was the disguise. Before the company recovered from the surprise of their appearance the music struck up a lively waltz, and round and round the couple went, faster and faster went the music, and faster and faster flew the strangers. It was not until in the fury of the whirling dance, with hoop skirts flying horizontally, that twinkling amid the white drapery beneath, the well-known boots of von Borcke betrayed the first suspicion of who the lady was. As suddenly as they had come they vanished, waltzing out through the open door and followed by convulsive roars of laughter from the delighted audience. Nothing would satisfy the company but their reappearance, and in they came arm in arm to enter into conversation with their friends. The skill of their disguise and their acting was now even more remarkable than at first. It was really difficult to detect their personalities even then.

Von Borcke and myself were great friends; every one has faults and weaknesses and he had his like the rest of us, but he had many attractive qualities, *particularly on the surface*. Having been bred a soldier and born an aristocrat he was at heart proud and imperious, but he had himself thoroughly under control and could be, and generally was, very agreeable. He never spoke of his country or his high social position there unless asked about it, and then, if he found real interest was felt, he would be communicative and very entertaining about it. He had more tact than any young man I ever knew, and could adapt himself to any company. Among the private soldiers he was *very* popular, adopting a frank air of good fellowship which won their good will without sacrifice of dignity. In female society his manners were exceedingly fine, and among his comrades of the staff he was generally liked, though he became a little spoiled by the admiration he received in society wherever we went. General Stuart was very fond of him at first but got a little tired of him towards the last when he became affected by the praises which Stuart had been mainly instrumental in bringing to him. He owed everything to General Stuart and it was a debt he was inclined sometimes to forget latterly. I remember now many little things which I did not then see through clearly. He got General Stuart to place the body of couriers detailed at headquarters, some forty or fifty men, under his command and to give him the title of Chief of Staff in consequence. We could not conceive why he was so tenacious of this trifling matter until his book appeared after the war in which he calls himself Chief of Staff of the Cavalry of the Army of Northern Virginia. This position, Chief of Staff, in European armies is second in importance to that only of the General himself. In our army there was no corresponding position, the Chief of Staff in this case being only the officer who managed the domestic affairs of the military family at headquarters. The General himself controlled directly all movements of troops. This, and appropriating many achievements of other staff officers and greatly exaggerating his own were some of the weaknesses of character which were developed in the exceedingly interesting series of papers he wrote for *Blackwood's Magazine*, which were afterwards published in book form.

Many and many a long night on the march have I drawn von Borcke out about his country, and much valuable and interesting information did I receive thereby. Von Borcke and his servant were perpetually in trouble. Whatever restraint he exercised over himself towards others was omitted in the case of his servants, of whom he had an endless succession, no one being able to remain with him long. Under Gilbert's faithful care, my domestic comfort was particularly well cared for in our camp life, and von Borcke proposed one day at The Bower that I would share my tent with him. I did not like the idea much, and Gilbert still less, but it was difficult to refuse as von Borcke's domestic infelicity and discomfort were the laughing stock of the company. I at last agreed and he moved in, bag and baggage, the last consisting, besides his saddle and what was carried thereon, of a tin wash basin and small valise. The basin was duly mounted on one side of the tent door, like mine on the other, on three stakes driven into the ground, and close at hand was planted a tall stake with numerous prongs, from which dangled towels, a sponge and a small looking glass corresponding to a like toilet table on my side of the house.

But it was in the close contact of roommates that such natural asperities of temper as he had could not always be covered by the smooth mantle of art, and von Borcke and myself soon had a quarrel. It was about some trifle; I scarce remember what — the tin wash basin, if I am not mistaken — but it was no less a quarrel and a hot one, though it lasted only a short time and was the only break in our friendship that ever occurred. He was a man whom it would not do to allow to encroach, and after this was clearly impressed upon him there was no further trouble. The absurdity of the thing kept us both quiet about the matter; we had ceased speaking to each other for several days and no doubt would have made up in time. We were both desirous particularly that General Stuart should not hear of the coolness between us, as such things were very painful to him when occurring in his military family, and particularly between two he was so fond of. Ill luck, however, would have it otherwise. Major Fitz Hugh, our Adjutant General, one of the best fellows in the world, happened to be present when the difficulty occurred, and was the only member of the staff who knew of it. A night or two afterwards an expedition was to be sent out which two members of the staff were to accompany. We were all sitting around the campfire in front of the General's tent when Fitz Hugh came out of the office tent and asked the General which two officers he wished him to detail on this service, and he told him von Borcke and Blackford. Fitz Hugh coughed and signaled to the General who got up and followed him into the tent, and presently the written orders were issued for two others to go in our stead.

The next morning General Stuart called von Borcke into his tent and asked him about our disagreement; he said it was nothing and that he was sorry for it etc. etc. The General then came to my tent and told me what von Borcke had said, and I told him I had none but the kindest feelings towards the Major and was quite willing to make it up. So the General called von Borcke in and we shook hands and never quarrelled afterwards. I have mentioned this insignificant affair to illustrate the kindly feeling of General Stuart towards his staff and his great aversion to all personal disagreements around him.

We had at headquarters a capital band of singers who were accompanied by Sweeny on his banjo, Bob, the General's mulatto servant, on the bones, and occasionally by a violin and other instruments. But the main standby was Sweeny and his banjo, and every evening at the Bower this formed a part of the entertainment.

As soon as we all got settled I got General Stuart to give me an escort of five men and I went across the mountain to near Dranesville to get Comet, whom I had left at a farm house after his wound. The enemy were in occupation of the country where he was, but we went in at night and brought him off safely, being absent only two days. The wound in Comet's neck was running and was fearfully offensive. It would explode at times squirting the contents across the road against the fences as we rode rapidly along. Having an opportunity soon after, I sent him home where he remained in pasture for the rest of the war.

Our camp life now was very comfortable. A long table under an open fly was our dining hall where the General and his staff took their meals and where we were seldom without guests. The country abounded in provisions at this season and we lived delightfully. Ten days of delightful rest and enjoyment slipped rapidly by, but on the morning of the 1st of October we were reminded that *we* were still in this world, and not in a soldier's paradise, by a call to arms. The enemy had made a vigorous attack upon our outposts at several points, while the sun was scarcely above the horizon, and our cavalry camps were instantly the scene of quick preparation for meeting it and for falling back upon the main body of the army should it prove a general advance in force.

Couriers came dashing in frequently with dispatches from the extended front we covered, and General Stuart awaited further developments to see to which point to repair in person. Our light headquarters camp was struck and everything put in the wagons to await further orders, while we of the staff, with horses saddled, waited also. At the Bower all was consternation and tears, but we assured them it would soon be over and that we would not all be killed.

Towards the middle of the day it became evident that the main attack was from towards Shepherdstown and General Stuart and the rest of us proceeded thitherward at a gallop. It was an attack of cavalry, supported as usual by infantry, under Pleasanton. Upon our General's appearance a general advance of our lines was made in splendid style and the enemy retreated in a panic, followed at full speed by our cavalry, and we drove them across the river at Shepherdstown in great confusion, capturing many prisoners and killing quite a number, General Stuart as usual leading his men with great gallantry and inspiring confidence and enthusiasm wherever he went.

It was near midnight before we returned to the Bower but the family was still up awaiting our return with their hospitable board spread with a substantial repast, to which our busy day's work enabled us to do full justice, while the narration of the events which had transpired was eagerly listened to by our admiring and sympathizing friends.

Von Borcke was sent next day with a flag of truce and some dispatches from General Lee to McClellan about some business or other, about exchanges of prisoners I believe, and on his return entertained us much by his account of his trip within the enemy's lines — he having gone, by a strange oversight on their part, to headquarters of the army. He tells a story well, particularly when he can draw a little upon his imagination, as he could in this case, since he was alone. He was gotten up in great style in a new uniform and really did look a superb specimen of the soldier.

We again returned to our charming life of social enjoyment among the lovely maidens of the Bowser, and deep were the wounds of Cupid's shafts in the susceptible hearts of the gay young fellows at cavalry headquarters with their General in the lead; in love as well as in war always among the first. Oh ye huge shady trees along the rippling banks of the moonlit Opequan! how many tales ye could tell of those good old days. Pelham was badly struck as he always was. Three girls went in mourning for him, poor fellow, when he fell. But it was impossible to help being wounded by such darts under such circumstances. There was a feeling, as von Borcke, before he had become familiar with the language, expressed it, of "Let us enjoy ourselves, Blackford, today for we know not that we shall live until tomorrow yet." This he said one day when I remonstrated with him for ordering all the delicacies we had in our headquarters mess to be cooked at one time. After so many narrow escapes each one of us began to think it was only a question of time and chance when his time would come, though up to then only one of us had fallen, and that we had as well be happy while we could. I could see by now that the war had no end that was apparent, and I had little thought that I would survive until its termination.

We were now to engage in the most daring and brilliant affair that the cavalry of our army had up to that time attempted, an expedition up into Pennsylvania under Stuart with cavalry alone. To realize the boldness of this movement it must be recollected that the Potomac could only be crossed at fords that were by no means frequent and that the country was filled with railroads and telegraph lines to give notice of us and to intercept us by movements of troops, and that being in a hostile country, all information that the country people could give of our movements would be contributed to those engaged in our pursuit. The remarkable success of the expedition was to be attributed first to the shrewdness and sagacity and boldness of its leader, and secondly to the luck of the weather being so favorable. For a large part of the time it was misty, preventing signal stations from seeing and communicating intelligence of our movements.

A detail of eighteen hundred men selected from the whole cavalry force was divided into three bodies under the command respectively of General Hampton, Colonels W. H. F. Lee, and Jones ("Grumble Jones," my old Captain), and four pieces of artillery under Pelham. Only picked men and horses could go. Von Borcke of the staff had to remain in camp as his horses were in poor condition and unequal to the trip and we were sorry to lose him. I notice in his book he says he was left in Stuart's place, while he was away, but the real reason was that his negligence in attention to them and his unmerciful treatment of his horses had rendered them unfit for use at this time. He had always, I suppose, had grooms who attended to his horses without looking after them, and his only idea of riding was to dash about at full speed, regardless of his horse.

The force assembled at Darkesville and camped that night above Williamsport to cross at daylight on the 10th at McCoy's ford, and we captured the picket at that place. A large infantry force had just marched by, going westward, as we came to the great National turnpike, the road which, before the B. &. O. B. R. was built, was the great avenue to the West. The luck of not encountering this force at the outset was a source of congratulation for it might have caused such delay as to have made the trip impracticable. A signal station was also captured by surprise, and our movement thus concealed the longer. General Stuart had capital guides, soldiers of our army from Western Maryland who knew every foot of the country and many of the people. Finding that the enemy had a large force at Hagerstown, the General determined to push northward to Chambersburg. At Mercersburg I found that a citizen of the place had a county map and of course called at the house for it, as these maps had every road laid down and would be of the greatest service to us. Only the females of the family appeared, who flatly refused to let me have the map, or to acknowledge that they had one; so I was obliged to dismount and push by the infuriated ladies, rather rough specimens, however, into the sitting room where I found the map hanging on the wall. Angry women do not show to advantage, and the language and looks of these were fearful, as I coolly cut the map out of its rollers and put it in my haversack.

Our line of march was as follows: one division of six hundred men formed the advance and another of six hundred the rear guard, while the third division of six hundred occupied the centre and were to do the collecting of horses along the line of our route. General Stuart determined to take nothing but horses, as cattle would have delayed our movements. That part of Pennsylvania was full of great, fat Conestoga horses of the Norman breed, most valuable animals for artillery purposes but wholly unfit for cavalry mounts. Everything was arranged, but no plundering was to take place until we had crossed the Maryland border. The men were wild with enthusiasm, and eagerly watched for the line across which the fun would begin. The middle division was arranged so that parties of half a dozen or a dozen under an officer were to dash out right and left to the farm houses and bring in the horses, which were then tied by their halters three together and led by a soldier riding alongside.

As good luck would have it the day was cloudy with occasional showers, and the thrifty Pennsylvania farmers were assembled in their huge barns threshing wheat. From every direction through the mist our foraging parties were guided to the spot by the droning hum of the threshers with which all these Pennsylvania barns are provided. For the fun of the thing I joined in several charges of this kind and in every case was rewarded by amusing scenes, to say nothing of the raids we made upon the well filled pantries at the houses. These Dutch farmers live well, and there was no end to the stores of good things they had on hand. The prevailing custom of baking their bread once or twice a week in quantities was a godsend to us, for it supplied all our eighteen hundred men wanted and a vast deal over. Riding up to the humming barn a rap at the entrance with a sabre hilt would bring the surprised owner to the door. Sometimes our presence would be accounted for by claiming to be U. S. soldiers pressing horses and then we would be entertained by a general cursing of the Government, the army and the war in general. The horses were all hitched up to the machines; so we brought off harness and all, which was no doubt very convenient to our batteries as no collar we had would have fitted these huge, bull-necked animals.

After allowing the farmer to air his patriotism awhile, our men would admit they held the same unfriendly opinion of Lincoln, and then tell the astounded fellow who they were. Generally he would not believe the statement at first and the expression of his face, and the faces of the men working with him, as the truth broke upon them, was very amusing. Some seemed paralyzed by fear, but the greater number accepted our assurances of safety in good part and took their loss good humoredly, after they knew it was not done by their own people. After getting the horses the pantry was inspected; where there was such abundance the men became choice and would take only freshly baked bread, leaving behind in exchange any less fresh they might have on hand from previous collections. The returning party would present a vista of roasted turkeys, hams and rounds of beef strapped to the saddles, brown rolls peeping out from haversacks and crocks of cream and rolls of butter carried in the hand for the refreshment of friends in the column who had not yet gone out foraging.

If the day had been fine and the people out in the fields, the news of our coming would no doubt have spread and not nearly so many horses would have been collected. A clean sweep of all on the place was generally made, but I remember that in one case I made an exception in a rather curious manner. It was at a house whose occupants were evidently more cultivated and refined than usual for that part of the country, for though the average Pennsylvania farmer is the most prosperous agriculturist in our country, he does not know nor care for the refinements of life usually. We had just taken an unusually nice looking lot of horses out of the barn when quite a genteel looking old lady came out and asked that we would let her keep her old driving horse, which she assured us was in the thirty-fifth year of his age. She said she had owned him from a colt and knew him to be that old, and that he had long since done nothing but work in her buggy when she wanted to go anywhere, and that he would be of no use whatever to us. I asked her to point out the animal. It was a handsome dark brown which at a little distance with head up and fine prominent eyes looked like anything but the horse she represented. On closer inspection, however, gray hairs could be seen all over the glossy, well groomed hide, and around the eyes and nose they gave a distinct tinge to the prevailing color. But the moment I opened his mouth I saw the old lady's account was true, his teeth were worn off level with the gums. This was an animal whose age was as seldom reached by his kind as that of a hundred and twenty-five years would be by a human being. Bowing to the old lady I returned her faithful and noble favorite, to her great delight.

During this long day's march everything indicated our coming to be unexpected, and not a shadow of opposition appeared. The truth was that their cavalry were afraid to meet us and gladly availed themselves of the pretext of not being able to find us. Up to this time the cavalry of the enemy had no more confidence in themselves than the country had in them, and whenever we got a chance at them, which was rarely, they came to grief.

It was after dark, at the close of a march of about forty miles, that our advance guard reached a hill close to the town of Chambersburg where General Stuart expected to pass the night. There was every reason to think, however, that troops might have been thrown into the town, and our General naturally felt anxious about it. Artillery was placed in position quickly and a small party sent in with a flag of truce to demand the surrender of the place. All the local authorities had fled, however, and we had to take quiet possession from some citizens who appeared. As we rode in the people came to their doors freely and some spoke kindly. General Hampton was placed in command of the town for the night, the troops were distributed around it, and the men snatched a few hours' rest in the drizzling rain and chill. General Stuart occupied a house in the edge of the town and after carefully providing for Magic, I got a little uncomfortable sleep on the floor of a room, in my wet clothes and with arms buckled on, ready for instant service. It doesn't look as if it ought to take any time to buckle on a sabre and put on a field glass and haversack, but when suddenly called to arms in the night it is very distracting and something is apt to be left behind, so I always slept completely equipped when on active service, and slept the sounder for feeling ready for any emergency.

We were now immediately in rear of McClellan's army at Harpers Ferry, about forty miles from the Potomac where we had crossed, above McClellan, and double that distance from the river at the fords below his position. No one knew when day broke what our movements were to be, as General Stuart had preserved absolute reticence upon that subject. To return by the route we had come would be nearer, but would it be the safer? The march to the lower fords would take us for a long distance very near the main body of the enemy, and below the river was deeper and the fords less numerous. But the enemy would be expecting us above and would not be expecting us below, for he would never dream of our attempting to cross below and so near him. But in war an axiom is, Never to do what your enemy expects if you can help it.

Just as the sun rose the command moved out of town and until the head of the column turned eastward, no one knew which direction it would take. Even then by marching some miles towards Gettysburg, Stuart produced the impression that he was going to attack in that direction, but after proceeding far enough for this purpose, the line of march was turned southward towards Leesburg, and the men knew they were to make a second grand circuit of McClellan's army, greater than the first on the Chickahominy on account of the greater distance and because it was through the enemy's country.

A detachment under Col. M. C. Butler was left behind to burn the depot and cars, and some stores of government arms and supplies in the town, after which they followed us.

Just as the column cleared the town, General Stuart asked me to ride on ahead with him a little way so as to be out of hearing, and then followed a conversation which made an indelible impression on me, and is now as fresh in my memory as if it had occurred yesterday. He said, after a long pause in which he was plunged in thought, "Blackford, I want to explain my motives to you for taking this lower route and if I should fall before reaching Virginia, I want you to vindicate my memory," these were his exact words I think, for they impressed me strongly by the unusual earnestness with which they were spoken. He then took out his map and explained all I have already said: how Cox's command which we passed behind on the National road would be halted to wait for him, and how from its hilliness that upper country could be so easily defended, while below they would not be expecting him, the fords were not easily defended from the rear, the country was level and open and everything was to our advantage except the much greater distance and passing so close to the enemy at Harpers Ferry. These two last difficulties he would meet by quick marching and precautions against information reaching them. He then asked me if I understood his reasons and what I thought of them. I told him I understood them perfectly and agreed with him fully in thinking this a wise movement, and if the contingency he spoke of arose and I survived him, I should certainly see that his motives were understood aright. I felt much touched by this mark of confidence, and both his eyes and mine filled as we closed the conversation and began a march which for length, speed and boldness has few equals in cavalry annals.

From a point about forty miles in rear of the enemy we were to march to a crossing of the Potomac ten or fifteen miles below his position, passing within less than ten miles of his main body, so that for the greater part of the day we were going directly towards their camps. The march was the longest without a halt I have ever experienced. Starting from Chambersburg that morning we marched all that day, all that night and until four o'clock the next day before reaching Leesburg in Virginia; ninety miles with only one halt of half an hour to feed the horses the evening of the first day. It was only by riding captured horses and resting their own that the men could keep up, though I myself rode Magic the whole time without change, fearing to loose her, in case of a sudden attack. I found opportunity, however, to rest her occasionally during the night by walking and leading her. During these walks I also broke up ears of green corn and fed her with them, she eating cob and all most ravenously. This march, it must be recollected, was preceded by a day and a half of hard marching before reaching Chambersburg.

The column, by the time we got all the horses we wanted, was about five miles long. First there was the advanced guard of one squadron, preceded by three videttes at a distance of a hundred and fifty yards ahead; a couple of hundred yards behind the advance guard came a division of six hundred men with a section of artillery, then six hundred men leading the horses, and then six hundred bringing up the rear with a section of artillery, followed by a squadron for a rear guard, about the same distance behind that the advanced guard was in front, and behind them again three men for videttes. General Stuart usually rode at the head of the 1st Division, sending his staff frequently back along the column to see that everything was closed up and in order. My place usually was with the advanced guard and I generally rode with the three videttes in front so as to report to the General at once anything we might encounter. Having my powerful glasses, I could see exactly the character of any body of men we came in sight of, and thus could tell whether those we saw at a distance were armed men or only country people and thus saving much delay in approaching them. General Stuart issued orders that no firearms were to be used in attack, nothing but the sabre alone until further orders. This was to prevent as much as possible the noise from giving intelligence of our position. If the enemy appeared on either side of the column the Colonel of the Regiment then passing should instantly and without further orders charge. So long as we were in Pennsylvania the collection of horses continued, but it ceased as soon as we crossed the line into Maryland.

Unlike the day before, the weather now was clear, but there was no dust fortunately, owing to the rain, and signal stations at a distance could see nothing of us, which they would have done had the great cloud of dust usually hanging over a cavalry column been present.

It seemed almost incredible that the enemy should not have discovered our position as the day wore on. Why their cavalry had not hung upon our rear and given intelligence of our route is unaccountable. The truth was, no doubt, that their cavalry was afraid of us, for up to that time our superiority in that arm of the service was unquestioned, and they seldom ventured within our reach, and whenever they did they invariably came to grief. But why a small party should not have followed us and given information can be attributed only to bad management, for they could have gotten the information in a friendly country without ever making an attack, by means of the citizens along the roads we passed. But so it was, as appears now from their official dispatches, that up to our reaching the river on our return, they had no exact intelligence of our movements. They knew early in the day by a dispatch from Colonel McClure, the editor of the *Philadelphia Times*, who was in Chambersburg, that we had left there going eastward, and General McClellan inferred *we* would attempt a crossing below him. He sent all his cavalry to intercept us and some thirty miles from the river we passed within four miles of General Pleasanton and his large body of cavalry, but he knew not of our presence. The details of this march are well given in H. B. McClellan's book, *The Campaigns of Stuart's Cavalry*, and as I only attempt in this narrative an account of my personal observations, I will refer the reader to this book for a careful and accurate history of the movements on both sides.

The success of the expedition was largely due to the excellent guides General Stuart had provided himself with; until now Logan and Harbaugh, who had lived in Pennsylvania, acted, but as we approached Maryland, Capt. B. S. White became the guide; his residence in that part of Maryland made him thoroughly acquainted with every road in it. It was very pleasant to get amongst friends once more upon crossing the line into Maryland, though we could not take their horses.

The first place we came to was the little town of Emmitsburg which we reached about sundown, thirty-one miles from Chambersburg, and still forty-five miles from our crossing place. If we had fallen from the clouds the people could not have been more astonished than at seeing us come from the direction we followed, and their demonstrations of delight at seeing us were unbounded. An hour before our arrival a detachment of Rush's Lancers, a scouting party of a hundred and forty men, sent to look for us, had passed through the town, and hearing of this, General Stuart had issued orders to overtake and capture any one attempting to leave the place while we were in it. Just as the advanced guard entered the street, a young lady rode out of a yard of a house before us, and seeing, to her dismay, a body of soldiers, which she took for Federals of course, she dashed off out of town towards her home some miles in the country. Our men called upon her to halt, but this only made her whip up her horse the more, and being reluctant to use their firearms, the only thing to do was for two of the best mounted to overtake and capture her. It was an exciting race for a mile and the poor young lady was, as she told us, scared almost to death, but finding she could not escape she pulled up and surrendered in great terror. But when she and her captors appeared leisurely riding back they were in high good humor, laughing and talking over the adventure. The young lady returned to the house she had been visiting and was requested to remain there until we had been gone an hour. Though only a mile or two from the Pennsylvania state line, the people here seemed to be intensely Southern in their sympathies and omitted no opportunity of showing us attention during the short half hour *we* passed among them.

Our long, terrible night march was now to begin. It is no small tax upon one's endurance to remain marching all night; during the day there is always something to attract the attention and amuse, but at night there is nothing. The monotonous jingle of arms and accoutrements mingles with the tramp of horses' feet into a drowsy hum all along the marching column, which makes one extremely sleepy, and to be sleepy and not to be allowed to sleep is exquisite torture. Only thirst, with water in sight but out of reach, is so bad. The night was not dark and through the uncertain light my tortured imagination, becoming strongly excited by loss of sleep, presented in the lights and shades of the forest, castles and beautiful houses along the road, which dissolved into thin air time and again as I drew nearer. Over and over again I made sure I could not be mistaken; there was the lawn, there the towers, and bay windows and gables as plain as could be, and yet in a moment it was nothing but a clump of trees, and the same illusion was experienced by many of my friends. It was a great relief to get down and walk, and this I did often during the night. Many of the men went fast to sleep on their horses and snores loud and long could be heard all along the column.

Once during the night I had an adventure with a dog which amused General Stuart and my comrades of the staff no little, though it was not at all amusing to me. Passing a country house, General Stuart told me to go in and find out if the man had seen or heard anything of the enemy. Lie waited at the gate of the yard while I dismounted and went in. The house stood fifty yards from the road, and half way to it a large bulldog dashed out and made a furious attack upon me. We were now very near the camps of the enemy and it would not do to use firearms, so I received the dog on the point of my sabre, inflicting a wound in the shoulder which, though arresting his first attack, placed him upon his guard and only infuriated him the more. He circled round and round just out of reach of my thrusts, uttering savage growls which showed plainly enough what he would do if he could get hold of me with his teeth. Stuart roared with laughter and called out continually, "Give it to him, Blackford," for he had an instinctive love of fighting and enjoyed seeing the battle, and but for the order about firearms I would have made quick work of it with my pistol. Soon, however, the man came out and called off the dog, and gave us all the information he had, which was nothing. I represented myself as a Federal officer and first inquired if any rebels had been seen or heard of by him and then what Union (our) troops had passed that way. But no troops of any kind had been seen or heard of by him. Knowing that many of the inhabitants were Union men I thought it safer to assume the part I did and to leave the man under the impression that we were Federals.

When day dawned on the morning of the 12th, we entered Hayattstown, having made sixty-five miles from Chambersburg in twenty hours. It was this great speed which baffled the enemy who had by this time found out in a general manner that we were moving southward, and were crowding all their available troops towards our supposed route to intercept us. Stoneman and Pleasanton with their cavalry were in hot pursuit, infantry was strung along the river at every ford, and a large force was placed on trains of cars at Monocacy crossing ready to move to any point at which they might be needed. The most of these facts were discovered by Stuart from intercepted dispatches, and his sagacity, boldness and quickness were taxed to the utmost to meet the occasion. By changing horses frequently the artillery was enabled to keep up during the tremendous march we had made, but there was still twelve miles between us and the river, within which twelve miles the ruin of all our hopes might lie.

It was now that the services of Captain White as a guide became so valuable. This was where he had lived all his life and every by-road was well known to him. By marching down a road towards a lower ford to deceive the enemy and then suddenly turning down through a cart track in the woods White led the column to a ford that was little used and where we were little expected. While on the main road we overtook a scouting party of the enemy, the first troops we had met in the whole expedition, and charged them, putting them to instant rout.

When the head of the column reached the river at the ford we were aiming for, called White's ford, we found it occupied along the wooded banks by what appeared to be a regiment of infantry. Preparations were instantly made for attacking them by dismounting the men and placing the artillery in battery, but as their position was a strong one, Gen. W. H. F. Lee, who was in command of our party, thought he would try a demand for surrender. So he sent in a flag of truce stating that Stuart with his whole force was there and he would give them fifteen minutes to surrender before an attack would be made. At the end of that time the advance was begun, but, as General Lee expected, they were in full retreat down the river under cover of the bank, to our unbounded satisfaction. A serious resistance from such a force, in such a position, at such a time, must have caused considerable delay, and possibly enough to have enabled the large forces near by to assemble and destroy us.

There was nothing to be done now but get the command across as quickly as possible, for General Stuart found to his great relief that the flood produced by the late heavy rains had not yet reached the place. A force was posted above and below to oppose and hold in check the enemy who was advancing from both directions, while Pelham pounded away with two guns first one side and then the other, with great spirit, on the heads of their columns in full view of us. It was of the utmost importance that the crossing should be effected without delay, and the captured horses were so famished for water that there was great danger of the narrow' ford becoming choked with them while drinking; so General Stuart sent me to the ford with orders that no man should stop to water his horse while crossing the river. It was necessary to repeat the order to every company commander as he came by and to see that it was enforced, for sometimes the horses would stop in spite of everything and plunge their heads up to their eyes into the water to take deep draughts of what they so much needed.

Some guns were trotted across first to go into battery on the opposite bank to cover the crossing of the main body and the long line of cavalry, and then the great horses which we had captured came rapidly past, led in couples. These captured horses presented rather a gaunt appearance, for they had been without a mouthful of food or drink for twenty-four hours and it was only by vigorous applications of the wagon whips captured with them that they could be forced on without stopping to drink. The ford was so wide, however, and the water so deep, that the horses managed to drink all the water they wanted without stopping before they passed out on the other side.

The last files of the last division were entering the water when General Stuart rode down the bank to where I was and in a voice choked with emotion, and his eyes filling as he spoke, said, "Blackford, we are going to loose our rear guard." "How is that, General?" I asked in surprise. "Why," said he, "I have sent four couriers to Butler to call him in, and he is not here, and you see the enemy is closing in upon us from above and below." This was Col. M. C. Butler of South Carolina, afterwards U. S. Senator, who was in command of the rear guard that day. "Let me try it, General," said I. He paused a moment and then, extending his hand, said, "All right; if we don't meet again, good-bye, old fellow." As I started off he called out, "Tell Butler if he can't get through, to strike back into Pennsylvania and try to get back through West Virginia. Tell him to come in at a gallop."

This interview made a strong impression on me and every word that passed was what I have stated. Now was one of the occasions when Magic's tremendous powers of endurance became so valuable. With all the extra distance I had made backwards and forwards along the column with orders, she had travelled nearly one hundred miles since leaving Chambersburg, and yet when I turned her head and spoke to her she dashed off up the bank with a snort and a toss of her crest, as full of spirit as ever. As I rose the bank I passed Pelham who with one gun, kept back for the purpose, was rapidly firing alternately up and down the river at masses of the enemy plainly in view not over a quarter of a mile away. We waved our hats at each other as I passed, and then I settled down in my saddle for a long heat. Knowing it would not do to let Magic in her then condition go as fast as she would if given full rein, I held her in to a good stiff gallop, which I thought she could keep for several miles without killing herself, and away we went. Courier after courier was passed coming back, who said they could not find Colonel Butler. The route along the obscure by-roads we had marched over was clearly marked by our trail, so there was no danger of missing it. The place where I expected to find Butler was passed, and on and on I went. One, two, and over three miles, until I gave up all hope of getting to him in time to save his command; but to find him I was determined, and kept on. At last at a sudden turn of the road I dashed right into the rear guard, halted and facing to the rear. Going on to where Butler was I called him aside and explained the situation to him. In a moment we were in motion at a trot, but I leaned over and told Butler we must move faster or we would be cut off, that General Stuart said he must come in at a gallop. It was necessary of course not to make the men nervous by letting the situation be known. Butler then put his command at a gallop and on we came at good speed. There was a gun with the rear guard and there was some doubt of the team being able to move fast enough. I told Colonel Butler we must abandon it if there was to be any delay, otherwise the command would be lost. He was very reluctant to abandon the gun, and to our surprise and pleasure the horses held out and brought the gun in safely.

We could hear the boom of Pelham's gun in the distance and so long as that continued in action, I knew the way was still open. As we approached the ford Colonel Butler got everything ready for a charge if it should be necessary to cut our way through to the ford, and with drawn sabres we dashed into the field where the entrance to the ford was. There stood Pelham with his piece and there the enemy, just as I had left them, with an open gap between for us to pass through. In a moment we were at the ford and Pelham's gun rumbling along after us into the water.

We were not half across when the bank we had left was swarming with the enemy who opened a galling fire upon us, the bullets splashing the water around us like a shower of rain. But the guns from the Virginia side immediately opened on them and mitigated their fire considerably, and we soon crossed and stood once more on Virginia soil. The march was continued a few miles farther to Leesburg, where we encamped that afternoon as weary a set as ever dismounted. Magic retained her strength and spirit to the last and would bound forward at the slightest touch of the spur, as full of fire as ever. I sat up until ten o'clock to give her a third heavy feed of corn, making thirty-six ears of corn that she ate in about six hours. There was some danger in giving her so much, but I gave her plenty of salt and she suffered no inconvenience.

The General unfortunately lost two of his horses during this trip, "Sky-lark" and "Lady Margrave," which Bob, his servant, was leading. Bob fell asleep in a fence corner and was captured with his charge.

There is one incident of our night march which I have omitted that was a delightful variety to its monotony. One valuable source of information which General Stuart always counted on was from ladies who had been left in the lines of the enemy. When we were in Urban a our headquarters were near the house of Mr. Cocky, in whose family there were some charming young ladies with whom we became very well acquainted. Our line of march passed within a few miles of Urbana, and on reaching New Market General Stuart rode up to me and said laughingly, "Blackford, how would you like to see the 'New York rebel' tonight?" This was the name he had given a beautiful young lady, a kinswoman of Mr. Cocky, who was staying at his house, who was a great friend of mine while we were there. I told him I should be delighted and he said, "Come on then," and off we started with several members of the staff and some of the couriers, making a party of about a dozen persons. The night was light enough to see very well and the roads were perfectly familiar to us from our experience during the Maryland campaign; so there was really no danger of capture even if we had fallen in with a force of the enemy, for we could have scattered and rejoined the command. A little after midnight the party halted in front of Mr. Cocky's house and General Stuart and the members of his staff present dismounted and entered the yard. Our knock at the door was answered from an upstairs window by a frightened female voice, "Who is there?" "General Stuart and staff," was the answer. The head peeped out and with a little scream disappeared again followed by hurried sounds of rushing about the room and questions from other frightened and incredulous voices as to who it was. Some did not believe the report and another pretty head in curl papers peeped out, "Who did you say it was?" she asked. "General Stuart and staff," shouted the General with a ringing laugh, "come down and open the door." Down fell the window and a general hustling on of dresses followed, succeeded presently by the sounds of the steps of those who had gotten on their shoes. Then came a rush down stairs, bolts and bars rattled and our lovely friends appeared in the moonlight, their kind faces beaming with pleasure at this unlooked for and pleasant meeting. Our time was limited, and in half an hour we had to tear ourselves away and gallop across to the line of march again.

This raid of Stuart's has been much criticized, and it has been charged that too much risk was run for the resulting gain. It must be recollected, however, that at that time the prestige of our cavalry was such that the opposition of their cavalry was considered of very little account by us. Their infantry alone we regarded as any serious obstacle, and this of course could not stop cavalry in an open country where there was room to march around them. They could only afford serious trouble by occupying the fords of the Potomac in superior numbers at every point. This General Stuart knew was impracticable for them on such short notice as they would have; so although we were very fortunate in avoiding an engagement entirely, yet the success of the expedition would not have been placed in jeopardy by even very considerable opposition. We had a picked band of the very best of our cavalry, every man thoroughly armed and equipped, eighteen hundred in number, perfectly drilled to fight either mounted as cavalry or dismounted as infantry. It would have been a cold day for any force of their cavalry which they could bring into action then to have placed themselves in the way of men such as ours, fighting towards home. The destruction of supplies in Chambersburg amounted to $250,000 worth, and besides paroling several hundred prisoners we brought off twelve or fifteen hundred horses. While capturing some horses on a farm in Pennsylvania our party was about to turn loose, as too young for service, a splendid two-year-old colt of the Percheron breed of horses; the filly was about fifteen hands high, which for that age was very large, and her form was very fine; so, knowing I would have an opportunity by the person I was to send Comet home by, I concluded to bring her along, and I sent her to the Meadows where she became a valuable work horse.

Leaving the troops to come on at their leisure, General Stuart, accompanied by his staff, pushed on to headquarters where we were received by the family at the Bower with great demonstrations of joy. They had been of course very anxious about us. To our great delight we found Maj. N. R. Fitzhugh at headquarters, just exchanged as a prisoner of war. He had been captured at Verdiersville just before the 2nd Battle of Manassas as heretofore mentioned, the first capture of any member of our staff. We listened with much interest to all he had to tell of the morning he was taken and how uneasy he was at seeing how near General Stuart was to capture as he passed the place, a prisoner, where the attack was made on our party; and when he saw General Stuart's hat and haversack which they got he said his heart sank within him until he found that the owner had made his escape. They treated him very politely, the commanding officer inviting him to ride with his staff.

Several days of delightful rest and enjoyment followed our return, and on the loth a grand ball celebrated our return to the Bower, where Von Borcke and Brien contributed greatly as usual to the entertainment by their dances and tableaux.

The next morning early a courier arrived in hot haste from the front with a dispatch stating that the enemy in considerable force of all arms had crossed the river and was marching southward. General Stuart accompanied by his staff was soon moving rapidly to the front where he found at least a division of infantry and strong forces of the other arms in proportion, engaged with our retiring outposts. All day long we skirmished with them, falling slowly backward, until it began to look like it was a general advance of their army. When within a mile of the Bower and late in the evening, a halt was made, they withdrew a mile and went into camp. Satisfied that this was all for that day General Stuart made the proper dispositions of his force and we returned to the hospitable Bower, its cordial welcome and its cheerful fireside. Here we found two Englishmen come on a visit to headquarters. The Hon. Francis Lawley M. C. and Mr. Frank Vizetelly, correspondent of the *Illustrated News*. Mr. Lawley was the correspondent of the *London Times*. These gentlemen were often after this our guests, and we all became very fond of them.

The next morning fighting was renewed and General Lee came up with Hill's division to support us, but before our infantry arrived the enemy began retreating. While crossing from one part of the field to another with orders from General Stuart, I felt my horse, a captured animal I had mounted that morning, stagger in a suspicious way, and I fortunately pulled up in time for him to come to a halt before he fell. The next moment he fell over dead, very nearly catching me under him, with a musket ball through his body. I had been galloping through a pretty sharp fire but was not aware of the moment the ball hit him. It was a lucky thing that I had not been on one of my own fine horses. Borrowing a horse for the remainder of the day from a courier, who took my saddle and bridle back to camp, I was enabled to remain on duty. But the enemy turned back, making, it appeared, only a reconnaissance in force and not a general advance as we thought. While the advance was in progress and the lines not over a mile from the Bower, General Stuart had ordered everything to be packed and held in readiness to move, but this order was followed later by one to repitch the tents and unpack, and on our return we again resumed our merry evenings at the Bowser.

Vizetelly was the most interesting narrator I have ever listened to around a campfire. He had been in all parts of the world, and in several campaigns as a correspondent, and what he did not see and enjoy of social life of every grade was not worth seeing. There was not a disreputable or reputable place of prominence in the civilized world that he did not know all about, and his accounts of his gallantries in Paris and other parts of the world were as interesting as a novel. We had a shrewd suspicion that he drew a little on his imagination for his facts, but what difference did that make to us. Late into the night we all sat around the embers of our fire out under the grand oaks listening to the fascinating tales he told, his expressive countenance and gestures giving full effect to his words by their play. Mr. Lawley was an exceedingly intelligent and refined English gentleman and in another style we enjoyed his instructive conversation very much, but Vizetelly was fascinating. At his request I made him some sketches of scenes in Pennsylvania during our late raid which he said he would embody in some he was making for the *Illustrated News*, but I have never seen copies of the paper of that period.

Our time at the Bower was now drawing to a close, and marching orders came at last. The enemy was moving eastward and on the 29th camp was moved. We all rode down to the house to take a last, sad farewell of our kind host and his charming family, whose tears fell fast as they bade us good-by.

General Lee moved his army across the Blue Ridge to interpose it between the enemy and Richmond, the cavalry as usual covering his front. There now began an endless series of skirmishes with their advance guard, their cavalry always appearing heavily supported by infantry and our cavalry depending upon itself alone, excepting of course the support of the artillery. All along through Loudoun and Fauquier counties we fought them day by day, falling back slowly from one position to another.

On the 3rd of November during a severe skirmish near the little village of Union, I received the first and only wound I got during the war, a slight one from a musket ball in the leg, which was not severe enough to compel me to leave the field. The ball passed through my boot inflicting a slight flesh wound. The nervous shock, however, was so great as to make me sick at the stomach, and I vomited. With three horses hit under me and about a dozen bullets through my clothes and accoutrements, two of my friends hit while I was talking to them, and three other men shot down at my side, it is strange that I should have escaped with this slight reminder of the war. I was as usual examining and reconnoitring the movements of the enemy. Our troops had been withdrawn and I was awaiting on a hill the appearance of their forces from some woods in the valley to form what estimate I could of their numbers and plans. I had dismounted to use my glass to better advantage and while standing with it to my eyes a skirmisher came out and took a shot at me.

On November 7, McClellan was superseded in command by Burnside and we were prepared for some extra effort on the part of the "new broom" which is said to sweep so clean. It soon became evident that the route to Richmond by Gordonsville was to be varied by a deviation towards Fredericksburg, towards which place their whole army was discovered to be in full march, and our army quickly followed, General Stuart establishing cavalry headquarters five miles from town near Massaponax creek, on the telegraph road.

There being no likelihood that the enemy would attempt a winter campaign, and the season for cold weather coming on, I was very desirous to see my dear wife and children; so I applied for a furlough of twenty days to visit them, and replenish my wardrobe. Leaving headquarters in Culpeper I went out to Abingdon where my wife was, and did not get back until our camp had been moved to Fredericksburg. The quiet and delight of domestic life made me look to the unsatisfactory life we led in the army with disgust. I did not mind it while still in camp, but after going home the contrast was striking. It certainly spoils a soldier to have a wife and children.

On my return through Richmond, an incident occurred which I must relate. At that period lights were dear, and the cars were not supplied with lamps. I occupied a seat near the end of the car, placing a large bundle I carried on the seat beside me. This bundle contained blankets, winter clothing and a pair of new cavalry boots, things which were hard to get then, and the loss of which at that season of the year in camp would have been exceedingly unpleasant. As the train stopped I stood up to await the passing of the stream of returning furloughed soldiers going out of the car and, when they had all passed, stooped down to lift my bundle, but to my dismay it was gone. Some rascal had stolen it as he passed. The chance of recovering my property was slender indeed but I determined to make the effort. From the Danville depot for several squares there was only one route up into the town, the bundle was too large to conceal, and it was, moreover, wrapped in a blanket of a peculiar color with large round circles on it, so it could be easily recognized. Getting out on the side opposite the depot and moving quickly along past the train I succeeded in passing, on the opposite side of the street, the whole column of passengers just landed; I then crossed over to the side they were on and took my stand under a street lamp to wait for and watch all who came by.

That part of the town was occupied by business houses only and was entirely deserted at night; there was only one dismal lamp on each square, and the drizzling rain that was falling confined the light of this to a narrow area. The long line of passengers had passed under my close scrutiny and the street was again empty, but still I waited in my vexation, in the hope that my bundle might still appear. Half an hour had passed and I was about to give it up when I saw a figure approaching through the gloom. It was a tall, powerful looking soldier, and under his arm with the cape of his overcoat thrown over it he seemed to have something large. He did not appear to see me standing behind the lamp post in the deep shadow. I could not see the bundle he carried until he had gone by, and then there appeared a glimpse of the white rings on the blue ground of the blanket in which my bundle was sewed up so nicely.

The chances of seeing anything of the thief had been so slender that I had not taken the precaution of drawing my pistol from my belt, for in those war times pistols were carried habitually. There was not time to draw it now, for the fellow might escape by a quick run if he took the alarm; so I sprang upon him from behind, passing my left arm around his neck, and then began feeling for my pistol. He struggled violently to get loose and pulled me out half way across the street, dropping the bundle on the sidewalk, but then, having gotten out the pistol and cocked it, I rammed it into his ear and ordered him to surrender which he did at once; and making him clasp his hands together over his head and keeping him covered by the pistol I marched him back to where my precious bundle lay on the sidewalk.

What to do now was a puzzling question. If I carried the bundle the man might get away before I could draw on him, and if I made him carry it he might run off down a dark alley with it and risk the chances of a shot in the dark. I was so incensed at the rascal that I was determined not to let him escape, and I felt a good deal like leaving him there on the street with a pistol ball through his head. While pondering the question I heard footsteps approaching and a couple of the railroad officers from the depot joined me. After I stated the case they kindly offered to carry the bundle for me up to the Spottswood Hotel, which was then the principal hotel in the place, and I marched the man on in front, turning him over that night to the police, giving the particulars and my address. At the Spottswood I fell in with my old friend and schoolmate Dr. Gray Latham, who sat with me while the policeman was being summoned, for with all this delay it was now one o'clock in the morning.

The next day I returned to the army, finding General Stuart's headquarters, as before stated, on the Telegraph Road five miles from Fredericksburg. The day following, a summons from the police court in Richmond was served upon me to appear in the trial of my captured thief, and General Stuart who had been much amused and delighted at the capture laughed heartily and said I was "playing old soldier" with a vengeance, and that he never had heard before of such a trick for getting another furlough. But a five days' leave was granted, and I went back to Richmond in high glee, greatly to the envy of my mess-mates. The fellow, however, escaped from the worthless old jail and I had my five days of uninterrupted enjoyment in the city.

Burnside's army occupied the north bank of the river with quantities of artillery crowning all the hills commanding the town. General Lee's army lay opposite, a mile from the river across the low grounds, holding the town with one small brigade only. The cavalry lines extended along the river twenty miles below and thirty miles above the town, to give notice of any attempt to flank our position.

We had been ready for many days but still the attack was deferred. At headquarters we were having a pleasant time enough. The weather was intensely cold, but we had plenty of wood and we had drawn good new tents from the quartermaster. In anticipation of a battle, Mr. Lawley and Vizetelly, the correspondents respectively of the *Times* and *Illustrated News*, paid us a visit, also a Captain Phillips of the Grenadier Guards stationed in Canada who was on leave of absence to visit our army. Of the two first I have already spoken, and the young English Captain was a fine fellow whom we all liked. During the battle he was so desirous to see everything that he went under fire freely and showed perfect coolness, though it was his first experience. Two weeks passed in this manner, General Stuart going down once or twice to the extreme right near Port Royal to shell some gunboats with the horse artillery, and almost every day we went to the lines in our front to see what the enemy was about.

They were mounting great numbers of guns on the hills over the river commanding the town and were evidently preparing for a general advance. From information obtained, General Lee issued a circular urging the citizens of the town to leave there, for the place would soon be shelled. The exodus began about the 8th of the month, and it was a pitiable sight. The hard frozen roads were lined day and night with carts, wagons, and carriages of every description, and crowds of people on foot, old men, women and children. Many were camped in the woods and everywhere would be heard the cry of children of all ages, shivering in the cold.

On the night of the tenth, one of our couriers who lived near Chancellorsville invited General Stuart and staff and guests to attend a party at his house. General Stuart concluded to decline, as the battle, he thought, could not be postponed much longer, and he did not like to be away; but he said we might go provided we returned before daybreak. We started soon after supper on a six-mile drive over the frozen, rough country roads in the headquarters ambulance drawn by four spirited mules, Phillips, von Borcke, Terrel, Pelham, Dabney and myself, together with the musicians. Yon Borcke and Terrel undertook to drive and away we jolted at a furious rate. Expecting that we would upset, I let down the tail gate and took my seat on the straw, letting my legs hang out behind ready to jump if we went over, a position which as it turned out was unfortunate for me. All went merrily until within a couple of miles of the place, when the hind axle snapped off at the wheel while we were in rapid motion, letting the end on that side fall on the ground with a fearful bump. My legs, striking the ground, dragged me out full length on my back and pitched all the rest backwards down out of the vehicle. I would not have been hurt but for the wheel which, severed from the axle and left by the ambulance, toppled over and fell upon my head, knocking me senseless for a few moments and cutting my head severely. When I came to myself all the party were collected around looking very mournful, for the profuse bleeding and my being unconscious led them to think I was seriously if not fatally wounded. Rolling the body of the ambulance aside, the fore wheels were brought up for me to mount and thus, followed on foot by the jingle of the steps of the booted and spurred party, I reached the house.

Great was the pleasure among the rustic beauties assembled at our arrival for they had given us up. I managed to mingle in the dancing until supper, for our cold ride had given me a keen appetite, and the supper was excellent, but then I begged leave to retire, for I did not feel equal to returning to camp that night, and I was furnished with a delightful feather-bed by our kind hosts.

The party had come on wheels to save the exposure of the horses to the cold by remaining out all night, but a messenger had been sent back to camp for them and our servants arrived in time for all except me to return in time. The next morning by daylight I was conscious of a booming, jarring noise mingling with my dreams which quickly aroused me to the fact that the long expected battle had begun. I bounded out of bed, much mortified that I should have been caught away from my post on such an occasion. Knowing that General Stuart would have left headquarters before I could reach there and that I would find him at the front, I took the direct road for Fredericksburg and galloped rapidly to meet him there, reaching our lines a few moments after he did.

The fog lay thick upon the valley as I reached the hill near the Telegraph Road where were assembled General Lee and his staff and Generals Stuart, Longstreet and Jackson with their staff officers, besides some of the Major Generals whose divisions were near the place. This hill having been occupied by General Lee all through the battle as field headquarters, it has borne his name ever since.

The artillery fire which had opened the day had ceased, and the silence was only broken by the muffled rattle of musketry in the town half a mile distant, where Barksdale's brigade occupied trenches and rifle pits along the river bank with deep zigzag covered ways leading back from them through the town for the safe withdrawal or reinforcement of the men in the works. Our army occupied a line five miles long enclosing the valley in which Fredericksburg was situated. The line rested upon the river half a mile above the place and ran out farther and farther from the river along the crest of the hills bounding the plain below. Our infantry right was a mile and a half from the river and rested upon Massaponax Creek near Hamilton's crossing and from that point to the river the cavalry occupied the ground.

Totally unable to cope with his able adversary in an open field by manoeuvring, Burnside had placed himself in a position which was secure from attack, and then hoped under cover of his guns to engage successfully our forces, secure from serious disaster in case of failure. To make this attack he moved forward in two columns, one to cross at Fredericksburg, the other below opposite Hamilton's crossing. It was no part of General Lee's plan to engage him close to the river, and only rifle pits along the bank were to oppose the laying down of his pontoons. The position of these below was not particularly favorable and but little opposition was there made, but, in the town, the houses affording cover during withdrawal, the opposition was made with great spirit to the last moment by Barksdale's brigade, their rifle pits, or rather their trenches, being so well built that little loss was sustained. I was exceedingly anxious to see what was in progress there; so the General gave me leave, with his usual cheery caution of, "Look out for yourself, old fellow," and I galloped into the town, leaving my horse in care of a courier on Main Street, three of my regular men for this duty having come with me. Taking the other two men with me, I entered one of the zigzags leading from Main Street to the river a little below the Island. It was the first time I had ever entered a fortified work in action and it felt very comfortable to hear the bullets whistling and hissing and pattering about against the earthworks above my head so harmlessly. Right in front of us a pontoon bridge had been laid a third of the way across the stream, the nearest boat not a hundred yards distant, and upon it lay several dead and wounded men. Time after time had the foolish attempt been made, and time after time had the working parties been swept away by our riflemen in the trenches dug on the crest of the bank. Our men in the pits were highly elated and swore they could hold the place against the whole Yankee nation. They had evidently given up laying the pontoons for the present and I could see preparations being made for loading boats with men to cross and charge the pits, and knowing this would probably be preceded by a bombardment as soon as the fog cleared I concluded to withdraw while I could.

I had scarcely returned to the hill and made my report before the fog began to rise, revealing the cool, gray masses of old, time-stained roofs and walls of the town between its white, rolling clouds. It was now about ten o'clock. The town was clearly in view when the slackened rattle of Barksdale's rifles was drowned by a roar like Niagara. In an instant every hill on the other side of the river was a bank of clouds, and shells of every tone, from the keen whistle of the rifle shot to the coarse howl of the heavy shell, were tearing their way through the houses, and bursting with deep detonations within their walls. It was a fearful but a grand sight. Numerous dark columns of smoke soon arose in various parts of the town from fires kindled by these shells, from which red tongues of flame gleamed as they leaped higher and higher, licking up all within reach, while the very ground we stood upon shook like an earthquake. For two hours the cannonade lasted, and ceased as suddenly as it had begun, our batteries taking no part whatever.

In spite of all warnings many people had remained in the town. When the cannonade began many of them came pouring out in great fright, but even after the bombardment some remained and some of them were ladies. We naturally felt uneasy about Barksdale's brigade, but no sooner had the roar of the cannon ceased than we could hear the rattle of their rifles in full fire, for the enemy was attempting to force the passage in boats. Having no idea of making serious opposition, General Lee gave orders for Barksdale to withdraw and the enemy proceeded at once to lay their bridges and hurry over their forces. Not seeing them active below the town where they had been concentrating troops all the morning and appeared to be preparing to cross near Mansfield, General Lee told General Stuart to find out what they were doing. Stuart sent me. It was necessary to use some caution in approaching the river as the opposite banks were lined with the batteries which had already driven away our pickets there; so I got into the valley of Deep Run, a stream along which I had fished when a boy, and leaving my horse concealed near the mouth, crawled along the ground to Mr. Alfred Bernard's house close to the high banks of the river and near the Run. The house was abandoned when the battle began and it had been a good deal damaged by the cannonade. As I entered from the rear the scene of confusion was striking. The whole house was strewn with feathers, the bedrooms, the passages, and the parlors, for where cannon balls pass through feather beds they set them flying, which was the case in this instance. Furniture was torn to pieces, and great gaps in the walls showed where the shots had passed through and through.

From the upstairs windows I could see all I wanted, for right below, within a stone's throw, they were busily at work laying the pontoon bridge, and across the river not over one hundred and fifty yards away was the head of their column awaiting the completion of the structure to cross. With this information I hurried back. The rest of the day was spent on Lee's hill, as it is now called, watching the slow movements of the enemy.

Before day, in the bitter cold, over the rough frozen roads, General Stuart and his staff, accompanied by Captain Phillips, the English officer who was on a visit to our headquarters, rode to the field where we expected certainly the battle would soon begin. All day we lay and waited and waited, but the enemy did nothing but march and countermarch, getting his vast force into position; so after dark we returned to our snug quarters to talk over the events of the day, and speculate on those of tomorrow, for certainly the morrow we thought would be the day.

The day of the long expected battle had at last arrived. Stuart with his cavalry and horse artillery covered our right flank and the enemy attacked in two columns, one from the town and the other four miles below, near Hamilton's crossing.

I discovered near the mouth of Massaponax creek between the lines and in flank and rear of the enemy, a high hill from which a fine view of all their movements could be had, and reported the fact to Stuart, proposing that I should occupy this hill as a post of observation. He was delighted with the idea, and sent twenty couriers with me, telling me to send him a report every fifteen or twenty minutes. By approaching cautiously I reached the spot unobserved, and leaving most of the men at the foot of the hill I took three with me on foot to the top. Here for the most of the day I remained undisturbed, but occasionally they would turn their batteries upon the hill and shell it furiously for half an hour at a time. We would then get down on the off side and wait for the storm to blow over. They did this more as a preventive I think than as against us, for I do not think they could see me as I was very careful to keep out of view, but they realized the importance of the point as an observatory.

From here I could see all their preparations which were completely concealed from the view from our position on the line of battle, and I gave notice of each attack they made by sending a report in writing to General Stuart, which he forwarded to Jackson. I was not over five hundred yards from their outposts and with my powerful English double glasses I could tell the rank of the officers as they rode about.

When the last general attack was about ready to start, having sent off all the couriers, I went myself to General Stuart to inform him. In returning von Borcke volunteered to accompany me and I was glad to have his company, and he spent the remainder of the evening with me. Imagine my surprise when I saw in his published memoirs that he spoke of having done all this himself, and that *I* volunteered to accompany *him* to the place where *he* sent the reports etc. etc.

Watching the battle from this splendid point of view was interesting and grand in the highest degree. Von Borcke became so excited that in spite of all I could do to prevent it he stood up and of course drew upon us a severe shelling. One of these shells passed right between our heads as we sat on a log on the rear slope of the hill at what we thought a safe distance down. Von Borcke dodged so that he lost his balance and rolled down the steep slope, to our great amusement.

A curious complication occurred when this shelling began. I had hitched my thoroughbred mare, Magic, to a hickory sapling seven or eight feet tall a little way down the hill, and I found that the shells were passing close enough to the ground where she stood to hit her, so I went to get her away. She was in great excitement, rearing and plunging, and as I reached her she plunged forward against the sapling, getting it under her between both fore and hind legs. She then went forward until the reins drew her head down like a martingale, and her hind feet got hooked in the branches so I could not back her out. The shells came ploughing and tearing through the bushes nearer and nearer and to save the mare I had to cut the reins.

The great battle had been fought and we did not know it. We could have fought a battle like this every day for a week. Yet Burnside had given it up. All the next day and the next again, we lay expecting a renewal of the attack but it never came.

Early the second day following, General Stuart sent me out to see what the enemy was about, and, in the thick fog, the only way to discharge the duty was to approach their lines until some skirmisher in a rifle pit fired at me.

Riding across the space between the lines at a canter in a zigzag course, so as to make them take a side shot flying, my attention was arrested by some figures on foot moving in the same direction. These proved to be men of my brother Eugene's battalion of sharpshooters from Rhodes' brigade, and I soon found Eugene. He had been sent out on the same errand I was on, so we joined company. Presently we came to rifle pits but they were empty, and proceeding farther we ascertained that the enemy had recrossed the river during the night. I at once sent a courier to General Stuart with the news and then Eugene and myself rode on into the dear old town — the town where both of us were born. In passing along the streets, being the first Confederates to enter the town, we picked up quite a number of stragglers who had slept in the houses and came out too late. Not caring to be encumbered with prisoners we made them face our lines and told them to double-quick in that direction, and if they looked back or stopped, we would shoot them dead, and as soon as they got a good start we went on. In the suburbs of the town we met our brother Charles, a Captain in the 2nd Virginia Cavalry, who had been sent on the same errand. Our old home had been used as a hospital. The room in which we were born was half inch deep in clotted blood still wet, and the walls were spattered with it, and all around were scattered legs and arms. The place smelt like a butcher's shambles.

Our uncle, Mr. John Minor, had lived here until his death not long before. He was an antiquarian in his tastes, and being an old bachelor in easy circumstances he had surrounded himself with a fine library of rare books and many works of art, and curiosities of all kinds. These books and valuables, it seems, had been used for the amusement of the troops during their occupation, and what they had not carried off were scattered all over the town.

We traced the track of a shell on the place that was rather remarkable. It entered a window, taking out a pane of glass clean, without breaking the sash, then, after passing through a brick partition wall, it cut through the back of a book-case, passed between two shelves and out through a glass panel without breaking the door of the case. It then took out a panel of an outer door. It then struck the ground just under the front gate, ploughing a trench but not touching the gate. Tired apparently at doing no mischief so far, it then flew upward and struck the roof of a house opposite, tearing it nearly off. The whole damage on our lot would not amount to over a couple of dollars. The other shells had done but little damage, though some had scarred the walls.

How many memories of my boyhood came crowding into my mind as I wandered through the rooms, every corner of which was so familiar to me, and how strange it seemed that I should now see them under such circumstances. In the old "cuddy," as it was called, a garret where all household lumber was stored, there was at that moment a dead man, but we did not know it; he had been firing at our lines from that retreat when a bullet laid him low. His body was not found for weeks in that dark, lonely place.

We found some citizens of the town who had remained throughout the bombardment, and among them our old friends the Miss Thoms, two old maiden ladies, who could not believe that the bearded, weather-beaten soldiers they saw before them were really "Willy", "Charlie" and "Eugene" Blackford, but as the fact dawned upon their minds their welcome was most cordial. The enemy were swarming on the other bank of the river but did not fire upon us as we rode along our side of the stream, and they answered by a jolly laugh when we called out to inquire why they had not continued their march on to Richmond.

The field opposite Marye's hill had been the scene of the greatest slaughter. We rode over it and examined it carefully. I saw it the day after the fight, and from the heights it looked as blue as if it had been covered with a blue cloth. At no one spot during our war were there as many bodies on the same space as here.

We now settled down into winter quarters. Many visitors from time to time came to us, among them Lord Hartington accompanied by Colonel Leslie of the British army and Mr. Lawley, all of them members of Parliament and charming men. They spent a week with us. It was the first time I had been brought into contact with civil rank and I made a little mistake at table in consequence. At our mess table the General sat at the head and I usually at the foot. Mr. Lawley, who was past middle age, sat next to me and Lord Hartington next to him. In carving I passed the plate to Mr. Lawley first as the oldest guest but with a polite bow he handed it to Lord Hartington who was quite a young man. After that I always helped "my Lord" first. They were all unassuming, and thorough gentlemen. I could not think, however, that Lord Hartington was a man of talent sufficient for the high positions he has since held. Von Borcke and I went with them down to Mosses Neck, the old homestead of the Corbin family, to introduce them to General Jackson, and they were very much pleased with him. It was one of Jackson's peculiarities that when visitors came to see him he would insist upon taking their hats. In a tent or in a room with only camp furniture there was no place, of course, to hang a hat and every one held it in his hand; but General Jackson would jump up and collect them all with, "Let me have your hat, sir," and then he would realize that there was no place but the floor to put them. I told our guests about this and they could scarcely keep their countenances when he went through the performance.

In the beginning of the war Jackson was very careless of his dress and appearance, but after the battles around Richmond when he became so famous there was a marked change in him in this respect, and he dressed handsomely and rode fine horses. It may have been, however, owing to his receiving so many presents of uniforms and horses, principally from the ladies. His manners in company though quiet were always refined, but he had little conversational powers. I suppose, however, he felt during time of war that he had to be on his guard so much that it formed the habit of not expressing his opinions. He was in the office at Mosses Neck, a little house in the yard hung with pictures of race horses and gamecocks, for, like most of the Virginia planters of olden time, the Corbins had been keen sportsmen.

In the course of the winter my dear wife paid me a visit, I having secured rooms for her at a house in the neighborhood. She only brought Lizzie with her as the accommodations at this house were limited though comfortable. It was desirable to have her as near headquarters as possible, so I preferred this house near, to more spacious ones farther away.

As the spring advanced we were destined to suffer many losses among our military family at headquarters, which as yet had been remarkably exempt from casualties, considering the exposure we had undergone in so many actions.

During the winter Pelham and I had become more intimate than we had ever been before. Our tents were next each other and we had built our stables together. Pelham had some fine horses and, like myself, liked to see them well cared for. I had five and he had three. Two of mine were furnished me together with a wagon and driver, by the quartermaster department for the transportation of my engineer's office equipment, and the others were my saddle horses. Gilbert, my faithful body-servant, together with the driver of the wagon, Tom, gave me ample comfort in the way of service, and I kept everything around my tent and stable in excellent order. Frank Robertson and Tom Price had been commissioned Lieutenants in the Engineer Corps and assigned as my assistants, and I was now prepared to keep up a complete set of maps of the country we operated in, and Frank became my tent-mate.

Pelham and I had been reading aloud to each other Napier's "Peninsula War," and the day he left us to go to Orange C. H. on a little pleasure trip I marked the place we stopped and I have never had the heart to read more in it since. A sudden advance of the enemy was made just as he reached there and he went out to the field and was killed at the very opening of the engagement.

He had been wanting to go to see some friends in Orange for some time, and the night before he persuaded the General to let him go, nominally under orders to inspect the Horse Artillery. Fitzhugh made out the order and gave it to him, and fearing that Stuart would countermand it, he concluded not to wait for breakfast the next morning but to get his breakfast at the camp of a battery on the road; so he was off before daylight. General Stuart loved him like a younger brother and could not bear for him to be away from him. So the next morning at breakfast the General asked where Pelham was, and when he heard he was gone, and expected to breakfast at the camp on the road he told Fitzhugh to order him back.

These and the curious combinations of little incidents which follow show on what slight circumstances important events sometimes hang. Any one of these might have been different, and Pelham would not have met his death at that time.

Fitzhugh wrote the order and the courier started. But Pelham knew the General well, and feared he would do exactly this thing; so when he got to the camp of the battery he did not tarry but took a cup of coffee and pushed on. The courier did not overtake him until he had nearly reached Orange C. H. late in the evening, and of course he had to go there to sleep that night. The next morning a locomotive came in from Culpeper C. H. for ammunition with news that the enemy had advanced his cavalry in some force, and Pelham, knowing Stuart would sanction such a violation of orders, jumped on the engine and returned with it. The troops had marched out to meet the enemy before he arrived and with great difficulty Pelham borrowed a horse and followed. The roads were heavy and when he reached the field the Horse Artillery had not yet arrived,[6] so Pelham rode down to the skirmish line to reconnoitre and select a position for the guns when they reached the field. A light skirmish fire was going on and an officer had his horse hit. He was a friend of Pelham's and he pulled up to talk to him and advise about the treatment of the horse. The officer asked Pelham a question, but receiving no answer looked up and saw his saddle empty. Pelham was stretched on the ground with what his friend supposed to be a bullet through his head. It was, however, only a tip from the ball which did not enter the skull. Thinking Pelham dead, his friend threw the body across a saddle in front of a man and with his head hanging on one side and feet on the other he was taken several miles to the rear before meeting an ambulance; a treatment sufficient to have almost killed a well man, and yet Pelham did not die for twelve hours. If Pelham had stayed for breakfast at headquarters or at the horse artillery camp as he intended; if the locomotive had not come for the ammunition; if Pelham had not gotten a horse; and if his friend had not sent him to the rear as he did, Pelham would not have lost his life when he did. What a pity it was that none of these things had happened differently. His remains were sent home to Alabama, and lay in state several days in the capitol in Richmond, where many people went to see them and place flowers on the bier.

Not long after this Capt. Redmond Burke and Lieutenant Turner of our staff were killed while on scouting duty. Burke was a man of great presence of mind and courage and had done some deeds of desperate gallantry. This made four killed from the staff, and the campaign scarcely opened.

As the weather got warmer the health of the camp, which had been on the same ground so long, was impaired. I felt its effects, and was glad when we moved up to Culpeper C. H. Burnside had been removed after his disaster at Fredericksburg and Hooker succeeded him. Hooker was burning to distinguish himself and began to show signs of activity early in the season. He had improved their heretofore worthless cavalry a great deal and from this time on we were to have more and more trouble with it, partly from its improvement, and partly from our declining efficiency owing to our inability to supply remounts. We now felt the bad effects of our system of requiring the men to furnish their own horses. The most dashing trooper was the one whose horse was the most apt to be shot, and when this man was unable to remount himself he had to go to the infantry service, and was lost to the cavalry. Such a penalty for gallantry was terribly demoralizing.

---

6   This account of his death I heard at the time, but it since appears that he was killed in a cavalry charge. — Wm. W. B.

It was on the 9th of April that our headquarters camp of the Cavalry Corps near Fredericksburg, where we had spent the winter, was broken up, and in high spirits at the prospect of a more active life in a more attractive country we moved to Culpeper C. H. The immediate cause of the move was that the enemy had concentrated a large force of cavalry opposite that point, and with this force we were destined to meet in another of the many cavalry combats which came off on the plains around Brandy Station. In the meantime while watching our opponents we made the best use of our time in the enjoyment of the social pleasures which the society of the place afforded. We received a visit at this time from a countryman of von Borcke's, Captain Scheibert, who spent several weeks with us, and proved to be a most accomplished though somewhat eccentric gentleman and one to whom we became much attached.

As spring advanced I was taken with a fever and given a twenty days' sick leave. My wife met me in Lynchburg and we returned together to the Meadows, her father's place near Abingdon. The mountain air and the comforts of home soon restored me and in ten days I was well again. Before, however, my leave was out, the enemy were reported moving and General Lee issued an order recalling all who were on leave. I at once started to rejoin the army but reached Fredericksburg the day after the battle of Chancellorsville was fought; this being the only general engagement of the Army of Northern Virginia that I missed during the whole war.

Stuart has never received the credit he deserved for his conduct in the battle of Chancellorsville, for it was under him that it was mainly fought. After the first attack by Jackson, little resistance was made for the remainder of the day; early in the night Jackson fell and A. P. Hill had command an hour or so, until he was wounded; then Stuart took command about eleven or twelve P. M. on the night of the 2nd of May and the main battle was fought on the 3rd of May by Jackson's corps under Stuart's command.

When we consider the fact that Stuart was several miles away when summoned to take this command, that he knew nothing about the positions of the lines or the plans of attack, that it was night in a thick, dark pine forest, and that belonging to another arm of the service he could not have known the troops, or the special capabilities of their officers, can a more trying position be conceived than the one in which he was placed? Under such circumstances, to have inspired confidence and enthusiasm, and to have led the troops to victory in a battle where the odds were more heavily against us than in any battle of the war except Sharpsburg, displayed a military genius and heroism surpassed by few characters in history.

Our staff had to mourn another loss in the person of Maj. R. Channing Price who fell in an action preliminary to the battle of Chancellorsville on the 2nd of May. Though very young, not over twenty-one or -two years of age, he filled the important post of Adjutant General of the Cavalry Corps in a manner which attracted the admiration of every one. Repeatedly have I seen while on a march General Stuart dictate two or three letters to him, giving orders to the commanders of the different columns. Each one of them would state by what places the columns were to move, at what hours they were to leave these places and where they were to concentrate. Price would listen, and without asking him to repeat a single thing, or taking a single note, he would ride out to one side of the road, dismount, take his little portfolio out of his haversack and write the letters ready for the General's signature; and it was rarely the case that any alteration was made when Stuart read them and affixed his signature.[7]

Lieutenant Hullihen of the staff was wounded in this action. Our losses in killed to date were Lieutenant Stuart, Captain Burke, Lieutenant Turner, Major Pelham and Major Price.

As I landed at Hamilton's crossing five miles from Fredericksburg, the infantry was returning from the field of Chancellorsville to their old winter quarters as full of life and spirit as ever, singing, laughing and joking. It was only after they settled down and saw the bunks of so many of their comrades empty that a gloom spread over the camps which hung over them until they moved out, a week or two after, to begin the great Gettysburg campaign.

---

7 This development of this remarkable faculty in Price was cultivated by his having acted as the secretary of his father who was a merchant in Richmond. In the latter part of his life he became blind and dictated his correspondence to his son. — Wm. W. B.

Lieutenant Thos. Price, one of my assistant Engineer officers and brother of Major Channing Price, had met with a misfortune during my absence. Lieutenant F. S. Robertson and Price had been sent to build a bridge above Chancellorsville a few days before the battle, and when the advance was made Price lost his luggage and in it his diary. Price was in Europe when the war broke out, at a University, in Berlin, I believe it was; he had remained there for nearly two years and only returned during the fall before the battle of Fredericksburg. Through General Stuart's influence Price had, though so late a comer, received a commission in the Engineers and been assigned to duty on Stuart's staff. Reaching our muddy, winter quarters camp, and all the discomforts of a soldier's life, fresh from the luxuries of a student's life in Europe, Price was disgusted with soldiering and everything connected with it. Unfortunately Price kept a diary and in this he unfortunately wrote all he thought and felt about camp life, and still more unfortunately wrote his reflections upon the character of General Stuart in a way not at all complimentary to the General. Whatever his peculiarities may have been, General Stuart had saved Price from being conscripted into the ranks as a private soldier, and this at least should have made him silent. We all noticed that Price regretted the loss of his diary more than we thought the thing deserved, but this was fully accounted for one morning by our seeing in a Northern paper, sent to General Stuart, extracts from the captured diary. *"Oh for Berlin."* *"General Stuart in his usual garrulous style exclaimed"* so and so, and remarks of like character were there in plain print. Poor Price! General Stuart felt this deeply for Price was a kinsman of his and the families were very intimate. There was only one thing to be done now, and that was for Price to leave the staff; so a few weeks after he was assigned to duty elsewhere.

We now moved headquarters to Orange C. H. and a most charming time followed for some weeks. The cavalry had been much strengthened by the return of the men sent home to recruit their horses or to get fresh ones, while a concentration of detached bodies of cavalry had been effected. Among these latter was a fine brigade from the valley commanded by my old Captain Wm. E. Jones, now a Brigadier General. The grass was beginning to grow long enough to afford our horses pasturage which soon improved their condition wonder-fully.

It was here we heard the news of General Jackson's death, May 10th, from the wound he received at Chancellorsville. It threw a gloom over the whole command, and I felt as if I had lost a near and dear relative. This was the first serious loss among our Generals, and it was a heavy one indeed.

Captain Scheibert, whom I have mentioned, was a Captain of Engineers in the Prussian army sent over to observe our military movements. He had been at General Lee's headquarters some time, and now at General Stuart's urgent invitation came to us. His simplicity of character and odd ways amused, as well as attached, all who came in contact with him. The Captain had some skill in painting, and the wife of one of our Generals, Mrs. W. H. F. Lee, had availed herself of his offer of assistance in touching up some of her sketches. There occurred one day a most amusing scene which I must relate.

Mrs. Lee was on a visit to her husband and was boarding at a house in town. Headquarters were a short distance out of the village, and Scheibert had gone by appointment one evening to touch up an oil sketch of a small-size female head which Mrs. Lee had just finished, while General Stuart and the members of the staff were stretched out on their blankets on the grass enjoying the warm spring sunshine. Scheibert was dressed in a very short jacket and white trousers in which his fat person looked as if it had been melted and poured in, so tight was the fit. After working for some time touching up the head with the moist sticky paint the job was completed to their satisfaction, and they laid the canvas on a chair and entered into conversation. One of Scheibert's odd ways was that when he became interested in conversation he would start up on his feet, in the eagerness of his gesticulation, walk about the room and then pop down on any chair that happened to be nearest to him. The weather was warm and the blinds were partially closed. Unfortunately for Mrs. Lee's work of art, Captain Scheibert, in one of these fits of enthusiasm, after walking about the room sat down upon the wet picture unobserved by either himself or Mrs. Lee.

When the time came for him to go Mrs. Lee thanked him cordially, and told him she would keep the picture as a souvenir of their pleasant acquaintance, and turned to get the picture for him to take a last critical survey of it. Where was the picture? "Bless my soul!" said the Captain, "I laid it down on one of the chairs, but I don't see it now." Then they looked and looked. "Oh!" said Scheibert, "the wind must have blown it under the piano!" so down on his hands and knees fell the Captain to crawl under the piano. "Here it is," said Mrs. Lee, screaming with laughter, as she peeled the unfortunate picture from the broad seat of Scheibert's white trousers, leaving the lovely face, somewhat blurred, transferred thereto most conspicuously.

Scheibert backed out from under the piano and without taking leave, or stopping to get his hat, cane and gloves in the hall, bolted across the fields for our camp. We saw him coming, waving his arms wildly and roaring like a bull with laughter. He threw himself on the grass, still convulsed, rolling over and over, and every time he turned that side up there was a bright picture of a lovely face on the seat of his trousers. It was a long time before he could find breath to tell us about it, and then you may rest assured we enjoyed the joke.

Visiting at another house not long after, with some of the staff officers, the ladies were some time making their appearance. Scheibert took his seat at the piano and began playing a German piece of which he was very fond, and over which he became much excited. In his excitement he rose partially to his feet and then came back heavily upon the stool. The stool crushed under him and he fell backwards upon the floor. Just then the rustle of the ladies' dresses was heard coming down stairs. In an agony of terror and embarrassment Scheibert kicked a part of the stool under the piano and made a rush for a leg which had flown out into the middle of the room but just then the ladies entered and Scheibert put the leg behind him and stood transfixed with eyes and mouth wide open, a perfectly ludicrous picture of embarrassment. We were too convulsed with laughter to introduce our friend, and there stood the ladies in mute surprise, looking at the strange figure upon whose crimson face great beads of perspiration were forming.

Captain Scheibert was not much of a horseman and his awkwardness in this accomplishment was a never-ending source of amusement to us, but our jokes at his expense were taken with an unfailing good humor. Coming to our army in the capacity he did he could not of course bear arms, but he compromised between his conscience and feelings by serving as a staff officer in other respects, and was always ready to go into danger unarmed as he was. He had a way of attaching all his belongings to his saddle in separate packages by strings and straps, and not being skilled in the art, these packages, when his horse galloped, would flop wildly, and becoming loosened would often fall to the ground. On one occasion during one of the hot skirmishes we had while he was with us, Stuart sent him to order up reinforcements. It was in a country filled with scrubby timber and numerous private roads running in every direction, and our troops and the enemy were a good deal "mixed"; there was no telling for a time which was which, and the multiplicity of roads was confusing.

Scheibert received the order and in his headlong impulsive way dashed off with it at full speed, but to Stuart's horror took by mistake a road which led directly towards the enemy. Dreadfully uneasy for fear that his guest should be captured, Stuart ordered a courier to follow and bring him back. The man was well mounted and soon came in sight of the Captain with his bundles dancing up and down around him, and shouted for him to stop. Scheibert, as I said, was unarmed and seeing himself pursued took it for granted that it was by an enemy; so into the flanks of his horse went his spurs, and away he flew; a bundle coming loose fell to the ground at nearly every jump of the horse. The courier appreciated the position and knew that only speed could save the Captain; so he let his horse out, and closed with him just as they came in sight of the enemy. To retrace their steps and find the scattered property was no easy task but poor Captain Scheibert at last appeared, sadly crestfallen and greatly to the relief of Stuart's mind.

Our army was now formed into three corps instead of two as formerly under Jackson and Longstreet. The corps now being 1st Longstreet's, consisting of Hood's, McLaws' and Pickett's divisions; 2nd Ewell's, containing Early's, Rodes' and Johnson's divisions; 3rd A. P. Hill's, composed of Anderson's, Pender's and Heth's divisions. Each corps numbered twenty thousand men. The cavalry, having been strengthened by several new brigades from the south, was formed into a separate corps composed of three divisions commanded by Hampton, Fitz Lee, and W. H. F. Lee.

On the 18th of May, General Lee began gradually to move his army from Fredericksburg towards Culpeper and Orange, threatening Washington and moving on towards Pennsylvania, a move which ultimately culminated in the battle of Gettysburg, and a move which soon drew Hooker out from his position at Fredericksburg.

On the 20th of May we moved cavalry headquarters to Culpeper C. H. and our magnificent cavalry corps, then at its zenith of power and efficiency, encamped along the Rappahannock.

I was ordered while at Culpeper to make a reconnaissance of the Rappahannock River from Chancellorsville up towards Warrenton and to make a topographical map showing the strategical strength of positions along the banks with reference to forcing a crossing. General Lee was slowly moving his forces up the river, to draw Hooker out of his hole behind the deep part of the river, by threatening Washington. Hood's division was in the advance, and I was to report to him all I found out. I took Frank Robertson and an escort of twenty-five cavalry, picked men, with me. The banks on the other side were occupied by the enemy. As we ascended the stream it became smaller and smaller and the fords became more and more frequent. Usually the enemy occupied the hills back from the river, but at one place, where there was an important road crossing, they had built a fort right on the river bank at the toe of a horseshoe bend, with the concave of the bend on their side, and bold hills encircling it on ours, a most absurd location for a redoubt.

Not expecting anything of this kind so close to the river, which was there a small stream not twenty yards wide, I was riding unconcernedly at the head of my little party, along a path on the bank, when on emerging into an open field I saw the opposite side swarming with blue jackets. They were mostly outside of the fort strolling about at their ease, unconscious of the approach of an enemy. To get a good idea of their position it was necessary to pass along the path, and seeing how much off their guard they were I concluded to try it, counting upon their mistaking us for a party of their own men. Passing the order for my men not to fire nor to appear on their guard but to go on talking and laughing as usual, I moved on. It turned out as I expected it would, for seeing a squad of cavalry walking their horses along fifty yards from the fort they never suspected for a moment who we were, but exchanged good-humored jokes with the men of my party. There was a full regiment of them, eight or ten hundred strong, and if they had only known it a volley would have settled us pretty effectually. I was enabled to make an accurate sketch of the position, and seeing what a blunder had been made in building the fort where it was and seeing that this point gave the best possible place to force a crossing, I at once reported to General Hood, whose command was moving up the turnpike parallel with the river a mile or two back. It was sundown when General Hood, at my representation, came down to look at the place and at once saw its advantages. His chief of artillery was with him and he gave him directions to select positions for the batteries, as he would make the attack in the morning. Seeing how much off their guard they were, scattered outside the fort, he laughed and said, "Major, send a shell first over their heads and let them get in their holes before you open with all your guns." This was a piece of chivalry characteristic of the gallant Hood.

During the night General Lee ordered Hood to move on up the river and the attack was not made. Whether General Lee really intended to cross and attack Hooker in flank I do not know; he might have intended to cross a small force and threaten him with a general attack, to hurry him up about leaving Fredericksburg.

A grand review was ordered for the 5th of June and all at headquarters were exerting themselves to the utmost to make it a success. Invitations were issued far and near, and as the time approached every train came loaded with visitors. I wrote to the University, and Mary Minor and a troop of Charlottesville girls attended. I was very sorry that my wife could not attend, but she was over three hundred miles away in Abingdon, and dreaded the journey.

When the day of review arrived the Secretary of War, General Randolph, came from Richmond to see it, and many infantry Generals and prominent men. The staff was resplendent in new uniforms, and horses were in splendid condition as we rode to the field on the level plains near Brandy Station. The ground was admirably adapted to the purpose, a hill in the centre affording a reviewing stand from which the twelve thousand men present could be seen to great advantage. It must be borne in mind that cavalry show much larger than infantry, and that these twelve thousand mounted men produced the effect of at least three times their number of infantry. General Stuart, accompanied by his brilliant staff, passed down the front and back by the rear at a gallop in the usual way, the general officers and their staffs joining us as we passed, so that by the time we got back to the stand there were nearly a hundred horsemen, all officers, dashing through the field. Then the lines broke into column of squadrons and marched by at a walk, making the entire circuit; then they came by at a trot, taking the gallop a hundred yards before reaching the reviewing stand; and then the "charge" at full speed past the reviewing stand, yelling just as they do in a real charge, and brandishing their sabres over their heads. The effect was thrilling, even to us, while the ladies clasped their hands and sank into the arms, sometimes, of their escorts in a swoon, if the escorts were handy, but if not they did not. While the charging was going on, Beckham with the horse artillery was firing rapidly and this heightened the effect. It would make your hair stand on end to see them. How little did we then think that on this very ground a few days later just such charges would be made in reality in the greatest cavalry action of modern times.

That night we gave a ball at headquarters on the turf by moonlight, assisted by huge wood fires, firelight to dance by and moonlight for the strolls.

General Lee arrived rather unexpectedly and on the 7th we moved to "Fleetwood," an old plantation residence near Brandy Station. The next day we had another cavalry review for General Lee's benefit. This was a business affair, the spectators being all soldiers. Many men from Hood's division were present who enjoyed it immensely. During the charges past the reviewing stand the hats and caps of the charging column would sometimes blow off, and then, just as the charging squadron passed and before the owners could come back, Hood's men would have a race for them and bear them off in triumph. This was the last of our frolics for a long time, for on the morrow we were to begin the fighting which was kept up almost daily until two weeks after the battle of Gettysburg, and we were to begin it in a severe action.

Up to this time the cavalry of the enemy had not been able to stand before us, but during the past winter great attention had been bestowed upon that branch of their service and it had become much more formidable. We were to meet the next day in nearly equal numbers upon the plain around Fleetwood in the great cavalry action, Fleetwood Fight, June 9, '63.

General Stuart's headquarters, as I have before stated, were at Fleetwood, an old homestead, situated on a hill half a mile from Brandy Station and four miles from the Rappahannock, and our cavalry was encamped for the most part along the river in front. Pleasanton then commanded the cavalry of the enemy and had been encamped twelve miles north of the river, but under pressing orders from Hooker to find out something of Lee's movements, he had the night before moved down to the river with the intention of crossing at daylight the next morning to attack Stuart at the Court House. Thus each commander was nearer the river than the other thought. Pleasanton moved in two columns, one under Buford to cross at Beverly's ford nearly in our front, and the other under Gregg at Kelly's ford six miles below. Both of these columns bivouacked about two miles north of the river.

At daylight our camp was aroused by a rattling fire proceeding from the bank of fog which hung over the valley. Stuart awaited impatiently the news, and presently a courier from General Jones, who was opposite Beverly's ford, reported that the enemy had charged through the ford, had driven in the picket there and had attacked the camp with great fury. Jones had met them with dismounted men and held them in check until his command could saddle up, had then struck his camp, packed his wagons and sent everything to the rear and was awaiting further developments. A sharp action followed without further advance on the part of the enemy. They were disconcerted at meeting such a force at that place, and awaited the movements of Gregg with the other wing six miles away.

Everything remaining quiet, Stuart accompanied by his staff rode down to the scene of action about the middle of the day, having previously sent Gen. Beverly Robertson with his brigade off to our right towards Kelly's ford to guard against an advance from that direction. This move was made on general principles of military strategy, he not having at that time knowledge of the movements of Gregg's column,

106

and if General Robertson had done his duty we would have had ample notice of any advance on that flank. Major McClellan, our Adjutant General, had been left by Stuart on Feetwood hill with some couriers to receive any communications arriving and to forward them to him. Time rolled on, and Stuart with his shrewdness suspected that some scheme was brewing and sent one of his aides, Lieutenant Goldsborough, off to Colonel Butler near Stevensburg to find out if he knew anything of the enemy in his direction. Goldsborough was a fine, handsome and gallant young fellow but he had only joined the staff a few days before and was, as it turned out, inexperienced, and lacking in that habitual caution necessary for a staff officer in riding up to a body of troops on a battlefield; he must be sure who they are before he joins them, particularly in dusty weather when blue and gray are covered alike with dust so as not to be distinguishable. The roads were deep in dust and Goldsborough, poor fellow, had not gone far down the Kelly's ford road before he dashed full tilt into the head of a column of the enemy and was captured.

I must now explain how this force came to be there close upon our flank and we not to know of their approach. Gregg had crossed at Kelly's ford without opposition and had then divided his force, bringing two brigades under Sir Percy Wyndham, an Englishman, and Colonel Kilpatrick up to form a junction with Buford and sending Colonel Duffie with the other part on towards Culpeper C. H. General Robertson, most unaccountably, did not attack either of these forces but allowed Gregg to go on towards our main army and Sir Percy Wyndham to pass him and go on towards Stuart's exposed flank and rear, and it was this latter column Goldsborough met. The first intimation any one had of this attack in flank and rear was their appearance in sight of Fleetwood. McClellan at once sent courier after courier to notify General Stuart, and as good luck would have it he was enabled to make some show of resistance by finding a piece of artillery accidentally passing the road across the hill. With this he immediately opened fire, the boom of the guns reaching us just as the courier brought the news to General Stuart, and satisfied him that McClellan was not mistaken, which at first he thought must be the case.

There now followed a passage of arms filled with romantic interest and splendor to a degree unequaled by anything our war produced. The waste of war had removed the obstacles to cavalry maneuvers usually met with in our country — fences and forests; and the ground was open, level and firm; conditions which led to the settlement of the affair with the sabre alone. Fleetwood hill was the key to the position. Artillery upon the commanding ground would render the surrounding plain untenable, and for its possession the battle was fought over its surface and on the levels beyond. There was here presented in a modern battle the striking phenomenon of gunpowder being ignored almost entirely. Not a man fought dismounted, and there was heard but an occasional pistol shot and but little artillery, for soon after the opening of the fight the contest was so close and the dust so thick that it was impossible to use either without risk to friends.

General Stuart turned to me and ordered me to gallop along the line and order every commanding officer of a regiment to move on Fleetwood at a gallop. It was a thrilling sight to see these dashing horsemen draw their sabres and start for the hill a mile and a half in rear at a gallop. The enemy had gotten a battery almost to the top of the hill when they arrived. This was taken and retaken three times, we retaining it finally. The lines met on the hill. It was like what we read of in the days of chivalry, acres and acres of horsemen sparkling with sabres, and dotted with brilliant bits of color where their flags danced above them, hurled against each other at full speed and meeting with a shock that made the earth tremble. Sir Percy Wyndham after a gallant fight was repulsed before Buford, who was pushing Rooney Lee vigorously, could come to his assistance.

Col. M. C. Butler heard of Duffie's advance, and with great good judgment, without awaiting orders to that effect, threw his regiment in his front and arrested his advance, falling desperately wounded himself. The same cannonball which took off his leg killed Captain Farley of our staff who was riding by his side.

As soon as this repulse was completed, General Stuart told me to watch closely to see if the enemy showed any infantry support, for if they did I must at once inform General Lee or General Longstreet. It was not long before I found them with my powerful field glasses deployed as skirmishers and though they kept low in the grass I could see the color of their trimmings and their bayonet scabbards. Informing Stuart, he sent me to report the fact and after a hot ride of six miles I reached General Longstreet's quarters and reported the fact to him. General Lee then came down himself with some infantry but they were not brought into action. Gen. W. H. F. Lee charged and drove back Buford who was still advancing and then a final advance on our part pressed them back across the Rappahannock.

By all the tests recognized in war the victory was fairly ours. We captured three cannon and five hundred prisoners, and held the field.

Colonel Hampton of the 2nd South Carolina, and Col. Sol. Williams of the 2nd North Carolina were killed, while Gen. W. H. F. Lee, Col. M. C. Butler and many others were wounded. Our loss on the staff was Captain Farley killed, Captain White wounded, and Lieutenant Goldsborough taken prisoner. Goldsborough's fate was a sad one. Taken prisoner in this his first battle, he remained in prison two years; he was then exchanged, and in the first battle after his return, during the retreat from Richmond, only a few days before the surrender at Appomattox, he was killed. During his short stay on the staff he made warm friends of all of us by his gallant bearing and unassuming, attractive manners. He was a son of Commodore Goldsborough of the navy, and one of the handsomest young fellows in the army.

During the action, in galloping from one part of the field to the other carrying orders, friend and foe were so mixed together and all so closely engaged that I had some capital pistol practice, and emptied every barrel of my revolver twice at close range. I could not tell with certainty what effects my shots had, for galloping by one cannot take a second glance, but at a target I seldom failed to hit a hat at that distance and in that manner. Pistol practice from the saddle at a gallop was our favorite amusement on the staff and it is surprising how accurately one can shoot in this way.

After the engagement Stuart ordered headquarters camp to be pitched on the same hill from which it had been moved in the morning, but when we reached the place it was covered so thickly with the dead horses and men, and the bluebottle flies Were swarming so thick over the blood stains on the ground that there was not room enough to pitch the tents among them. So the General reluctantly consented to camping at another place. He regretted this, for as a matter of pride he was inclined to hold the field as he held it in the morning even in this particular.

The next morning we rode over the field and most of the dead bore wounds from the sabre, either by cut or thrust. I mean the field around Fleetwood; in other places this was not the case to so great an extent.

General Lee now began his march towards Pennsylvania. His proposed route was to cross the Blue Ridge and follow the valley of Virginia with his main army, while Stuart was to move on the east side of the mountains to cover his flank at least as far as Middleburg. Winchester was occupied by a strong force of the enemy and Ewell was sent on ahead to clear the valley. This he did gloriously, capturing four or five thousand prisoners and some thirty pieces of artillery.

Stuart pushed on up into Fauquier where Mosby met us. Mosby by this time had become famous. I had not seen him for more than a year and the change in his appearance was striking. When he was a member of my company and afterwards when he became Adjutant of our regiment, the 1st Virginia Cavalry, he was careless about his dress and mount and presented anything but a soldierly appearance. As we were riding along the road at the head of the column one evening we saw a horseman, handsomely dressed, gallop across the field towards us and lift his horse lightly over the fence a short distance ahead, and approach us. I could scarcely believe my eyes when I recognized in this dashing looking officer my old friend and the now celebrated guerrilla chief, Mosby. He had been scouting, and was fully posted as to the movements of the enemy whose cavalry was following us in a parallel line some miles to the east of Bull Run Mountain. During all this period Mosby and his men kept us thoroughly informed of all movements of the enemy in that country.

On the 18th of June we reached Middleburg and on the 19th their cavalry attacked us with great fury. The day before there had been several combats in which we had been in the main successful, capturing many prisoners. The fight at Upperville was a very hot one and at one time we were forced back. General Stuart with his staff around him was slowly leaving the field before the advance of a heavy line of dismounted skirmishers who were pouring their fire into us, the only group of horsemen they could see at that time. We were going up the side of a gently sloping hill and the bullets pattered around us on the hard, hoof-trodden ground like drops of rain. Just then I heard a thump very much like some one had struck a barrel a violent blow with a stick. I knew well enough what it meant, and I can never forget the agony of suspense with which I looked around to see which one of our group would fall. My first glance was towards General Stuart, but there he sat as firm as a rock in his saddle. I then saw von Borcke who was riding close by my side drop his bridle hand and become limp, his horse bounding forward as the rein was relaxed. I saw at once that his spur was going to hang in the blanket strapped behind his saddle, for he slowly slid sideways from his seat with both hands clutching the horse's mane. I spurred Magic up alongside instantly, and, leaning over, took his foot in both hands and threw it over, clear of the saddle. His feet fell to the ground and this jerked loose his hold on the mane, letting him down easily on his back.

Frank Robertson and myself sprang to the ground while someone caught the horse and brought him back. Seeing that our poor comrade was shot in the back of the neck I had little hope for him but determined to get his body off the field if possible. Von Borcke had often expressed his horror of filling a nameless grave and he once asked me, if the occasion should ever arise, to mark the place so that his friends could find it. The horse, as I have said, was brought to us but he was in a state of great excitement from the constant hissing of the bullets, for the approaching skirmish line, seeing the party halted, were bestowing special attention on us. I was at my wits' end to know how we were to throw our friend's body, weighing two hundred and fifty pounds, across the rearing, plunging charger, and how we were to keep it there if we succeeded in doing so. I then recollected a thing von Borcke had once told me was taught in the Prussian Cavalry schools for this very emergency, and I made a courier twist the horse's ear severely and keep it twisted while he led the horse off the field with von Borcke on him, the horse becoming perfectly quiet immediately. How strange that von Borcke's mentioning this little trick on a long night march in a general conversation to while away the time should have saved the narrator from capture, and quite likely from death from neglect in prison.

When we first lifted him von Borcke was as limp as a rag, but to our great surprise and pleasure he then showed signs of returning consciousness and stiffened himself on his legs enough for us to lift one foot to the stirrup, and then with a mighty effort to hoist him to the saddle, where with assistance on both sides he kept his balance until we could get him to an ambulance.

Von Borcke's strong constitution enabled him to survive this wound, though it was a very severe one. The bullet passed through the collar of his jacket an inch or two from the spine and entered his throat, and for months he coughed up pieces of his clothing which had been carried in. He was never able, however, to enter active service again with us. A few months before the surrender he returned to his own country and in the war with Austria held a position on Prince Frederick Charles' staff, though obliged to ride mostly in a carriage. In 1884 he visited this country and I dined with him at the Maryland Club in Baltimore, an elegant entertainment given in his honor at which there were present some twenty-odd old comrades of his, including Generals Wade Hampton and M. C. Butler of South Carolina, Gen. W. H. F. Lee of Virginia and Col. R. Snowden Andrews and Gen. Bradley T. Johnson of Baltimore. When I met him on this occasion he threw his arms around me and his eyes filled with tears. I spent a couple of days with him in Baltimore and we called to see the "New York rebel" who happened to be on a visit to the city at the time. She was still unmarried. This was the beautiful girl we met at Urbana, Maryland, during the Antietam Campaign in 1862, the one with whom I was dancing at our memorable ball when the wounded arrived. We had many pleasant memories to recall, but it was hard to realize that the middle-aged, matronly looking lady and the huge gentleman weighing between four and five hundred pounds were those who danced so gracefully then. Von Borcke told me he had not been able to reach his feet to tie his shoes for years on account of his corpulency. He was immense — his neck quite as large as his head, and all his manly beauty gone.

When he visited this country von Borcke had just lost his wife. He showed me her picture, and the picture of his two boys. She was a beautiful woman, judging by the photograph.

When Col. Chas. Venable visited Prussia, von Borcke invited him to his castle and ran up the Prussian flag on one tower and the Confederate flag on the other.

The improvement in the cavalry of the enemy became painfully apparent in the fights around Upperville. It was mainly in their use of dismounted men, and in their horse artillery, however, for they could not stand before us yet in a charge on horseback. Around Upperville the fields were much enclosed by stone fences which greatly favored dismounted troops, and greatly impeded the mounted men. They were much better provided with long-range carbines than our cavalry, which gave them an advantage dismounted. Their cavalry too had been largely recruited from the infantry and had seen service and been drilled as such, which of course was greatly to their advantage serving on foot, while our cavalry had served from the beginning in their branch of the service, and had been drilled mainly mounted.

In the series of combats from Aldie to Middleburg from the 17th to the 21st it must be borne in mind that we were following a *defensive* policy, Stuart's only object being to cover the gaps of the Blue Ridge. This of course places cavalry at a disadvantage as it is mainly an *offensive* arm of the service and our object was successfully obtained, for the enemy never even entered a gap of the mountain. From a captured dispatch Stuart found that a strong force of infantry was supporting their attack and he then called upon General Longstreet for a detachment. These reached us, or rather reached a point within supporting distance in Ashby's Gap, but were not brought into action, nor even in sight of the enemy, as shown by General Pleasanton's report of the action.

We were now about to start on an expedition which for audacious boldness equaled if it did not exceed any of our dashing leader's exploits; but before entering upon the subject we must take a glance at the position of the contending forces: Lee occupied the valley from Winchester to the Potomac, and Meade awaited his movements in Loudoun and Fauquier, the two counties opposite, on the eastern side of the Blue Ridge. Stuart, as I have stated, guarded the passes of the mountain, and occupied the space between the Blue Ridge and the low range of hills parallel thereto called Bull Run Mountain, with headquarters at Rector's crossroads. General Lee being now ready to begin his march northwards, Early crossed the Potomac with his division as the advanced guard on June 22nd.

The question now arose as to how Stuart was to reach the head of Lee's advancing column, now entering Pennsylvania. It was impossible for him to move along the eastern slope of the Blue Ridge between the mountain and Meade's forces, and all the roads leading northward through the valley were densely filled with the trains of artillery, and quartermaster, commissary and ordnance wagons, to say nothing of the infantry columns. Two plans were presented by Stuart and submitted to General Lee's consideration: one, to take the route through the valley, and the other, which Stuart was ardently in favor of, to sweep around the rear of Meade's army and dash northward past him, and between him and Washington; cutting his communications, breaking up the railroads, doing all the damage possible, and then to join Early in Pennsylvania. General Lee left the decision of the question to Stuart, and Stuart immediately prepared to carry it into execution.

It was clearly necessary to leave a strong force of cavalry to guard the passes until Meade had left his position, else their cavalry could pour through and fall upon Lee's rear. Stuart had with him about five thousand men. This force he divided, leaving Wm. E. Jones' and Robertson's brigades, three thousand men, under command of Robertson to hold the passes until their front was clear and then to operate with the main army as Gen. R. E. Lee might direct; and he took three brigades, Hampton's, Fitz Lee's and W. H. F. Lee's, the latter under the command of Colonel Chambliss, numbering about two thousand men.

These three brigades were ordered to rendezvous at Salem on the night of the 24th, and a little after midnight on the morning of the 25th of June we started. No one could ride along the lines of this splendid body of men and not be struck with the spirit which animated them. They knew they were starting on some bold enterprise, but their confidence in their leader was so unbounded that they were as gay and lively as it was possible for them to be, for up to that time no reverse had crossed their path and they believed themselves and their leader invincible. Often have I heard, when some danger threatened and Stuart galloped by to the front, the remark, "Ah boys! I feel all right now, there is General Stuart."

Mosby had reported the enemy still in their encampments the day before and Stuart expected to move eastward through Haymarket and thence direct to Fairfax C. H., but at Hay-market, early in the first day's march, he found Hancock's corps on the march occupying the road he wished to cross for many miles each way. After shelling them awhile and capturing some prisoners, he had to wait most of the morning for them to pass, and then by a detour he passed around their rear and by a more circuitous route pushed on, crossing the Occoquan at Wolf Run shoals, capturing a small force at Fairfax C. H., passing through Dranesville, and reaching Rowser's Ford of the Potomac on the night of the 27th. The ford was wide and deep and might well have daunted a less determined man than our indomitable General, for the water swept over the pommels of our saddles. To pass the artillery without wetting the ammunition in the chests was impossible, provided it was left in them, but Stuart had the cartridges distributed among the horsemen and it was thus taken over in safety. The guns and caissons went clean out of sight beneath the surface of the rapid torrent, but all came out without the loss of a piece or a man, though the night was dark, and by three o'clock on the morning of the 28th of June we all stood wet and dripping on the Maryland shore.

Oh, what a change! From the hoof-trodden, war-wasted lands of old Virginia to a country fresh and plentiful. The march for three days had been through a country naturally poor at its best, but stripped by war of all the little it once had. Not a mouthful of grain had even I been able to beg, borrow, or steal for my horses; and where I could not find it there was apt to be none to find. Poor Magic looked as thin as a snake but cocked her ear as gayly as ever. Manassas had been wounded during our attack on Hancock's corps at Haymarket, but could still do duty, though much in want of food. The necessity for stopping to graze the horses on this march had delayed us a good deal, both in the time it took and the weakening of the animals from such light diet. I rode Manassas on the march and had Magic led, saving her for the big battle that we knew was brewing. It was absolutely necessary, though time was so precious, to allow the artillery horses some rest and a chance to eat the fine grass around us after their hard night's work; so it was nearly the middle of the day before we reached Rockville, a pretty village on the main road leading from Washington and nine or ten miles from that city. We had just arrived when a long wagon train of a hundred and fifty wagons appeared on the road slowly approaching from the direction of Washington, and a detail from Hampton's brigade was at once sent to capture it, which I accompanied. Galloping full tilt into the head of the train, we captured a small guard and a lot of gayly dressed quartermasters, and over half the wagons, before they could turn round; but then those beyond took the alarm, turned and fled as fast as their splendid mule teams could go. After them we flew, popping away with our pistols at such drivers as did not pull up, but the more we popped the faster those in front plied the whip; finally, coming to a sharp turn in the road, one upset and a dozen or two others piled up on top of it, until you could see nothing but the long ears and kicking legs of the mules sticking above bags of oats emptied from the wagons upon them. All behind this blockade were effectually stopped, but half a dozen wagons had made the turn before this happened and after them two or three of us dashed. It was as exciting as a fox chase for several miles, until when the last was taken I found myself on a hill in full view of Washington. One hundred and twenty-five uninjured wagons were taken and safely brought into our lines, together with the animals of the others. Here was a godsend to our poor horses, for every wagon was loaded with oats intended for Meade's army and it did one's heart good to see the way the poor brutes got on the outside of those oats. After giving my horses all they could eat I slung half a bag, saddle-bag fashion, across my saddle for future use, and my horse seemed to know what this additional load was, for he occasionally turned an affectionate glance back towards it.

There was a large female academy in Rockville, and flocks of the pretty maidens congregated on the front to greet us, showing strong sympathy for our cause, and cutting off all the buttons they could get hold of from our uniforms as souvenirs. In passing along the street I saw a very duplicate of my little daughter Lizzie. Never have I seen so remarkable a likeness between two people. Frank Robertson was as much struck with it as I was. Twenty years after he met her there, a grown woman.

With the exception of a squadron of the enemy, encountered at Winchester, we met no opposition until Hanover was reached about noon on the 30th. It seems remarkable that the enemy should not have used more enterprise than this, for we were destroying his communications as we advanced. At Hanover, however we met Kilpatrick's division of cavalry and had a hot affair with them. We were just opposite

Gettysburg and if we could have made our way direct, the fifteen miles of distance to that place would have passed that day, and we would have effected a junction with General Lee the day before the battle began. It was here the wagon train began to interfere with our movements, and if General Stuart could only have known what we do now it would have been burned; but he knew nothing of the concentration which accidental circumstances were to bring about at Gettysburg in the next two days, and as he expected to meet Early at York very soon, he held on to them.

The 2nd North Carolina Regiment made the first charge through the town, driving the enemy out, but receiving strong reinforcements they rallied and drove the North Carolinians back in their turn in great confusion. As General Stuart saw them rushing out of the place, he started down the road to meet them, calling me to follow him. We tried to rally them, but the long charge *in* and the repulse *out* and the hot skirmish fire opened upon them from the windows on the street by citizens had thrown them into utter confusion, and in spite of all we could do they got by us, and before we were aware of it we found ourselves at the head of the enemy's charging column.

The road was lined on each side by an ill-kept hedge grown up high, but at some places, fortunately for us, there were gaps of lower growth. Stuart pulled up and, waving his sabre with a merry laugh, shouted to me, "Rally them, Blackford!" and then lifted his mare, Virginia, over the hedge into the field. I knew that he only said what he did to let me know that he was off, so I followed him. I had only that morning, fortunately, mounted Magic, having had her led previously, and Stuart had done the same with Virginia, so they were fresh. As we alighted in the field, we found ourselves within ten paces of the front of a flanking party of twenty-five or thirty men which was accompanying the charging regiment, and they called to us to halt; but as we let our two thoroughbreds out, they followed in hot pursuit, firing as fast as they could cock their pistols. The field was in tall timothy grass and we did not see, nor did our horses until close to it, a huge gully fifteen feet wide and as many deep stretched across our path. There were only a couple of strides of distance for our horses to regulate their step, and Magic had to rise at least six feet from the brink. Stuart and myself were riding side by side and as soon as Magic rose I turned my head to see how Virginia had done it, and I shall never forget the glimpse I then saw of this beautiful animal away up in mid-air over the chasm and Stuart's fine figure sitting erect and firm in the saddle. Magic, seeing the size of the place and having received a very unusual sharp application of my spurs, had put out her strength to its full in this leap and she landed six or seven feet beyond the further bank, making a stride of certainly twenty-seven feet. The moment our horses rose, our pursuers saw that there was something there, and it was with difficulty they could pull up in time to avoid plunging headlong into it, and their firing was of course arrested. This time Magic's activity had saved me from capture, but ten minutes later her quickness saved my life.

General Stuart galloped on up towards the top of a hill to direct the fire of a battery on the pursuing regiment, while I, wishing to get Magic cooled down away from the excitement of other horses, took a path which wound round the foot of the hill. I had just quieted her, so that she had put her head down and was walking with the reins on her neck, when I heard the clatter of a horse's hoofs behind me at full speed. Thinking it was someone who wished to join company, I did not turn to look until I found the horse was not going slower as it approached. I then looked back, and there, within a couple of horses' lengths, came dashing a Yankee sergeant bending low on his horse's neck with his sabre "en-carte" ready to run me through. It was the work of a second to seize the slackened reins, pull them over to the right and plunge my left spur into her flank. As quick as lightning Magic bounded to the right, so quickly that my left arm was lifted a little from my side, and at the same instant there gleamed the bright blade of a sabre between my arm and body as my pursuer made his thrust; but by the time I could gather the reins and turn, the man was fifty yards away. Then I heard some cheering, and looking up to the left, on a hill nearby saw a general officer and his staff, towards whom my man was making his way. It was evident that, seeing me alone, this man had made the pass as a little sword practice for the amusement of his comrades and his own glorification. I would have given anything if I could only have had half a minute's notice of his coming, for I don't think there would have been then anything for them to cheer. From where they stood it looked exactly as if he had succeeded in running me through, and he no doubt did not disabuse their minds as to the facts. I could only show my feelings upon the subject by shaking my fist at them as I moved slowly on to the battery on our hill.

It was night before we withdrew from Hanover, and Kilpatrick had been so roughly handled that he did not follow us on the first. On approaching York, Stuart found that Early had left there, moving westward, and he sent Maj. Andrew R. Venable of his staff on his trail to get orders from General Lee. Later in the day Capt. Henry Lee of Fitz Lee's staff was sent on a similar errand. During our night march the wagon train and nearly four hundred prisoners, who had been taken since the first batch of four hundred were paroled four days before, were a source of unmitigated annoyance. The mules in the captured wagon trains could neither be fed nor watered, and had not been for several days, while the prisoners fared nearly as badly. The consequence was great difficulty in moving them. Expecting to get rations in Carlisle, Stuart sent his commissary on ahead to make a requisition on the town, but since the withdrawal of Early the place had been occupied by the enemy. Stuart reached the place on the evening of July 1, and found it occupied by two brigades of militia under command of Gen. W. F. Smith. Of this officer he demanded a surrender, which was refused; whereupon Stuart opened his batteries and shelled the town and burned the barracks.

About midnight Venable and Lee returned with the first information we had received from our army and with orders from Gen. R. E. Lee for Stuart to march to Gettysburg at once. They also brought us intelligence of the successful combat of that day at Gettysburg.

We started from Carlisle about one o'clock A. M. on July 2, and effected a junction with our army at Gettysburg early in the day, Hampton becoming engaged in a sharp conflict with Kilpatrick's division before reaching there.

The brigades of Jones and Robertson, left at Upperville when Stuart started on his expedition, remained there long after the enemy left their front, and did not rejoin us until after the Battle of Gettysburg was fought and we were withdrawing towards the Potomac. Whose fault this was I cannot say, but certainly not Stuart's. If Robertson had not been a West Pointer he would have been deprived of his command for his inactivity in letting General Wyndham's command pass him as he did at Fleetwood Fight on the 9th of June, and the same qualities in the man which made him play such a part there may have been the cause of the delay on this occasion. General Robertson was an excellent man in camp to train troops, but in the field, in the presence of the enemy, he lost all self-possession, and was perfectly unreliable. But had he not sat upon the benches at West Point? Certainly he had, and he must consequently be made a general without ever having done one single thing in action to deserve that promotion. Our cause died of West Point as much as of any one thing. General Lee and General Stuart must have been convinced of his incapacity by this affair, for he was relieved of his command soon after and sent elsewhere.

It is easy enough to say that some other course would have been better than the one Stuart followed, looking back now with the knowledge of *what has since happened*; but is it fair to blame him for acting for the best with the *knowledge he then had*? If the Battle of Gettysburg had been won by us, as it very nearly was, this expedition would have been called a magnificent achievement. As it was the injury inflicted on the enemy by the diversion of troops was alone enough to justify it. Maj. H. B. McClellan gives a very able defence of Stuart on this point in his book, *The Campaigns of Stuart's Cavalry*, pages 332 to 336, and shows clearly that the effect of Stuart's movement accomplished as much, if not more, diversion and neutralization of the forces of the enemy as any plan he could have pursued.

Napoleon, I believe, once said that a dog-fight might bring on a battle, and General Heth says that the Battle of Gettysburg was brought on upon that spot by the stores in the town being well stocked with boots and shoes, for his division being in want of shoes, and hearing of those in Gettysburg, he marched towards the place to get them and, meeting Meade's advance, he was reinforced; thus was brought on the engagement at that place. There is a great deal of luck in war. Circumstances sometimes seem to combine, for or against, in a way that sets at naught all calculations, and at the Battle of Gettysburg half a dozen things may be enumerated, any one of which might have given us the victory if we had been "in luck" at the time. It is not within the scope of these pages to give a history of the battle, but I wish to record one circumstance which came under my own observation, one which I can but think had a good deal to do with its loss, and a circumstance I have never heard alluded to since.

In the supreme hour of battle the Commander in Chief is the soul of an army, that is, if he is worthy of the army he commands. This being so, anything which affects his physical condition at that time must have a powerful influence upon events. We all know the desperately weakening power of severe diarrhea, and this General Lee had, as I know. When Stuart arrived upon the left flank on the morning of the 2nd, there followed several cavalry combats, and during the evening I was sent to General Lee to report what had happened. I found General Lee at his headquarters near the town, but he was in his tent and I was told by one of his staff that I could not see him; so I gave my report to this officer, either Venable or Taylor, I think it was, who took it in to General Lee, and then I sat half an hour with them telling of our expedition. When coming on errands of this kind before, I had usually given my report to General Lee in person, but on this occasion I supposed he was too busy to see me. I was a little surprised therefore to see him come out of his tent hurriedly and go to the rear several times while I was there, and he walked so much as if he was weak and in pain that I asked one of the gentlemen present what was the matter with him, and he told me General Lee was suffering a good deal from an attack of diarrhea. This was the evening of the 2nd day's fight and the day before the final contest. Now who in such a condition would not be affected in vigor of both mind and body, and will not this account for several things which were behind time, or not pushed forward as they should have been the 3rd of July?

After leaving General Lee's headquarters I rode along our lines towards the right, meeting many friends on the way; among them I remember Hearing, who then had an artillery command but was afterwards a Brigadier General of cavalry. On returning I rode through the town of Gettysburg towards our left flank and was delighted to find that my brother Eugene's battalion of skirmishers from Bodes' division was there. They held the range of two-and three-story brick buildings on Main Street on the side next Cemetery Ridge, through the back windows of which they were keeping up an incessant firing into the enemy's lines nearby. It was the first time I had seen warfare carried on in this way, and wishing to find my brother, I was glad to have the opportunity of examining into it. Leaving my horse in charge of the courier who accompanied me, at a place in the street somewhat sheltered from the shells which at times came tearing through the houses, I ascended a handsome stairway to the second floor. This floor along the whole block had been used in each house for parlors, sitting rooms and dining rooms, and the floor above for bedrooms, while the lower floor was occupied mostly by stores. Eugene's men had cut passways through the partition walls so that they could walk through the houses all the way from one cross street to the other. From the windows of the back rooms, against which were piled beds and mattresses, and through holes punched in the outside back wall, there was kept up a continuous rattle of musketry by men stripped to the waist and blackened with powder. It was a strange sight to see these men fighting in these neatly and sometimes elegantly furnished rooms, while those not on duty reclined on elegant sofas, or stretched themselves out upon handsome carpets. I was surprised to see in some houses feathers scattered everywhere in every room, upstairs and downstairs, and found it had been done by shells bursting in feather beds on the upper floor. Fools of blood in many places marked the spots where someone had been hit and laid out on the carpets, and here and there a dead body not yet removed, and many great holes in the walls, showed where artillery had been brought to bear upon this hornets' nest when their sting became too severe for endurance. I enquired for Major Blackford and was directed to a room in the middle of the block where I found him and some of his officers lolling on the sofas in a handsome parlor. On a marble table were set decanters of wine, around which were spread all sorts of delicacies taken from a sideboard in the adjoining dining room, where they had been left, in their hurry, by the inhabitants when they fled before our advance the day before. Outside could be heard the cannonade and the growl of the musketry around Cemetery Ridge, and echoing through the house the reports from the deadly rifles puffing their little clouds of light blue smoke from the back windows, while the room was pervaded by the smell of powder. After I had partaken with great relish of the refreshments, Eugene showed me over his fortress. From the back windows, by keeping duly out of sight of the watchful men in the rifle pits a short distance beyond the houses, I could see all that part of the lines of the enemy and could form an idea of the strength of the position luck had given them. If General Lee had been in his usually vigorous condition of health the day before, I believe he would have followed up our success in the first day's action and occupied this ridge, or he would have withdrawn to a more favorable field; but suffering as he was how could he be as active as usual? It was then he missed *Stuart*, as McClellan says, and not the cavalry. But if he had been on the spot himself he would have seen it all at a glance. Such are the little things which in war, as in everything else, sometimes lead to great results. General Lee's sickness may have been sufficient to cause the loss of the battle.

The next day all was quiet for a long time; hour after hour passed and scarcely a gun was heard. Stuart moved his command forward on the York road a couple of miles and placed it in a position to cover the left of our main line around Gettysburg as well as to threaten the enemy's rear, but still no enemy was in sight in our front. Wishing to know what was going on in the main body of the army, Stuart sent me with a roving commission to find out. All was as quiet as if there was not a soldier within a hundred miles, and the country looked so calm and beautiful, dotted over with thrifty farms, that it was hard to realize that nearly a quarter of a million men were met together to settle their "difficulty" upon "the field of honor."

Seeing everything so still, I made no effort to hurry my mission, but rode through our army seeking acquaintances and picking up what news I could on the left wing. I then passed the town, and was behind a clump of woods when it seemed like "hell had broke loose," as a soldier near me expressed it. Every cannon in both armies opened and three hundred brazen throats joined in such rapid accompaniment that individual reports could not be distinguished. In a moment the lines were wrapped in clouds of thick, white smoke, and I knew that the general and perhaps the final action had begun. I stood for some time watching the scene and was sorely tempted to stay and see what was going to happen, but my duty clearly called me to return to General Stuart; so I reluctantly withdrew and a short time after, Pickett started on his memorable charge. I have never ceased to regret that I did not witness this historic event, but I did not.

Soon after I left Stuart, the cavalry of the enemy had made an attack upon him in force and a severe conflict had ensued, the closing scenes of which I got back in time to witness. Stuart held his ground, however, and the enemy withdrew after about as bloody and hot an affair as any we had yet experienced The cavalry of the enemy were steadily improving and it was all we could do sometimes to manage them.

At the close of the day we did not know how the result stood, for both armies held exactly the same ground they did in the morning; but during the night our army concentrated on the hills west of Gettysburg, drawing in the left wing, and offered battle all the next day, the 4th, but scarcely a gun was fired and no attack was made upon us. The fact was they had been very nearly beaten, and I believe Meade is said to have at one time actually issued the order to retreat. They certainly were well content to let well enough alone, for they never disturbed us again while we remained north of the Potomac. All day on the 4th did we await the expected attack, as I have stated, but another and greater danger now threatened in the rains which set in that day. We were nearly forty miles from the Potomac, whose fords were deep and wide at their best, and now the water rose beyond all possibility of crossing and swept away the pontoon bridges which had been laid across the stream at Falling Waters.

General Lee issued his order of march on the 4th, and that night we took up the line of march in retreat towards Virginia, the cavalry keeping up the campfires and covering the movement. The Battle of Gettysburg in its *results* was a great victory for the Federal cause, but Lee's army did not feel at all like a beaten one. There was no rout or confusion; not even a pursuit to remind us that our invasion had come to an end, and all the silly stuff we read in the Northern accounts of "flying rebels" and "shattered army" are pure fictions prepared for the Northern market.

It was ten days after the Battle of Gettysburg before we crossed the Potomac on the night of the 13th of July. There had been numerous cavalry actions and a part of Ewell's train of wagons had been captured, but it was not until the 12th that Meade brought his infantry in sight of our main body, now strongly entrenched, and awaiting the fall of the raging river behind them to cross back into Virginia. On the night of the 13th, orders were issued for the crossing, the infantry drawing out of the entrenchments and the cavalry taking their places; then as soon as the infantry had crossed the cavalry followed. Longstreet's and Hill's corps crossed on pontoon bridges, which had been rebuilt, at Falling Waters, while Ewell's corps forded at Williamsport and the cavalry all forded at Williamsport also. The ford was very wide and still almost past fording. I witnessed the passage of Ewell's corps and it was a strange and interesting sight. On either bank fires illuminated the scene, the water reached the arm-pits of the men and was very swift. By the bright lurid light the long line of heads and shoulders and the dim sparkling of their musket barrels could be traced across the watery space, dwindling away almost to a thread before it reached the further shore. The passage of the wagon trains was attended with some loss, for the current in some cases swept them down past the ford into deep water. It was curious to watch the behavior of the mules in these teams. As the water rose over their backs they began rearing and springing vertically upward, and as they went deep and deeper the less would be seen of them before they made the spring which would bring their bodies half out of the water; then nothing would be seen but their ears above the water, until by a violent effort the poor brutes would again spring aloft; and indeed after the waters had closed over them, occasionally one would appear in one last plunge high above the surface.

In crossing even on horseback the cavalry got almost as wet as the infantry, and they were worse off afterwards, for they had to sit in wet saddles without the warming exercise which walking gives. Having been greatly exposed to the weather during the ten days of rain following the Battle of Gettysburg and then having to take this cold bath in the middle of the night, I felt the next morning very badly, but kept up until we reached the hospitable home of our friends at the Bower, Mr. Stephen Dandridge and his family. Our camp was pitched at the old place in his park and our pleasant, gay life was resumed, with the lovely daughters and nieces of our host. A shade of sadness hung over our meeting, however, when we thought how many who were with us during our former visit were dead or absent from wounds.

We had scarcely gotten settled, however, when my malady increased and I was glad to accept Mrs. Dandridge's kind invitation to come to the house. There I was put to bed, the Doctor pronouncing mine a case of camp fever. I was stuffed with quinine until I was nearly crazy, and after a few days was glad to hear our surgeon say I must go to the rear to a hospital. An ambulance was fitted up and a courier detailed to accompany me as far as Staunton or farther if needed, and I bade farewell to my kind friends at the Bower and at headquarters. Our surgeon, Dr. Eliason, gave me plenty of physic to take on the road and a supply of nice rations suitable for an invalid. The first day I chucked all the physic out of the window and by the time I reached Staunton I was well enough to travel alone; so I sent the courier back with the ambulance and concluded I would avail myself of my sick leave to visit my wife in Abingdon. Telegraphing to her I was coming, I reached Lynchburg, where I intended spending a few days with my father and mother, and found to my delight that Mary had come to meet me there and accompany me back to Abingdon. Long before my leave was out, I was well again and enjoyed extremely the delights of home.

After Lee crossed the Potomac, Meade moved southward, occupying Harpers Ferry and Loudoun County, thus threatening Richmond; so Longstreet moved down the valley and then across the mountain to interpose in his front, while the rest of the army followed at their leisure, our cavalry holding the line of the Rappahannock. There then followed a period of rest, which was occupied by a reorganization of the cavalry into two divisions, with Hampton and Fitz Lee promoted to Major Generals commanding. The organization became as follows:

J. E. B. Stuart Major Gen.
Hampton's Division.

Jones' Brigade (Brig. Gen. Wm. E. Jones).
6th Va. Cav. — Lieut. Col. J. S. Green.
7th Va. Cav. — Col. R. H. Dulany.
12th Va. Cav. — Col. A. W. Harman.
35th Battalion Va. Cav. — Lieut. Col. E. V. White.

Baker's Brigade (Brig. Gen. L. S. Baker).
1st N. C. Cav. — Lieut. Col. J. B. Gordon.
2nd N. C. Cav. — Lieut. Col. Robinson.
4th N. C. Cav. — Col. D. D. Ferebee.
5th N. C. Cav. — Col. Evans.

Fitz Lee's Division.

Lee's Brigade (Brig. Gen. W. H. F. Lee).
1st S. C. Cav. — Col. J. L. Black.
9th Va. Cav. — Col. R. L. T. Beale.
10th Va. Cav. — Col. T. Lucius Davis.
13th Va. Cav. — Col. T. R. Chambliss.
Lomax's Brigade (Brig. Gen. L. L. Lomax).
5th Va. Cav. — Col. T. L. Rosser
1st Battalion Md. Cav. Lieut. Col. Ridgely Brown.
11th Va. Cav. — Col. O. R. Funsten.
15th Va. Cav. — Col. W. W. Ball.
Wickham's Brigade (Brig. Gen. W. C. Wickham).
1st Va. Cav. — Col. R. W. Carter.
2nd Va. Cav. — Col. T. T. Mumford.
3rd Va. Cav. — Col. T. H. Owen.
4th Va. Cav. — Lieut. Col. W. H. Payne.

On the 13th of September active operations began again in what is known as "The Bristoe Campaign." Urged on by public opinion at the North, an effort was to be made to improve the victory of Gettysburg by pushing on towards that goal of all their hopes, Richmond, and a series of hot cavalry fights followed, some over the famous Brandy Station fields. Meade had occupied Culpeper County, but there he seemed to be at a loss what to do, for he made no further move until his wily adversary made a movement similar to that practised upon Pope the year before by turning his right flank.

Stuart moved on the 9th of October to Madison C. H. and the army marched the next day, the cavalry covering the movement effectually. General Lee had determined to push his adversary back from the front on the line of the Rapidan, and under cover of the cavalry he moved to Warrenton without the knowledge of his adversary and there concentrated his army. There now occurred one of the most extraordinary events of the war.

On the morning of the 13th Stuart received orders from General Lee to make a reconnaissance towards Catlett's Station on the Orange and Alexandria R. R. He immediately sent Lomax on to Auburn, a cross roads two miles from the railroad, at which place a country road, running parallel to the railroad, crosses the road from Warrenton at right angles, and Stuart followed soon after with seven guns under Beckham and two brigades of cavalry, Funsten's and Gordon's.

Leaving Lomax to guard his rear, Stuart pushed on and sent me to reconnoitre the railroad to which we were moving. On coming in sight of the open country along the railroad I found it filled with a vast park of wagons and the enemy in strong force. Leaving our horses with one of the men who accompanied me, I took the two others and by creeping in some places succeeded in reaching a clump of trees on a knoll from which their whole encampment could be seen, and I then wrote a note to General Stuart telling him where I was and what I saw. In a short time he came himself to the spot and was examining it carefully when a courier came in hot haste to announce that the enemy were in our rear.

We hurried back to find that a large body of the enemy, two army corps, the 2nd and 3rd, were marching on the road we had crossed at Auburn. Their advance had driven Lomax away and there they were steadily marching across our rear, enclosing us between themselves and the corps on the railroad, but entirely ignorant of the fact. The ground to the north of us was steep, broken and wooded, and to the south as ill luck would have it there was a wide and deep canal or mill race reaching parallel to the road we were on, and a hundred yards from it, all the way from Auburn to the railroad. It was thus impossible for us to escape on either side and to break a way through could not be thought of, except as a last resort. With the inspiration of his genius Stuart grasped the subject in an instant and adopted a plan as simple as it was effective, by which the command was extricated without the loss of a man. He found almost in sight of Auburn the mouth of a little valley opening on the road and covered with woods, and finding this valley large enough to hide his command in, he marched it in there, just about dark. On the road were stationed two strong pickets of dismounted men twenty yards apart who were kept concealed in the bushes and were to remain so if any large body of troops passed in the night; but if single horsemen, or a small body, approached, the first picket was to keep low until the second stopped them and then the first was to rise and cut off the retreat. In this way several dispatches were captured during the night, giving us valuable information of the enemy's movements and showing that our position was unknown to them.

On the little ridge between the valley and the marching column of the enemy there was a cleared, grassy field from which we witnessed the march all night long. Their column was not over one hundred and fifty yards distant and we could hear their conversation. Almost every man, it seemed, carried a lantern which gave the scene a very picturesque effect in the dark, still night. I had stretched myself out a little way down the slope to watch the scene when General Stuart threw himself down by my side and laid his head on me and in an instant was fast asleep. Hour after hour passed and the General's head on my middle became rather heavy for comfort, but I was reluctant to disturb him. It got so bad at last that I was compelled to move it gently to another part of my body, but this awoke him and I then snatched a few hours' sleep. We were so close to the enemy that it was necessary to place a man at the head of every mule in the ambulances to keep them from betraying our presence, for the poor beasts needed food and water, and often we would hear an incipient bray brought to a premature close by a whack over the head from a sabre scabbard.

Five picked men were chosen and sent by Stuart to General Lee to report the predicament he was in, and to ask that an attack might be made in the morning at daylight to serve as a diversion in his favor, and all of these men passed through the column safely and made their reports. A little before daybreak the marching column halted and drew off on a hill nearly opposite us on the other side of the road, and lighted fires to cook breakfast. This proved to be the rear guard of the two corps which had been passing us all night. When day broke Stuart waited with great impatience for the sound of the hoped-for attack from the troops near Warrenton, but it was delayed until the sun was half an hour high. In the meantime our guns were loaded and placed just back of the hill we were on, so they could be run up by hand at the proper moment, and at the first light rattle of musketry from the force approaching for our relief we opened fire from seven pieces on the breakfasting party two hundred and fifty yards away. Great was the consternation on that hill, where we could see coffee pots upset and men running hither and thither from the storm of shells pouring upon them. They threw forward a line of skirmishes, but Gordon charged and scattered them and then Stuart marched the command out and moved off. Just after this charge, or rather while it was yet going on, Stuart sent me to General Gordon with some orders, and as I rode up to him the whole breast of his uniform was covered with blood. He had not noticed it and was at a loss to account for it at first, but then found his nose was bleeding fast. This had been caused by a bullet which passed so close across the bridge of his nose that it was sore to the touch for several days but had not broken the skin. Gordon was a good deal relieved, and so was I that it was no worse, for we both thought at first that he was seriously hurt. For all the good they did, the force sent down from Warrenton might just as well have stayed away, but they said afterwards that our shells impeded their advance.

The withdrawal of the enemy from Culpeper County having been effected by General Lee's manoeuvre, he advanced no farther than Warrenton, but Stuart with his cavalry followed them up, with frequent collisions with their cavalry as far as Bull Run. We then turned back and on the 19th of October we inflicted a severe blow on their cavalry which was called ever after the "Buckland Races." Stuart was falling back with Hampton's division, on the road which led through Buckland, before Kilpatrick's division, while Fitz Lee's division was within supporting distance on our left towards Auburn. Fitz Lee suggested that Stuart should withdraw past Buckland and that he would attack Kilpatrick in flank, and at the first gun Hampton should wheel and attack him in front, and Stuart at once acceded to the arrangement. A mile and a half from Buckland the road crosses a low range of hills, and behind these Stuart placed Hampton and then awaited the sound of Lee's guns. It was a broad, straight turnpike road, and as far as the eye could reach their column of splendidly equipped cavalry came marching on with flags fluttering and arms glittering in the bright autumn sunshine. Hampton's division was formed in two columns, each heading at a gap in the ridge, and all before them was smooth, firm ground.

We waited with breathless impatience the boom of Fitz Lee's cannon. Not seeing us, the enemy was just ascending the little rise behind which we were, not two hundred yards distant, when rapid firing of cannon in Lee's direction announced his attack, and at the same moment our two columns were let loose, and at them we went.

Attacked in front and flank, they did not wait for us to get halfway to them before they broke, and then it was a race like a fox chase for five miles. Next to that after the Lancers near Cold Harbor in the seven days around Richmond, this was the most exciting sport I ever had. They were well mounted and the country being so open, we only got two hundred and fifty prisoners and eight or ten ambulances. Among the latter was one containing Custer's baggage and correspondence. Some of the letters to a fair, but frail, friend of Custer's were published in the Richmond papers and afforded some spicy reading, though the most spicy parts did not appear. We chased them back upon their infantry supports and captured some of these in the confusion of the entry into their camp.

Stuart now rejoined the main army around Culpeper C. H. His capture of prisoners during the ten days this campaign lasted numbered thirteen hundred and seventy (1370) as reported by the provost-marshal, Maj. G. M. Ryals.

I omitted to mention that for a month before starting on the Bristoe Campaign our headquarters had been at the house of Dr. Andrew Grinnan near Orange C. H. The family consisted of Dr. Grinnan and his sister, and to the mutual advantage of the parties we clubbed messes with them, we furnishing such supplies as their garden and dairy did not supply. We took our meals in the house, occupying one or two rooms also as offices. It was here I wrote the song called "The Cavalier's Glee" which was immediately taken up by our singers at headquarters and became generally known and sung throughout the cavalry.

Urged forward by the home demand for "rebel blood," Meade made another advance soon after our return, forcing a passage of the Rappahannock on the 7th of November.

General Lee had withdrawn his army across the Rapidan and had put them into winter quarters. We had barely gotten pretty well fixed when again we were called into active service by an advance on the part of the enemy. An "on to Richmond" movement which turned out so absurdly that it cost Meade his head — officially speaking — and is known as the Mine Run affair.

On the 26th of November, Meade put his army in motion, crossed the Rapidan at Ely's and Germanna fords, and moved up to Lee's position on the 28th. Lee had selected a strong line along me west bank of Mine Run and there awaited his adversary; but when said adversary appeared what did he do? Instead of *attacking* he went to *entrenching* — was there ever anything so absurd? There was Richmond nearer to him than to us, he having assumed the offensive; and yet as soon as he found the enemy he sought he sits down to digging dirt. The weather was intensely cold, but there was plenty of wood on Mine Run, and as we were only five or six miles from our winter quarters, our servants came down every evening with cooked rations and kindled a log heap thirty feet long, along the sides of which General Stuart, his staff and couriers spent the nights very comfortably, wrapped in our blankets and stretched on banks of pine tags scraped up around us. For four mortal days did Meade remain digging for dear life all the time, and keeping up a spiteful skirmish fire with our lines. Following the example set them, our men dug away too into the frozen earth and soon had formidable entrenchments, which became at last impregnable to direct attack.

Each day the attack was expected, we mounted and rode down to the front a mile distant and whiled away the time as best we could inspecting the ground and chatting with friends on the lines. Stuart's headquarters were on the main road a few hundred yards from Gen. R. E. Lee's, and this was about the centre of our infantry front, the cavalry occupying the flanks; but like their comrades in the infantry the cavalry remained on the defensive and we did not disturb them. Rather a curious incident happened one day between the infantry lines, which at that place were about three hundred yards apart. About midway there was a farm house and around it wandered a solitary turkey which a Yankee skirmisher shot and then ran forward to secure amid cheers from his side; as he stooped to pick up the turkey one of our men shot him dead and ran forward to get the prize amid cheers from our side. Just as he stooped to pull the turkey from under the Yankee, a shot from their side killed him and wild cheers from their side arose; and there they all three lay one on top of the other, neither side wanting turkey any more. Men in the infantry have such a hard time of it and see so little fun that when a chance offers they are just like children. I certainly pitied the poor fellows in the trenches at Mine Run, for huddled together in a narrow ditch and under constant fire they could not keep fires going very well to warm by. This was nothing, however, to what it was afterwards in the trenches at the siege of Petersburg, for there they had no wood.

A soldier will steal food for himself or his horse when he can't get it any other way, and I must confess I was no exception to the rule; and yet it is disagreeable to be caught at it as I was one evening during the freezing four days. Gilbert came down one evening reporting that no forage was to be had at Orange C. H. from the quartermaster, and Magic was hungry. Hearing from one of the couriers, in confidence, that there was a cornfield a few miles off that had not been gathered, I took him with me to collect some. I had filled a bag on which I sat, mill-boy fashion, and we were returning, when just as we had left the field a little way, a man met us and asked quite politely where I had gotten that corn, and thinking he was a cavalryman, I told him. "Well," said he. "Sir, that is my corn." But before he could say another word a touch from the spur sent Magic flying down the road defying all pursuit, and I landed it safely in camp. And how Magic did enjoy it! And I sat by her while she ate, to keep the other fellows from stealing it.

I slept alongside the General, and one night a scout came in about three o'clock in the morning with a report of great interest. General Stuart called to me to listen, for he wanted me to take the report to General Lee. This young fellow, whose name I forget, had spent the night riding about in Meade's army. He had been to Meade's headquarters and had talked with the sentinel and had tried his best to get him to leave his post and get him a drink of water, so he could pull down and bring off the headquarters flag. All this he told us afterwards, but the value of his report was that the enemy were moving their whole army backward, as far as he could judge. To get back to General Lee with this information as soon as possible it was necessary to follow some distance a road occupied by marching troops, and this the audacious fellow did at a rapid trot, holding an official envelope in his hand and calling in an authoritative voice to the men to make way for him as he carried an important dispatch, holding up the envelope as proof of the fact. The men gave way right and left and in a short time he was with us.

General Stuart asked me if I had heard it all and then told me to go and tell General Lee. The interview which followed will never fade from my memory. The house General Lee occupied was a small frame structure on the side of the road and I found him already up and partially dressed, though it was still long before daylight. The room contained little else in the way of furniture than the General's camp bed, a small camp writing table and some camp stools. He was walking backwards and forwards in his shirtsleeves before a bright wood fire, brushing his hair and beard. He spoke to me cordially and listened attentively to my report; then, as he had a way of doing with young officers with whom he came in contact, he began asking me questions, and every word he said impressed itself so firmly on my memory that I can give them now just as he said them. *"Well, Captain,"* said he, *"what do you think they are going to do?"*, pausing in his walk before me, and holding his hair brush in his hand: I told him I thought they were going to attack. *"Well"* said he, *"where do you think they will make the attack?"* I told him I thought they would turn our right flank. *"Why do you think so?"* said he. I told him I thought the ground on that flank was the only part of our line where they could possibly hope for any success, as it was leveler and more favorable in every way. He then resumed his walk and the brushing of his hair for a while and then faced me again and said, *"Captain, if they don't attack us today we must attack them!"* slapping the palm of his left hand with the back of the brush. "*We must attack them, sir!*" slapping his hand with the back of the brush more sharply, and stamping with his foot, while his eyes flashed with excitement. "*And you young men must exert yourself! You must exert yourselves, sir!*" slapping with his brush again. I assured him I would do all I could, and then took my leave, much impressed by the personal magnetism of our great commander. I wish I could have his picture as he stood before me that night, his handsome face all aglow, and his eyes fairly flashing fire as he brandished his brush. When I stepped out of the house the road was filled with a column of marching troops — troops that were to make the attack which he had already planned before I saw him. But this was not to be, for Meade had withdrawn and that day, December 1, we returned to our snug winter quarters near Orange C. H.

My time in the cavalry was now drawing to a close. General Lee had long felt the need of a corps of sappers and miners in his army, and measures were now being taken to organize such a corps under the name of Engineer troops. General Stuart had often tried to get me promotion on his staff, but the War Department would not give the Chief Engineer officer of the cavalry corps a rank higher than that of Captain. General Stuart told me of what was contemplated about this regiment and said that Maj. T. M. R. Talcott, of Gen. R. E. Lee's staff, would command it, and though he would be very sorry to lose me, I could be made next in rank to Talcott, he thought, if I desired it, and that he would do all he could to promote my interests in the matter. I thanked him and told him I should be very sorry to part with him, but that promotion like that I ought not to decline, and that I would be much obliged to him for his influence. So about January 25, I received notice to come to Richmond, and there was ordered to report to Lieutenant Colonel Talcott as Major of the 1st Regiment of Engineer troops.

Before entering upon my duties in this new field, I went back to headquarters to get my horses and effects, and take leave of my dear friends, the General and his staff. General Stuart was not at home the day I spent there, but I was glad he was not when it was the means of my receiving a farewell letter that I prize very highly and give below.

(Copy of General Stuart's letter.)

Headquarters Cavalry Corps A. N. Va.

Near Orange C. H. Jan. 80th, 1864.

Dear Major:

I regret that I was not here to participate in the parting scenes of your late visit to these headquarters. To say that I part with you with regret is a poor expression of what I feel. To no member of my staff have I felt the same bond of attachment: dating to the ever memorable First Manassas. But your long-merited promotion is to some extent a palliation for the severance of those ties which grew so firmly by association. We do not part, as those who part to meet no more — often on the battlefield, at the bivouac, or the bower — I trust we shall meet again, with no tears to shed, but glad in the sunshine of victory, till peace shall encircle with her rainbow the Independent Confederate States. May we live to celebrate that bright epoch, is the prayer of your comrade, messmate, and sincere friend, J. E. B. Stuart.

Maj. Wm. W. Blackford,

Corps of Engineers C. S. A.

My parting with General Stuart was a source of deep regret to me, but so many of the old members of the staff were dead or disabled that I felt somewhat like that "last rose of summer." John Esten Cooke was the only one left of those who constituted the staff when I first joined it. Of the later members, Dr. Fontaine was a fine fellow and so was Theodore Garnett, but it takes time to knit a friendship like that I felt for those who were no more with us. I was tent-mate with Fontaine when I left there. Poor fellow, he was killed the next fall near Petersburg, and Stuart fell three months after he wrote that letter to me.

My commission as Major was dated February 19, and that as Lieutenant Colonel of the regiment April 1, 1864, being a Major only six weeks, which was some compensation for having been a captain so long. The regiment was being recruited in Richmond. Colonel Talcott opened a recruiting office there, and sent me to command the camp five miles out of town until he completed his preparations. The conscript law was just then being enforced and a class of men were brought in by it which, by selection among them, afforded the very best of material for filling a regiment such as ours was to be. They were men from twenty-five to thirty-five, mostly married, and skilled in the use of tools in some way or other, mechanics of all sorts, and farmers, etc. With these the ten companies in the regiment were filled to about their full quota of one hundred men each, making a splendid body nearly one thousand strong.

The officers of the 1st Regiment Engineer troops were all appointed, no elections being tolerated for any position connected with it, and consequently the discipline of the regiment was superb. The field and company officers were civil engineers by profession, also most of the lieutenants, and the rest of the lieutenants and the non-commissioned officers were either well-educated men or men of special qualifications in some mechanical branch. We had miners, sailors, carpenters, blacksmiths, masons, and almost every other trade among them. We were armed and drilled as infantry, and in campaigns served as infantry unless there were military bridges or other works to construct. In sieges we served as sappers and miners. Two companies of the regiment were equipped as pontooners, each being furnished with a train of boats mounted upon wagons made for the purpose, and these companies were drilled in the art of taking up and laying down these bridges across streams until they became experts at it. The wagons would gallop up to the bank of a stream, slide off the boat and planks which, before another could do the same, would be placed in position in the water and connected with the shore by the flooring; then another, and another boat with floor laid across from one to the other until the farther shore was reached, and a crossing provided for the army. The men of the other companies were instructed in the art of making gabions, sap-rollers, chevaux-de-frise, and other siege material, at which they became very expert. During the siege of Petersburg this proved of great service.

During the months of February, March and April the organization and equipment of the regiment was pushed forward with all possible dispatch. Many of the recruits were raw men and I had my hands full in having them instructed in squad and company drill, and finally I had them out in battalion drill with fair success. The enemy, now under the command of Grant, were making vigorous preparations for the coming campaign and it was necessary for us to be ready to join General Lee's army as soon as it was possible for us to do so.

On the 8th of May we left Richmond, but on reaching Beaver Dam station, orders were received to halt there and defend the place against the enemy's cavalry, who were reported moving from Fredericksburg towards Richmond. This was Sheridan with all the cavalry of the army of the Potomac, twelve thousand strong. Finding that Mrs. Gen. Stuart was at Mr. Fontaine's, a short distance from the depot, I called to see her on my arrival and was invited to breakfast there the next morning, the 13th of May. We had received no news from the enemy except that General Stuart was hot on their trail and this made us feel quite content. Shortly after returning to our camp from breakfasting with Mrs. Stuart, I heard a locomotive come to the station from towards Richmond, and soon after a carriage drove rapidly from Mr. Fontaine's to the depot and the locomotive started back. Upon inquiry it turned out that this was an express sent for Mrs. Stuart to attend her husband who had been wounded at Yellow Tavern, five miles from Richmond, the evening before. The truth was that he was then dead, but we did not know it at the time.'

That our noble commander of the cavalry saved Richmond from falling into Sheridan's hands is a fact that history will confirm. By his great energy, and by a dash and courage unequaled in our cavalry service, he was enabled to harass this powerful column of twelve thousand superbly equipped men to such an extent during their march that when they reached the vicinity of Richmond they were almost worn out. Then he opposed them with such stubbornness that they gave up the game without ever reaching the fortifications of the city; and this Stuart did with a force not one-third as great as theirs. It was a heavy blow to our cause when he fell. My own feelings were as if I had lost a brother. It was so hard to realize that he was gone. Stuart had never been hit in any of the many actions he had been in since the war began, though always in the hottest part of them, and we of his staff never seemed to realize that he could be. We seemed to think, and I believe he did too, that it was a matter of course that he should escape. For three years I had been closely and intimately associated with him, and now my memory recalled all the stirring events we had passed through, and so many gay ones too, in all of which he stood the prominent figure. With many he had been at times harsh, but with me never, and during all of our long association there was never a break in our cordial relations towards each other. Seeing him as I did so often in moments of the highest excitement, his form, the expression of his face, and the tones of his voice were imprinted upon my memory so vividly that even at this writing, after twenty-odd years have passed away, I can close my eyes and bring him before me as vividly as though he were there in life. General Stuart had his weaknesses — who has not? — but a braver, truer, or purer man than he never lived.

From Beaver Dam our regiment marched on to join General Lee and took position on the extreme right of the line confronting Grant in Spotsylvania; and then began my first experience of infantry service in action. The fighting to our left was very severe for several days, and we began to find out that the new commander of their army, General Grant, was a man of determination if nothing else. Day after day he would hurl his troops against our lines to be slaughtered by the thousands, without gaining an inch, until the ground in our front was piled so with the slain that in those hot days of May the stench became so intolerable that he had to desist. In our own front there was only skirmishing. We threw up a good line of entrenchments and would have given them a warm reception if the fortunes of war had brought them into closer contact with us. With my cavalry experience I went out one day on a little reconnaissance to our right which revealed a large body of cavalry opposite our front, behind a wood, within easy range of the battery we were supporting. I at once galloped back and reported the fact to Colonel Talcott and then rode into the trenches to direct the fire of the guns upon them. As I was doing so with my body of course exposed above the parapet, several of the officers of the regiment stepped out of the trench on the bank behind, exposing themselves likewise, to get a better view. I was talking to them when the group attracted the attention of the enemy and a ball from the skirmishers hit Lieutenant Hood on the arm between the elbow and shoulder and spun him entirely around without his losing his footing. He was sent to the rear at once, and our talented young assistant surgeon, Dr. Murdock, under protest from our surgeon, Dr. Carrington, who wanted to amputate, performed what was then I believe the novel operation of *resection*. Three or four inches of the shattered bone were sawed off and the arm shortened of course that much, but otherwise it became as good an arm as ever, much to Lieutenant Hood's gratification.

Among the raw recruits of our regiment there had been some cases of desertion, and while at this place one occurred, or appeared to occur, of a rather singular character. A short distance to our front, between the lines, there was a farmhouse at which during the day was kept a picket post, but this was withdrawn during the night. Along our front, parallel with it and but forty or fifty yards distant, ran a bold rapid creek, one of the Mattapony branches (but which of the four I don't remember), dashing over the rocks in its bed; and across this creek there were stepping stones in the path leading to the farmhouse. One morning about daylight the sentinels along the trenches saw a man named Cates, from East Tennessee originally, leave the lines and start across these stepping stones. Not stopping when ordered to halt, the sentinels fired, the bullets splashing in the water around the man, who then turned and came back. Pie was arrested for desertion, but claimed that he was only going to the house for buttermilk, as the men had been in the habit of doing, and as he had done the day before; and that he did not know the picket was withdrawn; that he went that early to be ahead of anyone else. Pie said he had no idea he was doing wrong, or that he was outside of our lines until he saw the splash of the bullets; that the creek made such a roaring that he did not hear the order of the sentinels to halt, nor did he even hear the reports of the guns. Our Colonel, however, thought that the discipline of the regiment required an example to be made, and Cates was of rather bad character, and a poor soldier; so he was tried by court-martial and condemned to be shot. The execution was deferred until we reached Richmond, however, or rather our camp ten miles from there. Many of the officers of the regiment, myself among them, believed the man's story, and the morning of the day that it was to come off some of the captains came to me and asked if I would join in a petition to the President for his pardon. I told them I did not think the man intended to desert but that I would not sign unless Colonel Talcott thought his pardon would not injure the discipline of the regiment in the matter of desertion and that I would see him about it. The Colonel said he thought the man ought to be shot, but that if I preferred to do so he was perfectly willing for the petition to go in; so I signed it and so did all the captains, and a fleet messenger was sent on horseback with it to Richmond. The execution was to be at sundown. The grave was dug, and the drums were beating for the command to march out to witness it, before the anxious watchers saw a dust away down the road and a horseman appeared, waving over his head a large envelope. It was the pardon. Cates had sent to ask me, a short time before, to come to see him at the guardhouse, and was very much affected. He thanked me for my effort in his behalf and gave me messages for his wife in case the pardon did not come in time. Saving this poor fellow's life is among the pleasantest recollections of my life, for the captains said they would not sign the paper unless one of the field officers would head the list, and I suppose the pardon would not have been granted otherwise, either, and Major Randolph had refused to sign.

On the 21st of May orders came to break up our camp and march southward. Grant had given up his plan of breaking Lee's front by direct attack and was now making a wide detour around our right flank and moving towards Richmond. Lee marched his army in a parallel line abreast of him and in some places we could see the long columns of the enemy winding over distant hills. On reaching Hanover Junction, I became very desirous to see my cousins at Edgewood, the daughters of my late uncle Mr. Lucius H. Minor. Edgewood was ten miles off to our right, but Magic took me there in but little over an hour. The girls were overjoyed to see me, and to hear news of the army. I could only stay a short time. As I was moving away, Fanny insisted upon my taking some sweet potatoes to her brother, Berkely Minor, who at that time was a private in the Rockbridge Artillery. It was in vain I told her of the distance and the weight on my horse, and of the difficulty and uncertainty of finding the battery on the march; so I had to avail myself of her disappearance in search of the potatoes to gallop off, but saw her pursuing me in the distance with the bag in her hand. Fanny died some years after this. She was "My Cousin Fanny" of Thomas Nelson Page's story of that name. Not long after this I was delighted at being the means of getting Berkely Minor, her brother, a commission as Lieutenant in our regiment in a company whose Captain was on detached duty, so that Berkely had the command of the company for the rest of the war, a position he had richly won by his long and gallant service in the Rockbridge Artillery. He joined this famous battery as a private soldier, immediately after taking his degree of Master of Arts at the University of Virginia, had served with it ever since, and was wounded at Gettysburg.

Lee threw his army across Grant's line of march at Cold Harbor, and again the stubborn attacks were made day after day with the same useless loss of life. We here rendered valuable service in locating the lines of entrenchments, and as the process was an interesting one I will describe it. The work had to be done at night, of course, as it was in close proximity to the enemy. During the day the ground was thoroughly examined with our glasses, and as soon as it was dark enough, a long cord was stretched all along our front, and on this cord at intervals of a few feet white bits of cotton cloth were tied to render the position of the cord visible. Picked men held the cord in their hands at intervals of fifteen or twenty feet, and about one hundred feet distant from each other were placed Engineer officers. Each officer was directed to advance his part of the line a certain number of paces, these distances having been previously ascertained by daylight either by estimation or triangulation. The cord was thus carried forward silently, the men crouching low to avoid the incessant skirmish fire of the enemy. After the line officers had reached their assigned distances, by pacing, the line was then carefully inspected, and advanced or retired as was deemed judicious. After this was done, the fact was reported to the infantry commanders, and the working details bearing picks and shovels as well as their arms moved silently forward until they struck the stretched cord, with the little white fluttering tags, held up by the men of our regiment a couple of feet above the ground. Along the cord the infantry line was formed and went to work with a will getting themselves covered before daylight revealed their position to the enemy. As soon as the infantry line was formed, the cord was taken away and rolled up for use elsewhere. By this means the dangerous, irregular salient angles were avoided which came so near proving fatal to us in Spotsylvania, when one was carried by assault and all in it were either killed or captured, and a wide gap opened in our line of battle.

Grant fought at Cold Harbor as he had done before until our front was so covered with his dead, and the stench became so fearful, that he made another march around us and went to City Point on James River below Richmond, a point he might have reached with ships without losing a man. His losses up to that point, by their own reports, show a number equal to the whole force Lee had opposed to him. It was just as if every man in Lee's army had killed, wounded or captured one of the enemy. Lee's loss was considerable also but nothing in comparison, for he fought behind field works, receiving the attacks. In all the contests between Grant and Lee one is reminded of a fight between some powerful, awkward giant and a light, active and expert swordsman. But Grant was a man of strong common sense who knew what he *could* do and knew what he could *not* do. He knew that our resources were weakening and that he could afford to sacrifice three men to deprive us of one, and he did it. Grant took command of the army when it had been thoroughly disciplined by long service and was at its maximum of efficiency, with unbounded resources to keep it up to that point, while our army was just beginning to feel the effect of the exhaustion of our resources by constant and persistent bad management on the part of the government. What could succeed in times like those when our President insisted upon retaining direct personal control of every detail of every department, and placed only men in his Cabinet who were of abilities sufficiently moderate to consent to occupy the position under such restrictions? How differently Lincoln managed! But he, fortunately for his side, had not been educated at West Point. To a man of real talent such an education for war is certainly an advantage, but the trouble is that it makes many men of moderate ability so conceited that when placed in positions of responsibility nothing will convince them that they can act unwisely. General Lee would have been a great soldier without West Point, as his father was before him, before the school existed; and so with Stuart, Jackson and others.

We now had six weeks of rest in our camp on the Chickahominy, a time devoted to drilling and the instruction of the men in engineer duties. The long continuance of a salt-meat diet had given me a touch of scurvy, and it was with delight we found a farmer who had some capital cider vinegar which we drank with avidity at every meal, a treatment which soon cured the symptoms of this disagreeable disease.

During the march Magic had been stolen from a field where she was grazing and Gilbert was in despair of ever finding her, though he had ridden daily through every part of the army. General Lee had issued an order that all stray animals should be brought to his quartermaster's quarters, where their owners were to reclaim them, and knowing this I feared she had been sent away by the man who had her. One day, however, Gilbert came rushing into my tent in great excitement to tell me he had found Magic in the hands of a quartermaster's sergeant who was riding her along the road. Gilbert had claimed the mare in my name, but the man refused to give her up and threatened to shoot Gilbert if he did not go about his business, and say no more about it. But Gilbert followed him to his camp and then came to me. I at once rode to the place and found my mare in the camp of a quartermaster Captain and the man was his sergeant. If the man had not acted as he did I would have taken the mare and said nothing about it, but under the circumstances I preferred charges against the Captain and his sergeant, who were both cashiered by court martial for it.

My life now was a quiet one in comparison to that I had previously led, but pleasant enough. Colonel Talcott and Major Randolph were gentlemen whose society was agreeable and we had all the comforts that a life in the midst of the army would admit, though the chances to forage for fresh provisions were not like what we had in the cavalry on the outposts. We made a discovery in our mess which was the means of getting us many a good dish. No one thought that green tomatoes were good for anything, but when we found it out we had them every day fried with a little sugar sprinkled over them for breakfast, and they were good. Gilbert was instructed to keep the secret and in gardens surrounded by troops an ample supply would always be found.

While in this camp I had a large cross sixteen feet high made of cedar with the inscription cut on it in neat large letters, *Here fell Gen. J. E. B. Stuart, May 12th, 1864.* This I intended to take to the spot myself, but just as it was finished we were ordered off in a hurry to Petersburg, the "crater" explosion having made counter mines necessary, and I had to delegate the service to other parties who put it up suitably.

Grant had extended his left wing from the James River towards Petersburg and then around south of that town, facing the fortifications built there two years before, and had begun the famous siege of the town. At one of the salients a mine had been run under our lines and the salient with the battery it

126

contained blown sky-high. It appears that this scheme was devised and executed by an officer of Volunteers, a mining engineer, and of course West Point was insulted, and probably for this reason the attack after the explosion was not allowed to succeed. It looks very like something of the kind was the case, for if the attack had been made in full force and with vigor the Confederacy would have fallen that day. But Grant put his negro troops at the head of the attacking column and of course they wilted under the fire of our second line and gave General Lee time to bring up reinforcements, and time for our men to recover from the panic this new and startling mode of warfare occasioned. It was this event which caused the order for us to hurry over to Petersburg to countermine all our salients. I was now to begin a life as different from that I had ever led before as it is possible to conceive, and to engage in a mode of warfare strangely differing from the dashing cavalry service on the outposts. Instead of the movement and excitement of rapid marches, sudden attacks, and thrilling personal adventures, alternating with periods of gay social intercourse, I was now thrown into the very jaws of the grim death struggle in the trenches of a vigorously besieged town, and was to begin a strange sort of warfare under ground.

The weather was intensely hot and the roads deep in dust as we marched into Petersburg in July, 1864, the day after the explosion at the "Crater," as that salient was ever after called. As we approached, everything betokened the struggle which was in progress. The streets of the town were filled with army wagons and ambulances; the wagons bringing supplies of rations and ammunition, and the ambulances rattling along towards the front and returning with wounded men groaning, cursing and praying, with the drivers sitting on their seats smoking their pipes in a perfectly unconcerned manner. Along the sidewalks crowds of soldiers and citizens passed and repassed, shopping and attending to usual occupations apparently undisturbed by the constant cannonade and continuous rattle of musketry in the trenches outside, or of the crashing of shells through the houses. Certain streets seemed to attract the attention of the gunners of the enemy; these were not frequented, but on the very next streets to them everything went on as usual. Even ladies were not infrequently seen strolling along laughing and talking and pausing at a corner to watch the explosion of shells in the square beyond, and to listen to the deep, sepulchral sounds as they burst in the deserted chambers. These shells were fired from a mile distant and the slightest deflection of the gun would have swept the street they were on, and yet these plucky maids and matrons showed not the slightest alarm. Sometimes, in fact, a shell did drop out of the usual course along these streets, but it only caused a momentary pause, and then the tide of passengers rolled on as before. It is a curious thing, but nevertheless true, that the constant presence of death familiarizes people to the dread spectre and he loses his terrors.

Our Regimental headquarters and the bulk of the regiment were established a mile or two back of the town, while I took command of a detachment of two hundred men and occupied the slope in the rear of old Blanford church in front of the town, between the town and the trenches. The main body of the regiment was engaged in manufacturing siege material, particularly chevaux-de-frise to be placed just over the crest of the parapet of the trench. These chevaux-de-frise were pine logs ten or twelve feet long and eight or ten inches in diameter, along which at spaces of about a foot, holes were bored through at right angles. Through these holes strong poles were driven projecting three feet on each side and sharpened at the ends. The logs were fastened together end to end with chains and then rolled down the slope in front of the parapet to arrest a sudden dash of the enemy, and they made an exceedingly awkward thing to cross, with a line of muskets firing from the crest of the bank. Marvelous to relate though it be, the fire from the trenches of the enemy was so hot and so incessant, day and night, for months, that these structures had to be renewed frequently, being actually so cut to pieces by the bullets as to become useless. Our line extended across spurs of rising ground, and on these hills were the projecting portions of the trenches called salients, connected together by trenches of less strength called curtains. The curtains, being retired somewhat, were used mainly for passways from one salient to the other and for shelter for troops. The hot fighting was at the salients, for they commanded the line on each side. It was at these points the enemy made their closest approaches, their trenches being not farther than fifty or sixty yards distant at some of them. At six of these I was to countermine with the men of my detachment, they being relieved every week by men from the regiment. The shaft was sunk about thirty feet deep at a central point, in the trench, of the salient and then a drift was run out until ten feet outside the parapet above. Then galleries were run at right angles to the drift and parallel to the parapet above, extending across the whole front of the salient. Along these galleries four-inch auger holes were bored ten or fifteen feet towards the front at frequent intervals, some horizontally and some upwards, so that the approach of an enemy's mine could be discovered by the sentinels constantly pacing this gallery. In case the enemy struck one of these holes the guards on duty were provided with cartridges of combustibles the smoke from which would suffocate a man. These they were to run into the holes and fire by a fuse, closing their end of the hole tightly, and then, summoning the guard, they were to dig into and take possession of the opposing mine as rapidly as possible, giving another dose of suffocating smoke from time to time to keep the enemy out of his workings until they could dig into them. A working party consisted of one or two commissioned officers and twenty or thirty men. These were relieved every twelve hours and constituted two shifts which worked alternately every four hours. In this way the work could be kept moving constantly and rapidly.

The shaft was sunk by means of a windlass and bucket, and the earth was taken away in sacks unless there happened to be places where we could use wheelbarrows and not be exposed to the deadly rifle practice brought to bear on anything visible above the parapet. Below we used wheelbarrows. The shaft and all the workings were timbered securely', but even with these precautions the mouth of the shafts, the windlass and all the men around it would be blown sky-high sometimes by one of the mortar shells "our friends, the enemy" were continually dropping in our midst. These mortar shells were the most disgusting, low-lived things imaginable; there was not a particle of the sense of honor about them; they would go rolling about and prying into the most private places in a sneaking sort of way. They would be tossed over from the trenches of the other side just as if they were balls thrown by hand, not a bit faster did they come, and then they would roll down the parapet into the trench and if the trench was on a slope, down the trench they would roll, the men standing up flat against the sides or flattening themselves on the ground to one side of the shell's path, each moment expecting the deadly explosion of the nasty, hissing, sputtering thing. Then when one set of men were passed they would jump up and look down the trench at the track of the shell and shout with laughter at their comrades below whose turn had come to lay low. Then came an explosion, and then two or three dead bodies would be carried by and all go on as before. Very frequently men would pick up these shells and pitch them out of the trench, for which they would receive unbounded applause from their comrades. We had plenty of mortar batteries too and kept them as active as the other side did theirs.

The scenes along the trenches at night were grand beyond description. For miles the bright little flashes of the musketry in two parallel lines were the brilliants surrounding the brighter gems of the cannon flashes. Darting across with the rapidity of a meteor from side to side, in opposite directions, flew the lighted shells in almost horizontal lines, while high above all in the heavens in graceful, arching flight flew in flocks of six or eight at a time, the mortar shells, looking as if they were chasing and passing and re-passing one another in their eagerness to perform their deadly mission. The flocks of mortar shells from opposite sides sometimes crossed each other's paths and seemed for an instant tangled together, but then they would glide away and separate with the utmost grace. The flights of these missiles appeared astonishingly slow, indeed they did not seem to move faster than the flight of a bird; this was because there was nothing to compare their movement with except the "direct fire" shells below, which of course moved with great velocity. Smoke spread a lurid tint over the scene, sometimes obstructing the view of the flashes of the guns, but lighting up beautifully from them. This scene had its effect intensely heightened by the mingled sounds wafted through the night air. The crackle of the musketry in all degrees of intensity, from the clear, sharp reports near at hand to the distant, scarcely audible shots, made almost a continuous sound, so rapidly did they reach the ear; while the booming of the cannon closely followed by the screaming and bursting of the shells came in irregular bursts, sometimes drowning all other sounds and then dropping off for a moment almost entirely. In between these bursts of sound and mingled with the rattle of the musketry the shouting of the men could be heard like the voices of demons in the infernal regions.

The first duty I was called upon to perform was to get my men under cover in their camp. The hill was about forty feet high, just back of old Blanford church, and I selected a tolerably steep slope where by digging into the hill good shelter could be had from the shells constantly passing over our heads on their way to town. We soon had level benches cut into the hill for the men to pitch their flies on, and these were connected from one end to the other by a path made of the excavated material. While this was in progress I began work at the crater salient, where it was necessary to dig into and hold possession of the mine the enemy had used, to prevent them from using it again for the same purpose. But before describing our operations at this historic spot, I must give the reader an idea of the place when I first saw it, two days after the explosion, and a brief account of the attack. The mine which made the crater was well placed by the engineer who planned it, for it fitted the salient exactly, taking the trench completely away and blowing the men and cannon in it sky-high. A part of the parapet was left standing close on the brink of the chasm, and all around were piled huge blocks of the tough red clay, eight or ten feet square near the opening and diminishing in size the farther they fell from it.

When the attack was repulsed, many hundred negroes took refuge in this vast conical hole in preference to running back to their lines across the field swept by our fire. Here they were secure for a time until our mortar batteries got their range, and then they were slaughtered almost to a man by thousands of these deadly missiles dropping in among them. When our infantry entered to take possession, the bodies were thrown to the bottom of the pit and covered up with earth from the sides, making the level bottom about as high as the bottom of the trenches. This floor was afterwards raised a good deal higher, but this was what it was when I first saw it a few days after the explosion, as ascertained by careful measurement.

I began the countermine down on this level as close to the side next the parapet as possible and about centrally to the length of the crater, as I supposed the gallery they used must have been under this point. By the time this shaft was sunk eight or ten feet deep, an unexpected difficulty presented itself, which caused some delay. The explosion had opened fissures of course in every direction radiating from the mine chamber, and after a week or ten days of hot weather the decomposition of the hundreds of bodies buried there filled these cracks with gases of the most deadly character, flavored still by odors of powder smoke. The officer in charge of that countermine sent for me to see what was to be done, as his men fainted every time they went down into the shaft. On reaching the place I was disposed to think the difficulty exaggerated and that the fainting was more from the mortar shells falling in the pit than from the bad air; so I told them to let me down by the rope, taking the precaution, however, to tie myself around the body to the rope, and to take a lighted candle in my hand to give notice by its flame how pure the air was. I had scarcely reached the bottom, however, before the candle began to look sick, while I began to feel so too, and I had barely strength enough to call to them to pull me out. It was some days before I got the stench of that gas out of my lungs. We had then to send to Richmond for some wheat fans, and by connecting a long canvas bag or tube to the fan with hoops inside we got sufficient ventilation. But the fans made such a noise that the enemy let loose their mortars every time we worked them, and smashed several of them for us. It was weeks and weeks before we found the gallery used in laying the mine. We could not go to the powder chamber to begin on account of the bodies there congregated, and had to run galleries at random looking for it.

After getting the shafts down thirty feet at most of the salients, we began the drifts to run out beyond the parapets, and then started the galleries each way from it. As soon as the men got to working outside of the parapet there were constant alarms that the enemy was approaching with a mine. This was partly caused by their imagination and partly by the strange uncertainty there is in telling the direction of sound transmitted through earth underground. My orders were for the officer in charge to report to me at once any indication of the approach of an enemy, and I could generally tell from the report and from the character of the man who sent it, whether it was necessary for me to go to the mine or not. These reports invariably came at night, for in the day there was so much tramping and digging in the trenches overhead that the approach of an enemy, if there had been one, could not have been heard. After being aroused by the first report I generally waited for the second, and that was usually that it was a false alarm. But one night I got a note from an officer whom I knew to be a cool fellow, saying that the enemy was certainly near him with a mine, for he had heard the picks for half an hour distinctly. I immediately dressed, and buckling on my faithful revolver, proceeded to the spot. The trenches were approached by zigzag ditches called covered ways about eight feet wide and five or six feet deep, with the earth thrown on the side next the enemy for protection from his fire, thus making the protecting bank ten or twelve feet higher than the bottom of the ditch. When it rained these ways were deep in mud from the constant passing to and from the lines, and at night they were the most lonely and mournful places imaginable, the only sound reaching the ear being the firing in front and the weird shriek of the rifle balls flying through the air above; and through this desolate ditch I passed for a quarter of a mile.

On arriving at the mine I found the men in great excitement from the sounds of the pickaxe, which still continued. It certainly did sound as if the digging was going on just a few feet ahead of us. Before taking any steps, however, I concluded I would be sure the sounds came from nowhere else, and asked the officer if he was sure no one was digging in the trenches overhead. He said he was sure, for he had gone up there, and the men were all asleep, except the sentinels and those on duty. I then sent four men, very intelligent fellows, and told them to go two one way and two the other and to look closely for one hundred yards. Presently two came back and reported that there was a man digging himself a "bomb proof" in the side of the trench fifty yards down the line. I then sent them back and told them to strike, exactly at the same place he was at work, in three quick blows and after a pause one blow, then three quick, and one again, and to keep it up until I sent to stop them. We then waited with great interest the result. Presently there came the three quick blows and the one, and the same repeated many times, showing clearly that this was the source of the sounds which had caused the alarm. So I recalled the men and got back to camp just as the day was breaking.

It is very curious how soldiers become so familiar with one kind of danger, to which they have been exposed, as to disregard it almost entirely, and yet become demoralized when danger in a new form presents itself. Our men did not mind musketry and field artillery after the first two or three battles, but when they came under fire from the big guns on the gunboats below Richmond in 1862, they became nervous at seeing large trees cut off clean and whirled bottom upwards. To this they became accustomed. Then the mortar shells came, at the siege of Petersburg, and in time became familiar to them, but when the explosion at the crater occurred, a veritable panic ensued.

To have the very ground on which they stood blown up under them, without a chance for life or a chance to retaliate, was something so new and so terrible that the bravest turned pale. Every one of them was sure there were two hundred kegs of gunpowder right under his feet, and for days after the explosion not a laugh nor a song was to be heard along the trenches. Anyone familiar with troops can tell the spirit they are in exactly, by walking along the lines, and can catch from the conversation he hears in passing what is on their minds. In this case nothing was talked about but mines: whether a fellow would be killed when he was first lifted aloft, or whether he would know what was going on as he went whirling through the air, and how disagreeable it would be to fall from such a height on the hard ground. This continued until by an inspiration of some obscure individual, who ought to be immortalized, a simple device was invented which set every man at his ease. I never even heard the name of the man, nor do I believe it was ever known outside of his company or regiment. It was a case of necessity being the mother of invention.

The contrivance did not really render the position more secure, but it gave *hope* and satisfied the men, and this at that moment was all-important; for it would be weeks before we of the Engineers could get the countermines in working order. Some man in a battery who was a blacksmith, I heard, conceived the idea of making a simple boring tool by which holes could be bored with great rapidity to any depth along the trenches. These holes, kept full of water, would of course indicate with certainty whether the enemy was underneath, for if he tapped the hole with his mine the water would run out and as long as the hole remained full of water the men knew there was no danger. The contrivance was as simple as it was effective, working perfectly in that tenacious red clay, though in other soils it might not have answered. It consisted of a sheet of iron about one-sixteenth of an inch thick, bent into a truncated cone, about one foot long and about two and a half inches in diameter at one end and three and a half at the other, with the lap brazed together. Halfway there was cut a hole, and the lower edge was sharpened on the inside, with chisel edge outward, and into the smaller end was inserted a pole (securely fastened with nails) five or six feet long. The implement was used as follows: two men held it vertically and rammed it down by raising it a few feet and letting it fall. The clay would be cut by the edges and slightly compressed, so that to the depth it had gone the clay remained in the tool, another blow cut another depth and pushed the first cut higher up the cylinder, and so on until it reached the hole in the cylinder. The clay in the tool was then punched out by running a stick through the hole, and the ramming was then continued until the tool was again full and so on.

When the handle of the tool had sunk so deep that it could not be reached without stooping too low, a cord was tied to it and the blow given by jerking the tool up and letting it fall. In this way a hole twenty feet deep could be sunk in half a day or less. The movement of the cutting edge shaved off the inside of the hole until it became about half an inch larger than the diameter of the cutter, thus freeing it and making it work easily as it rose and fell.

The contrivance took like wildfire. Men sat up all night working at these holes. Every blacksmith's shop in the army was busy making the augers, and orders were sent to Richmond for hundreds of them. In a few days, all along the trenches for miles you could see the poles bobbing up and down and the foolish fellows were as happy and merry as ever. What cared they for the shot and shell when there was the hole full of water, and no mine under them. In any other service than ours the poor fellow who invented this would have been rewarded, but even his name is unknown, as I have said. The men seemed never to tire of sinking holes; at first they were sunk at wide intervals, twenty-five or thirty feet, then one would be put between these, then again and again the space would be halved until they were scarce two feet apart. It gave the men something to do, and diverted their attention from their hardships, for life in the trenches is hardship, in fact, of the worst sort.

One morning early I met General Stevens, the Chief Engineer of the army, in the trenches and he told me he had just received a report that a mine had been discovered under one of the salients, and that he wanted me to go with him to the place, for if it was so I must put a force to work at once to dig into it. When we reached the spot the men there looked perfectly ashy and hastened to give us the evidence. It seems that the night before they had been sinking a hole and had gotten twenty feet deep with it, but at bedtime they stopped work and put a box over the opening. In the morning, when they resumed their operations, in the first draught they brought up there was about a handful of sawdust. There was the auger and there was the sawdust in it, just such sawdust as gunpowder is packed in. It did look very like it came from a mine below — otherwise how could it have gotten there? I must confess I felt uneasy and could imagine sometimes I felt the ground under me starting heavenwards. General Stevens was a cool as well as a clever man, and he kept his wits about him. After examining the sawdust carefully he noticed it was from some unusual wood, one he had never seen used about ammunition before, and he called my attention to it. Then he asked if the hole had been covered in any way, so that nothing could fall into it. "Oh yes," said the men, "we had a box over it," and they produced an ammunition box. General Stevens' eyes brightened; he examined the box, but there was nothing in it. Looking around, he saw some other boxes like it, with cannon ammunition in them. He ordered one to be opened, and at once the mystery was solved, for they were packed with sawdust just like that from the bottom of the hole. The box turned up over the hole had some left in it and this had fallen to the bottom and had caused all the trouble. The men cheered Stevens lustily, and good humor was restored to these brave fellows immediately.

Grant, all this time, was extending his left, encircling the town more and more, and to extend his front proportionally Lee had to resort to every expedient to strengthen his fortifications so that he could draw off more men from them. At one place where a stream ran along our front a huge earth dam was built under the direction of the Engineer Corps, our regiment, luckily, having had nothing to do with its construction, the object being to form a lake along the front. One day, when the water had risen to the top, this dam gave way and a huge body of water came sweeping down the creek and into the Appomattox River above where we had a pontoon bridge laid. The bridge guard saw it coming but could do nothing, and it was a wonder the bridge was not carried away; but with some little damage it stood the shock. The dam was undermined by the water, the puddling ditches not having been sunk deep enough.

At the same time that Grant extended his left he sent strong expeditions from time to time against the Danville railroad, now the only communication left open for our supplies from the South for Richmond, Petersburg and the army. After the breaking up of the road by one of these, rations used to become pretty scarce with us. Once I remember a whisky ration was all we got, but somehow or other we managed to get on generally pretty well.

The enemy had been constantly increasing the size and power of their mortars, for at first they used only the small size for pitching shells four or five inches in diameter into the trenches; but now *we* saw in the Northern papers that three-hundred-pound mortar shells were to be used against us and we looked forward to their coming with some apprehension. The first of these three-hundred-pounders was connected with such an amusing scene at my quarters that I must relate it. I have before stated that my camp was back of old Blanford church, dug into the slope of the hill. From the camp to the church was an open, closely grazed field called the "common," sloping down towards the camp, and a favorite resort for cats from town at night. My fly was pitched in a dugout about ten feet wide dug back into the hill to a perpendicular wall about eight feet high. The back pole of the fly set against this perpendicular bank and reached three or four feet above the surface, so that there *was* an opening in the gable of the fly from the surface of the ground behind to the ridge pole, left in this way for light and air during the hot weather. One night a working party was to be sent out to start a mine in an exposed place and the officers who were to go with it, four or five in number, were sitting around a table in my tent, examining a plan of the work I had made and was explaining to them. We were all intently engaged on this when we heard approaching through the still night air what sounded like a railroad express train. We all knew what it was. It was the long-expected three-hundred-pounder; but no one spoke, all pretending unawareness, and I went on with my explanation. It must have been three miles off when it started and by a computation I made it must have reached an elevation of at least five thousand feet. It seemed hours that we were kept in suspense, though I suppose it was not really more than two or three minutes. Presently the sound came from right over our heads, apparently, and increased to a terrific roar, becoming louder and louder every second and I was sure it was going to fall right on my table. In spite of all I could do I felt my hand on the plan in which I held my pencil begin to shake; so I had to stick the end of the pencil into the paper to keep it steady, and I found my explanations were becoming not as lucid as they might have been, nor my voice as steady as usual. Just then a young Lieutenant sitting at the end of the table, a young fellow of not over eighteen or twenty, got so nervous that he slipped under the table; this started a titter among the others, which an instant later burst into an irrepressible roar of laughter from a most unexpected event. As I have said, the common above the fly was a resort for cats from the town at night, and these cats, hearing the fearful noise above them, and seeing the long stream of fire shooting towards them from the heavens, became completely demoralized and went scampering by as fast as they could run, back to the deserted houses where they made their homes. One huge tomcat, however, came tearing down the hill with eyes flaming, claws out, and hair on end, directly towards my fly. He was going so fast that he could not avoid the pit in which the fly stood, but came dashing, spitting and sputtering with one bound flop on the table, and with another clear out at the front and away.

The effect was irresistible. If we were all to go to kingdom come the next instant, laugh we *must*, and laugh we *did* until the tears ran down our cheeks. Even the young fellow under the table was relieved and came crawling out looking very crestfallen, and this convulsed us the more. But still that horrid sound came fiercer and fiercer, and nearer and nearer, and more and more directly above us. The laugh cooled down as suddenly as it began and we looked around at each other very gravely. Then to our intense relief came a tremendous blow nearby; the earth shook like an earthquake as the great shell struck the ground

132

twenty paces away. Then we waited and waited for the explosion, but it never came. The fuse had been extinguished by the blow.

The next day was Sunday and a squad of men, tempted by the price paid for reclaimed fragments of iron, dug all day in the hard gravel but were unable to lift the huge monster out after they reached it; and there it is, I suppose, to this day. From the surface of the ground to the top of the shell was thirteen feet by my own measurement, and to the bottom of the shell fourteen and a half, supposing the shell was only eighteen inches in diameter, though it was probably more. This penetration was through a hard gravel near the little branch which flowed by our camp.

I went out on the hill to witness the next shots, and the flight of the fiery meteors was very beautiful. They fell in the town and exploded in the houses with a dull muffled sound.

In the latter part of September, during the hottest day of the year, I had a duty to perform which overheated me, so that, my system being already charged with malaria, I suppose from sleeping six weeks in a pit in the ground, the result was an attack of sickness.

I started early one morning on a tour of inspection of all the countermines extending over about three miles of front. To get from one mine to the other could only be accomplished by passing through the trenches. The trenches were filled with men stretched out flat on their backs across the bottom, with blankets fastened to the sides of the trench on each side as awnings, hanging two or three or at most four feet above the men. It was necessary to move all the way in a half-bent position and frequently to crawl along under the awning, stepping over and between the prostrate men, much to their annoyance, and this in a temperature over one hundred degrees, without a breath of air. Never in all my life have I experienced such fatigue. Several times I felt like giving it up, but it was important I should make my report on the mines, and I kept on. Sometimes the men were close together and asleep, and I would have to waken each one where I wished to place my foot before I could make a step, and it took the whole day to accomplish my mission. Wet to the skin with perspiration, and desperately tired, I stopped in town as I passed through on my return about sundown at an ice-cream saloon and devoured eagerly two saucers of ice cream for which a fabulous sum in Confederate money was paid. I felt at once I had done wrong, for a chill came on and the day following, after a bad night, I had a high fever. The surgeon at once said I must go home, and nothing loth I went.

VI — 1865

I found on my return from furlough that the regimental camp had been established for the winter just across the river from the upper end of Petersburg in a sheltered little valley, and the men were all engaged in building cabins out of pine logs growing at the spot. The countermines were nearly finished before I went away, so the camp I had occupied back of Blanford church was broken up. Headquarters consisted of five tents, Colonel Talcott's, Major Randolph's, mine, the office tent and one for the Adjutant and Sergeant Major. We preferred tents to cabins, as anyone who has tried it will always do.

The duties of the regiment were now entirely the manufacture of siege material, for when the weather became bad drilling was out of the question. Having much leisure time on my hands during the long winter, I devoted it mostly to reading and occasional visits to friends in town. There was in Petersburg a public library to which I became a subscriber, and though there were no new books, there were some excellent old ones. One I remember was an English book on landscape gardening which I read with much interest. Many plans of houses and grounds were given as they were actually built, which not only displayed the beauty of the art but gave a good idea of the social life of the people who occupied them. I also went through a course of fortification, and read several books on other military subjects. Victor Hugo's books were then all the rage and I read them in Confederate type and binding, none of the best as may be supposed. I occasionally went over to Richmond where Mr. Robertson was keeping bachelor's hall most of the time in his house on Franklin Street, his duties as a member of the Legislature detaining him there, but the dearness of supplies in the beleaguered city, together with the uncertainty of the military situation, prevented him from having his family with him. Before proceeding to the description of the opening of the spring campaign which was to witness the collapse of the Confederacy, I must refer to the general situation of our affairs.

Grant was now Commander-in-Chief of all the armies, and under his orders Sherman was steadily pushing Johnston back from Chattanooga towards Atlanta, thus cutting the Confederate states east of the Mississippi in two. He had previously, by the capture of Vicksburg, cut off all west of that river. The advance of Sherman's column seriously affected our supplies in Virginia in men and all munitions of war, while the extension of Grant's left wing placed him in a position to threaten more and more our line of communication along the Danville road. The scarcity of supplies in the army and still more the suffering of the men's families at home produced a great deal of desertion which weakened our force seriously. Executions were frequent. I involuntarily witnessed one one day, and it shocked me a good deal. How strange that the death of men under some circumstances should produce such an effect on one who had witnessed so many deaths in battle. I was passing along the trenches and just as I walked around a "traverse" I heard a volley of musketry fifty yards distant and, raising my eyes instantly, saw five men fall into graves dug behind them with the blood spouting from numerous wounds. Then the officer in charge walked up and fired one or two shots from his revolver into the graves at such as were not done for, and then the dirt was shoveled in upon them. Their regiment was on duty in the trenches and these deserters had been sent there for execution. All these disastrous circumstances were steadily weakening us, and those in authority I suppose knew what was inevitable, but we in the army had not the least idea of it. We looked forward to beating the enemy when the campaign opened as a matter of course, and we would have been bitterly opposed to any compromise which would have involved the sacrifice of the independence of the Confederate States.

I remember that Colonel Boteler, who was then in the Confederate Congress, I believe, was at our camp one day and was full of suppressed joy at something which he said was going to happen in a few days and which he hoped would end the war. This was the conference that was proposed between Lincoln and Jeff.

Davis which never came off, Davis refusing to meet him on any other ground than independence. I think Colonel Boteler came over to the army to sound the sentiments of the men on this subject. If so he did not get much comfort from us at our camp. The politicians were the ones to bring on the war and many of them that were the hottest secessionists were the first to skulk.

The first bad news we got that spring was that of the fall of Atlanta. Mr. Davis relieved Johnston of the command of the army and put Hood in his place. I never shall think that Johnston did right in falling back so far without a general engagement, but it was a dangerous thing for Davis to remove him at the time he did on the eve of battle. Hood was a gallant man but weak in the upper story, and the position he placed himself in was ridiculous, leaving Sherman loose to march one way while he marched the other; was there ever such folly in the history of war? When Sherman was left unopposed it was only a question of month or two's march for him to sweep around in Lee's rear. Still we in the army thought at that time, knowing nothing about it, that it was all right and never troubled ourselves much about events so far away.

At this time a Richmond paper *The Examiner*, ably edited, was allowed to do as much harm as it was possible for any paper to do. Whether it was at heart treasonable I don't know, but its effect was in that direction. That the authorities should have allowed it to appear shows how little our President was adapted to revolutionary times. That a theory about "the freedom of the press" should have governed his actions at such a time shows what a visionary, unpractical man he was. When the lives of thousands of his soldiers were to be sacrificed it was in his opinion against the *Constitution* to shut up a foul, traitorous sheet which gave information to the enemy, and dispirited and dissatisfied our army. It makes my blood boil whenever I think of it: instead of doing this and many other things he ought to have done, there would come from him proclamations appointing days for *fasting* and *prayer*.

General Lee, we know now, wanted to give up Richmond several days before he did, but Mr. Davis would not let him. If this had been done, the contest might have been prolonged a little, at least they would not have headed us off at Appomattox; but we in the army did not know of this, of course, and what I am now to relate came like a clap of thunder. Our camp was in sight of the ridge on which General Lee had his headquarters. We were near the river, across which there was one of our pontoon bridges, and on the north side of it. On the south side and just below was the town of Petersburg. General Lee's headquarters were nearly opposite us across the river. It was Sunday, the 2nd day of April, 1865. All the morning there had been very heavy fighting along the trenches, but this was nothing unusual and some of us were thinking of going over to church in town, for it was a bright, sunshiny day. Colonel Talcott, Randolph and myself were standing in front of our tents when we noticed something unusual on the ridge across the river, horsemen galloping about and looking towards the trenches; presently men on foot appeared coming from towards the trenches, then more and more. Then came an order in hot haste from General Lee for us to burn the pontoon bridges and all the other bridges below, opposite the town, as quickly as possible. The enemy had broken our lines and was marching into the town. As soon as the bridges were destroyed we were to march westward parallel with the railroad.

At once everything was in motion. The excellent discipline of the regiment now showed its results. Every man knew his duty and did it. The enemy appeared on the other side, making directly for our pontoons, but we had them destroyed before they could stop us, as well as the other bridges below, as soon as our troops in town had passed over them. Then our wagons were packed and we moved off upon the great final retreat. Richmond was evacuated that day, and a great stream of people poured out, filling all the roads, leading westward. These columns we encountered as we proceeded on the retreat and a pitiable spectacle they presented. I remember the naval brigade particularly. The sailors did well enough on the march, but there were the fat old captains and commodores, who had never marched anywhere but on a quarter-deck before in their lives, limping along puffing and blowing, and cursing everything black and blue. Then came a perfect army of bureau clerks, quartermasters, commissaries, and ordnance officers all dressed in fine clothes and uniforms, with white faces, scared half to death, fellows who had for the most part been in these bomb-proof offices ever since the war began and who did not relish the prospect of smelling powder now, nor of having to rough it a bit like ordinary mortals in the field. Then there were citizens in broadcloth, politicians, members of Congress, prominent citizens, almost all on foot, but sometimes there were wagons and carriages loaded with them. Some ladies too might be seen occasionally and generally they were calmer than the men.

Why Jeff. Davis should have preferred to be kicked out of Richmond to evacuating it in a dignified manner I suppose he himself does not know. It was the egotistical, bull-headed obstinacy o the man, no doubt. He was sitting in church in Richmond when Grant broke our line. I suppose he thought praying would help him out of the scrape his folly had placed him in. In the confusion and panic resulting from the hasty evacuation, the lower part of the town was burned, where millions and millions of dollars' worth of property was destroyed. Here went up in smoke tobacco enough to have made things easy in the whole state. Many and many a family had put their all in tobacco, stored in the warehouses there and then burned. Burned by nothing else in the world than Davis' obstinacy in not retiring sooner so that order could have been secured.

During the retreat our regiment formed the rear guard on the road we traveled, breaking up the bridges as we passed and constructing new ones as much as possible in the advance. The enemy, however, did not annoy our rear much; he was striking for the head of the retreating columns. Once his cavalry appeared in small force on our flank and without dismounting poured a skirmish fire into the wagon train at a distance of three or four hundred yards. Here I had an opportunity of seeing the great advantage they had in the sixteen-shot repeating rifle they had recently introduced. These fellows galloped up and formed a line of mounted skirmishers on a commanding hill. Each one fired sixteen shots at our train in rapid succession, and were off before our infantry could move up and return the fire. They knocked down half a dozen or more mules in the wagons and hit as many men, produced some confusion and delayed the march perhaps half an hour. They might have done the same thing at another place as often as they liked without loss of a man, for our cavalry was not near us; but this was the last we saw of them. At Sayler's Creek, two days before we reached Appomattox C. H., the enemy made a vigorous attack and captured a considerable number of wagons, our headquarters wagon among them with all my private luggage. We were in sight of the place at the time but not engaged. When their line reached the field in which the wagons were parked, they made a rush for the plunder. Wagon sheets were torn off, and there was a perfect fountain of things rising in the air as the men threw out what was of no value to them, in search of trunks and private baggage. Our wagon was very near and I tried to save it but could not. The actual value of the articles I had was not much, but they were things I would have attached great value to afterwards as mementos of the war. During the winter I had contrived and had made in our regimental shops a camp desk which was a model of lightness and compactness, containing places for all the writing and drawing materials I needed and yet small enough to be transported easily. The outside dimensions were twenty by twenty inches and the depth ten inches. There were all sorts of little contrivances to pack a drawing board, triangles, a T-square and other instruments, besides places for sheets of drawing paper and everything needed for writing and preserving official papers. It was made of white pine dovetailed and banded and though very thin and light was very strong. All that was necessary to use it was to drive four stakes in the ground to set it on, like table legs, and place another for the lid to rest on. I also lost many drawings I valued highly of our mining works, and many sketches I had made of army scenes, also my full-dress Confederate uniform.

Even then I had no suspicion that matters were as bad off as they were. Great numbers of men had fallen out of the ranks from fatigue and hunger, but those who remained were as full of spirit as ever. Having lost our transportation, we were left without rations. The next day about noon we halted for what was supposed to be the midday meal; the midday was there, but the meal was not. The men were much exhausted, and I was sure that when the time came to resume the march some of them would be unable to move. While considering this matter with great solicitude, for in Talcott's absence at the time I was in command of the regiment, a little drummer boy attached to our regiment came running towards me breathless from the woods, with eyes sparkling, and said, "Oh, Colonel, there is a beautiful, fat heifer down there; don't you hear her bell?" Jack was a pet among the men, and whoever else suffered from short rations he at least was sure to be provided for generally; but now no one had anything to eat and Jack realized his painful situation. With wits sharpened by this, Jack's quick ears had caught the tinkling of the bell in the woods and had gone on a reconnaissance, with the result above stated.

I at once deployed a line of skirmishers two hundred strong and, guided by the bell, surrounded the unsuspecting animal, and by the time she caught the alarm they had contracted the circle until there was a solid wall of eager men to oppose her efforts at escape. Placing cartridge belts around her horns, we led off the prize in triumph to be slaughtered that night, for there was no time for it then. Hungry as everybody was, the capture of these rations acted like magic, and song and jest at once resumed their usual sway. The heifer was evidently a pet of someone, for she was as round and fat as a butter ball. But our good luck did not stop here. All the time during this halt, trains had been passing the road, mostly loaded with rations. I had made several efforts to get the commissary officers in charge to let us have some, but the reply had been invariably that they were needed by the commands to which they belonged, and the sight of these delicious loads of fat bacon and boxes of crackers had been an aggravation to us in our hunger. But, attracted by an unusual amount of swearing on the road, I saw something was wrong and I saw them unloading a wagon and found that a team had given out. The load was a mixed one of crackers and bacon which the commissary intended to send back for when they went into camp, but upon my representing our condition he agreed to let us have it. The men were wild with delight at this immediate relief to their sufferings, for there was enough to give a pretty fair meal to all, and the bacon in five minutes had disappeared down their throats without waiting for such a useless refinement as cooking. Then, with the pretty heifer at the head of the column, the march was resumed with all the wonted cheerfulness of our soldiers.

To my great delight soon after this I met on the road my brother Lewis, who was a Lieutenant of the Engineer corps, and as he had no prospect for supper he gladly accepted my invitation to spend the night at our bivouac. We were late getting in that night, and I was so hungry that when my share of the heifer came round, and a modest little steak it was, I swallowed it uncooked and unsalted hot from the shambles and without a mouthful of bread. I was surprised to find how good it was. Indeed I could discover no difference between this and rare beef steak, it was so warm and nice. For the last year or eighteen months of the war I never took the trouble to cook bacon on a march, indeed I preferred it uncooked. I generally managed to get a piece of thin side meat, and this is quite nice and delicate uncooked, and it was so much more convenient. I carried my ration of it wrapped in a piece of paper, and this in a piece of oil cloth in my haversack, with my hard bread or crackers; and when hungry all there was to do was to slice off thin pieces, take out a cracker and eat. But raw beef I had never attempted before, and to be relished I should say from this experience: take it hot and fresh. I was greatly amused at Lewis Blackford's horror at seeing the way I got outside of my ration. He worked away at his until he got it scorched over a green-pine wood fire, but I dare say it was not a bit the better for it.

On the night of the 8th of April we went into camp within a mile and a half of Appomattox C. H. and little did I dream that this was to be the last camping ground I should ever occupy as a soldier of the Confederate States army. So far as we knew everything was going on as usual. There had been fighting all day, but we knew nothing of the result. I remember while on the march some officer joined us and spoke despondently in the presence of the men, and I got quite angry, and he rode on to his own command.

The morning of the 9th of April was clear and bright and to our surprise we did not get marching orders as usual at daylight. We could hear cannon in front with some musketry occasionally. About nine or ten o'clock orders came from General Lee for us to move up to the support of a battery then in action on the edge of the little village of Appomattox, and the regiment marched on towards the place. When within half a mile we came in sight of the ridge on which the village was, and the smoke of the battery. We presented a splendid appearance, six or seven hundred men strong, marching in solid well-closed column, as we moved through the disorganized mass of stragglers crowding the road. It struck me as something strange that there should be so many men in this condition, but I paid little attention to it, as we were evidently now going into action. The battery on the ridge was firing at an enemy beyond and out of sight.

Colonel Talcott told me to ride ahead, reconnoitre the ground and select a place to put the regiment in rear of the guns; so off I galloped. Just as I reached the battery, a Richmond battery I think it was, they limbered up and began moving to the rear. I rode up to the Captain and asked him what was the matter, and told him we had been ordered to support him. He said he had received orders to remove his battery to the rear, but beyond that he could give me no information. I then asked him where I could find a general officer to get instructions, and he said General Gordon was there in the village, so off I dashed to find him. I could now see the open country beyond and the troops the battery had been playing on, and there were *very* large bodies of them, and nothing to oppose them before me. I found General Gordon sitting on his horse in the courthouse yard alone, looking at the enemy some four or five hundred yards distant. I rode up to him just as a body of some thirty or forty horsemen separated from them and came galloping towards us waving a white handkerchief tied to a sabre. Before I could state my errand he looked round and seeing none of his staff present he told me to ride down along a row of brick offices on the edge of the courthouse yard and tell the skirmishers occupying them not to fire on the flag of truce approaching. By the time I had done this the horsemen had entered the yard and halted. One officer then rode towards General Gordon, and, saluting, asked if this was General Gordon. Upon Gordon's replying that it was, he said, "I am General Sheridan." Gordon returned the salute and they entered into conversation. I stood a little way off and only caught part of what passed. I heard General Sheridan say something about "the terms of the surrender."

It struck me like an electric shock. All now flashed to my mind. The effect was like that of a stunning blow, and for a moment I felt dazed, staring at the short, heavily built, coarse-looking man before me in a bewildered manner. This was why the battery had ceased firing and moved to the rear, this was why we had received no marching orders that morning. The manner of the two distinguished men now conversing was as different as their appearance. Sheridan was in a plain undress uniform, and well mounted, but there was nothing striking in his appearance, while his manner was rough and not at all polished, while Gordon was a very handsome man, well dressed, well mounted and with that indescribable air of a gentleman which is unmistakable. All this passed through my mind as a sort of impression, but I was so stunned I could not follow the matter of their conference for a moment, but I saw that General Sheridan spoke very emphatically and Gordon in a dignified, reserved manner. Before I had recovered myself there came a crash of musketry and then a rattling skirmish fire off to our left half a mile and Sheridan turned sharply to Gordon and said, "What does this mean, General Gordon?" He replied, "I suppose, Sir, the order to cease firing has not reached them, but I will send at once." "Oh," said Sheridan with an impatient shrug of his shoulders, "let them fight it out." "No," said Gordon, "I will send the order at once," and turning to me he said, "Colonel, ride along the lines and tell those men to cease firing until further orders." I wheeled my horse and was about to dash off when General Sheridan said, "Hold on, I will send one of my staff with you to stop both sides." He called up a young man of his staff and we galloped off together. We introduced ourselves to each other. He was Lieut. Vanderbilt Allen, an aide-de-camp on Sheridan's staff.

We soon reached the scene of the skirmish, which was a cavalry affair. It seems a squadron of the enemy, either not having had the order, or wishing to make a display over a surrendered enemy, came charging into our lines and had gotten pretty badly worsted. Most of them who had not gotten killed or wounded had been captured, but there was still some fighting going on with squads who were trying to cut their way back. We, that is Lieutenant Allen and myself, rode on to find some officer of rank to give the order I bore to, but in the confusion of the melee it was hard to find one. Just then I heard the crash of a volley of musketry a little farther on in a pine thicket, and wishing to stop useless bloodshed and seeing there was little more going on where I was, I dashed off through the pines to this new place. As I got to the edge of the wood I found a line of infantry reloading their pieces, and a few paces in front a Yankee officer splendidly mounted, his uniform closely buttoned up to his chin, displaying a fine, large, manly figure. But from the closely fitting coat spouted a dozen streams of blood, and his horse was tottering with his hide riddled with bullets. Just as I rode up he fell, and the dying rider rolled off at the feet of the men, exclaiming, "My God, boys, you have killed me!"

138

What was my surprise to find this was my own regiment. After the battery moved off, Colonel Talcott had moved to the left and formed a line of battle confronting a body of cavalry who seemed about to charge. This Major of cavalry, as his friends told us afterwards, was pretty full of whisky that morning; he knew of the surrender and seeing this regiment forming he had galloped up to the line and, waving his sabre over the heads of the men, shouted, "Surrender, you damned rebels."

We had in the regiment quite a noted character, old Sergeant Smith, a man of education and a soldier of fortune, who had served in all the wars of his day in all parts of the world. He had been with Walker in Nicaragua, with Garibaldi in Italy and all through our war, and, though a man of sixty with gray hair, was as full of fire as ever, whisky having prevented his courage and talents from giving him what they deserved. Unfortunately for our Yankee Major he had waved his sabre right over the gray head of our fiery old sergeant and when he shouted, "Surrender, you damned rebels," old Smith replied, "Surrender! Hell!" and fired his piece into him. Then the Yankee wheeled and foolishly tried to gallop off, when the men, equally incensed at his insolence, let fly a volley and brought horse and man down.

I found Colonel Talcott and told him all that had happened and gave him General Gordon's order. Then to my horror I noticed that Lieutenant Allen was not with me, and very apprehensive that he might have come to grief among the excited troopers where I had seen him last, I hurried back to where I had left him. As I rode up he was in earnest converse with an officer who proved to be General Geary of South Carolina. "And you expect me to believe any such damned tale as that?" said Geary. "Where is the officer who brought you here? No, sir, you shall go to the rear with the rest of the prisoners!"

"I am the officer, General," said I, saluting him. Geary turned to me and paused a moment, his face becoming more and more troubled. Then beckoning to me he rode off to one side and said, "What does all this mean?" I said, "General, the army has surrendered." He quivered as if he had been shot, and sat still in his saddle a moment, and then, returning his sabre, which he held still drawn in his hand, he said, "Then I will be damned if I surrender!" And that night he passed out of the lines to join Johnston's army, I heard.

Lieutenant Allen and I then rode quietly back to the courthouse, where General Sheridan still was, and on the way chatted in a friendly manner about the situation, he displaying good taste and good feeling in all he said. I remember telling him that the want of rations was what had ruined us, which was of course a little stretching of facts.

I forgot to mention, as I rode up to the battery we expected to support, a lot of prisoners passed by, and three guns which General Roberts' Cavalry Brigade had captured that morning. This was consequently before the skirmish of General Geary, and the Yankee Major was killed after this skirmish was over, so there can be little doubt that the 1st Regiment of Engineer troops killed the last man who fell by the fire of Lee's army.

A few hundred yards back from the village there was an apple orchard where General Lee and his staff spent the day after the interview with Grant. After the surrender became generally known, quite a number of enterprising Yankee soldiers came wandering over among our camps seeking relics, and gossiping generally. To protect the orchard from intrusion of this sort, Colonel Talcott was ordered to surround it with a line of sentinels from his regiment and we in this way remained there all that day.

There were many details about the surrender to be attended to, one of which was getting rations for the army from General Grant's supplies, and officers were coming and going all day. General Lee's staff occupied the shade of an apple tree near the road where Colonel Taylor or Colonel Venable received the visitors. General Lee occupied the shade of a tree a little farther back, where he paced backwards and forwards all day long looking like a caged lion. General Lee usually wore a plain undress uniform and no arms except holster pistols. On this occasion, however, he had put on his full-dress uniform and sword and sash and looked the embodiment of all that was grand and noble in man. We field officers of the 1st Regiment occupied a tree near General Lee's staff. Colonel Talcott had been a member of General Lee's staff up to the time he took command of our regiment, and consequently there was a good deal of social intercourse between regimental and army headquarters; and during this day we were all much together, so we were kept posted pretty fully about all that was going on.

General Lee seemed to be in one of his savage moods and when these moods were on him it was safer to keep out of his way; so his staff kept to their tree except when it was necessary to introduce the visitors. Quite a number came; they were mostly in groups of four or five and some of high rank. It was evident that some came from curiosity, or to see General Lee as friends in the old army. But General Lee shook hands with none of them. It was rather amusing to see the extreme deference shown by them to General Lee. When he would see Colonel Taylor coming with a party towards his tree he would halt in his pacing and stand at "attention" and glare at them with a look which few men but he could assume. They would remove their hats entirely and stand bareheaded during the interview while General Lee sometimes gave a scant touch to his hat in return and sometimes did not even do that. I could not hear what passed, but the interviews were short. One practical result came from all this which was appreciated very highly and that was the arrival of a train of Grant's commissary wagons and the distribution of rations; for Lee's army was hungry. I did feel, however, a little choking sensation as I swallowed this food the first time. I had often lived for weeks on the best they had, but it was *captured*; this was *given* and it felt as if it would choke me when I thought of all it implied. But a hungry soldier doesn't choke *much* on sentimental matter, and after the first mouthful I made the best of the situation and dined heartily.

From this orchard, General Lee that morning accompanied by some of his staff rode over to meet General Grant beyond the village where the formalities of the surrender took place, and it was after this, upon his return, that the visitors mentioned above arrived. I suppose it was due to the fact that General Lee was in this apple orchard during the day that the report was made, and generally believed, that the surrender was made under an apple tree, for after we left there the tree General Lee stood under was carried off bodily by relic hunters. The surrender was actually made in a little country house beyond the C. H. where Lee and Grant met.

The behavior of General Grant and his army during the three or four days we stayed at Appomattox awaiting the paroling of the army was characterized by great forbearance and good taste. Except for occasional distant cheering in their camps, we received not the slightest reminder of our situation, and not a single insult or slighting remark could be heard as we wended our way in disorganized groups through their camps after all was over. Officers were allowed side arms and their horses, and this was extended to the cavalry so far as horses were concerned, when General Lee called Grant's attention to the fact that our cavalry horses were the private property of the men. But Grant had barely enough forage for his own animals and had no use for ours, so a very liberal course was pursued and almost all our animals were ridden off by our men. In fact any infantryman who bestrode a barebacked mule, who said he belonged to the cavalry, was allowed to pass. Many and many a poor infantry soldier went off on a fine C. S. mule which enabled him to make a crop that season for his starving family.

Towards sundown General Lee mounted his dapple-gray horse Traveller and started to his headquarters a mile to the rear; and now occurred a most remarkable exhibition of the affection entertained towards him by his army, and a display of deep feeling on the part of large bodies of men which I suppose has been rarely equaled in history. Along the road, on the hills on each side, between the orchard and headquarters, our army was encamped. The men had been lying in camp all day brooding over what had happened, and eating Uncle Sam's bread and meat. Being rested and fed, there was room for sentiment.

When they saw the well-known figure of General Lee approaching, there was a general rush from each side to the road to greet him as he passed, and two solid walls of men were formed along the whole distance. Their officers followed and behind the lines of men were groups of them, mounted and dismounted, awaiting his coming. I saw something unusual was about to happen, so I sprang upon Magic and followed, keeping a short distance behind, but near enough to hear what was said as General Lee passed. As soon as he entered this avenue of these old soldiers, the flower of his army, the men who had stood to their duty through thick and thin in so many battles, wild heartfelt cheers arose which so touched General Lee that tears filled his eyes and trickled down his cheeks as he rode his splendid charger, hat in hand, bowing his acknowledgments. This exhibition of feeling on his part found quick response from the men, whose cheers changed to choking sobs as with streaming eyes and many cries of affection they waved their hats as he passed. Each group began in the same way with cheers and ended in the same way with sobs, all the way to his quarters. Grim bearded men threw themselves on the ground, covered their faces with their hands and wept like children. Officers of all ranks made no attempt to conceal their feelings, but sat on their horses and cried aloud and among these I remember seeing Gen. W. H. F. Lee, Gen. R. E. Lee's son, much moved.

Traveller, General Lee's horse, took as much pleasure in applause as a human being, and always acknowledged the cheers of troops by tosses of his head, and the men frequently cheered him for it, to which he would answer back as often as they did. On this, Traveller's last appearance before them, his head was tossing a return to the salutes all along the line, which greatly added to the effect. Many expressions of confidence and affection were given which must have been very pleasant to General Lee. One man, I remember, extended his arms and with an emphatic gesture said, "*I love you just as well as ever, General Lee.*" After reaching his tent the men assembled around it and General Lee made them a short address, but I was not near enough to hear what he said.

The next two days were the "bluest" I ever passed in my life, and to add to the depressing effect the weather was rainy and dull. Four years of my life had passed away. Four years of its prime. And for what? Four years before I was on the highroad to prosperity and wealth, but now how different. The country ruined, all business stopped, and no career open before me. This was one side. On the other I was still alive, while so many thousands who entered the service when I did, at the very beginning, were dead, their bones scattered over many a battlefield, or buried in hospital trenches. Then I was as healthy and strong as ever, while so many thousands were disabled by wounds or disease. Then I could look back with pride to an honorable career where without previous military education I had risen from the rank of Lieutenant of Cavalry to that of Lieutenant Colonel of Engineers, while so many equally deserving had not advanced so far, or had not advanced at all.

It was a great consolation to know that I had served from the very first battle fought by the grand old army of Northern Virginia to the very last closing scene of its existence, without missing but one general engagement, and that when at home on sick furlough.

Thinking that it would be an advantage to me in my profession as a civil engineer, I wrote a note to General Lee apologizing for troubling him at such a time and asking him for a testimonial. In reply he gave me a very highly complimentary one which to my never-ceasing regret was burned some years after when my office was destroyed by fire in Lynchburg.

The paroling of the army having been accomplished, I took leave of Talcott and Randolph and all the officers of the regiment and joined a party going towards Lynchburg, among whom was my brother Lewis, who had been taken sick and was put in an ambulance. During the winter, field officers had been cut down to rations of forage for only one horse, and I had lent Frank Robertson my mare Lilly and had disposed of Manassas, keeping only Magic. At Sayler's Creek Gilbert had fallen into the hands of the enemy, but the faithful fellow made his escape and, meeting with Frank, had been placed in charge of Lilly. Frank, after General Stuart's death, had joined Gen. W. IT. F. Lee's staff and being in the cavalry could keep two horses. Gilbert made his way on as far as he could and then turned the mare over to a man who brought her safely home. Lilly was a superb thoroughbred which had been presented to General Stuart by some of his kinsfolk, the Hairstons, in 1862, they having paid at that time, it was said, $800.00 in gold for her. She was too light for the General and he sold her to Theodore Garnett of his staff, and I, wishing to have her for my wife's riding horse, traded a horse I had just bought named Brandy for her a short time before I left Stuart's staff. Not long after my return home, I sold her to Mr. Alex Stuart of Saltville for $500.00 in greenbacks, or rather for two carloads of salt which brought me that sum. This, together with the proceeds of three thousand pounds of tobacco in which my wife had been wise enough to invest some of the full supply of money I placed in her hands, was all my start after the war. Tobacco was selling very high and we got a dollar a pound for what was sold for cash, and a good deal more for that was used in paying off some debts I did not know I owed, and which my wife had several times tried to pay during the war but could not get the parties to render the bills. Those who held bills against those they thought good would not render them if they could help it, to be paid in Confederate money. To my surprise and irritation the doctors in Abingdon presented bills on my return, one for fifteen hundred dollars and the other for seventeen hundred for professional services rendered my family during the four years of the war, and what made it particularly vexatious was that most of it was for medical attendance on our negroes who were now free. I went to them and told them I thought they had acted badly towards me in not presenting their bills when repeatedly asked for, when they could have been paid easily, but that now it was a different matter and that I had a proposition to make; if they did not accept it I would not pay at all without a lawsuit. I offered each one a box of tobacco (100 lbs.) and they accepted the offer, so those two hundred pounds of tobacco cleared me of debt.

I also gave fourteen pounds of this tobacco for a little three-year-old donkey for my children to ride. The tobacco cost twenty cents a pound in Confederate money, so the donkey cost me $2.80 and the $3,200 doctors' bills were paid with $40.00. This donkey was ridden by my children until they all grew too large, and I then gave it to Frank and his children; all used it and it is still living.

The first night after leaving Appomattox we stayed at Mount Athos, Judge John Robertson's place, six miles below Lynchburg, on James River. Judge Robertson was a brother of my father-in-law, Governor Wyndham Robertson, and unlike him was the hottest kind of a secessionist, and being an ex-member of the U. S. Congress, he had much influence. In the discussions between them I have heard the old Judge, who was very profane, say he would be damned if he would not be willing to eat every armed Yankee that ever put foot on Virginia soil. This was in reply to Mr. Wyndham Robertson's expression of his opinion that secession would bring on a war. When we arrived at Mt. Athos, I could not help smiling as I thought of this and what a powerful digestion the old Judge would require to fulfill his promise. We were to meet under peculiar circumstances as I shall relate.

The house at Mt. Athos was then, for it has since been burned, a massive stone structure situated on a hill four hundred feet above James River, commanding a magnificent view of all the country round, and of the Blue Ridge Mountains and the Peaks of Otter, as well as of the splendid body of low ground (enclosed by a horseshoe of the river), which constituted the plantation where all the extensive farm buildings and negro quarters were0 The road approaching the house wound around the hill in easy ascent, while a footpath led directly up to the front. Our party consisted of three or four officers and as we neared this footpath we observed a Yankee soldier sitting by the way. We had nothing to do with Yankee soldiers then, however, and passed on, the man saluting us politely as we passed. We noticed that as soon as we got by he arose and walked rapidly up the footpath towards the house, but we paid no particular attention to him.

Riding up to the front porch, and not knowing whether anyone was at home or not, I called several times. Presently the old Judge came out and, glaring savagely at me, said, in his fiercest tone, and he could be very fierce in manner when he chose, "What do you want here now?" I was a little surprised that he, the model of hospitality at home, should greet anyone in this way; but I saw he did not recognize me and said, "Why, Judge, you don't recognize me." "No," said he, "I don't. Are you not one of those damned ruffians who have been plundering my house?" I then told him who I was, and as weather-beaten and dirty as I then was, I am not surprised he did not know me.

The old gentleman's face lit up with its wonted genial smile. "Good God Almighty!" said he as he hurried down the steps with both hands extended. "Excuse me — dismount, gentlemen, and come in. Here, Bob, take these horses to the stable." He then told us that a party of a dozen Yankee marauders from a camp not far off had just left the house: "And there the damned rascals go," said he, pointing to a squad of cavalry trotting across the low grounds. I at once asked if they had taken anything of value, for in that case I would go to their camp and lay complaint against them and recover the things. "No," said he, "they came stamping in without knocking, and ordered supper to be cooked for them, which I refused, and they were quarrelling about it when a man came in and told them something secretly and, strange to say, they all hurried off without getting anything at all." This explained the conduct of their sentinel at the foot of the hill who had given them notice of our coming.

I received a most cordial welcome from the family, Mrs. Robertson, Powhatan Robertson, the Judge's invalid son, and his charming wife. There was no end to the interest they took in all I could tell them of the momentous events which had transpired, and they richly rewarded our narrations by their kind attention to our wants. Such a table as we sat down to that night! It was a bright spot in the life of war-worn, half-famished soldiers. A genuine, old-fashioned, ante-bellum, old Virginia supper — none of your modern "teas" but a *supper*. This was the first contact Mt. Athos had ever had during the war with the enemy, and the Judge's ample means enabled him to live in all his usual comfort. Then such beds! and the luxury of taking one's clothes off to sleep, a luxury we had not enjoyed for weeks, and then a hot bath; my eyes fill with delight to think of it all, even now. No one used to all these things every day knows how to appreciate them.

Declining with many thanks the old Judge's considerate offer of a loan of money to help me on my way home, we started the next morning for Lynchburg, where *my* widowed mother and my sister Mary were living in our sweet old home on Clay Street. After a couple of days' rest I continued my journey on horseback towards Abingdon, where my wife was living at her father's place, the Meadows, near town.

The railroads were not running, all civil and military authority was at an end, and the country was filled with lawless bands of returning soldiers. I fell in with two or three officers going my way towards their homes in the South and we joined company for mutual protection, but Magic lost a shoe and fell lame; so after the first day they left me and I made the trip alone. Several times on the road I felt myself called upon to assert such authority as the stars on my collar yet gave me in the opinion of the soldiers, to put a stop to their plundering citizens. Once in Roanoke, I rode up to a house just as a party of three or four cavalrymen belonging to a Kentucky regiment were leading out of the stable the only horse a farmer had left. He appealed to me and I assumed such an air of such authority, drawing my pistol at the same time, that the men gave it up at once. It is curious how strong the force of habit becomes, and it was only from force of habit these men obeyed me, though they must have known I had no authority over them. Then too the force of habit gives an officer a tone of command that has its influence.

The first night I spent at Belleview, the residence of Mr. W. Holcombe in Bedford County, where I was most hospitably entertained. Mrs. Holcombe pressed me to stop at her father's house in Roanoke County, Oakland, which I was glad to do. Her father was Gen. Wm. Watts and her sister was my old friend Miss Alice Watts, now Mrs. Judge Robertson of Charlottesville. The next night I spent at General Watts' and they were very glad to see me, both as a matter of hospitality and for the information I could give of the state of affairs, about which they had received little except the general fact that Lee had surrendered. There was a party of officers, guests at the house, who intended starting the next morning to join Johnston's army, and among them Dr. Sorrel, a brother of General Sorrel, at one time on Longstreet's staff. They were guided by my advice and did not go, for I told them that Johnston would be obliged to surrender, and would probably do so before they could reach him. This house was a model of elegance and comfort and old General Watts and Mrs. Watts were as elegant as their home. I have rarely seen two more distinguished-looking old people than they were. It was the first time I had ever visited there, though often invited during the period before my marriage when Miss Alice and myself used to be such good friends. The perfect order in which this large household was kept, comprising some twenty-odd house servants, was a marvel. Everything seemed to move like clockwork, and on the rich and beautiful plantation all seemed equally well appointed. The next night I spent at Mr. Langhorne's near Shawsville, where everything that a cordial welcome could do to cheer a weary soldier was done, and all seemed never weary of hearing the particulars of the great events which had transpired. In Marion I was entertained at Mr. James Sheffy's most kindly and cordially. At all these places I think I relieved many forebodings of evil to come by telling of the consideration with which General Grant had treated us.

At last on a day in mid-April I rode limping along on my lame mare, Magic, up the street of Abingdon. What a contrast to the way I left the place with my splendid company of cavalry, one hundred strong, four years before. No one recognized me when I first spoke to them, but the news of my arrival spread rapidly and I had in a few moments a group around me shaking hands and giving cordial greetings. They told me the news of Lincoln's assassination, and my first feeling was that of intense gratification, though I learned to know afterwards that this event was a great misfortune to us. Then at last I held my dear wife in my arms once more, and my four lovely children upon my knee. It seemed as if all suffering was at an end and that come what might I would be content. The country gradually became filled up with returned resident soldiers and with this force to preserve order the danger of lawlessness from roving bands was much lessened, though it was many weeks before law resumed its sway. I had during this period two occasions for taking the law into my own hands for the preservation of society, which, as examples of the state of the country, I will relate.

I have stated before that among my first investments on reaching home was the purchase of a little donkey for my children. This little animal I had rigged out in quite a stylish manner, for having nothing to do I spent my time playing with my little ones. There was at that time, and had been for several years, a gang of "bushwhackers" and horse thieves in the mountains along the Tennessee line eight or ten miles from Abingdon who levied blackmail on the country round and ran off horses whenever they felt like it. It so happened that a party of six of these men was passing the road half a mile from the house one evening, and our little donkey with the pretty bridle decorated with rosettes had wandered out into the pasture near the road. One of the men stole the bridle, and I would never have known what went with it but for a negro boy who was returning from the mill and met the gang and recognized the bridle by the rosettes. As soon as he told me I determined I would follow and recover my property, not so much for the value of it as for the example. They had several miles' start and it was late in the afternoon, but mounting a horse I followed rapidly. Passing the houses of several returned soldiers whom I found ploughing their fields, I represented the case and they immediately joined me, so I soon had five men besides myself, but mine was the only pistol in the party. These men knew the men we were following and where each one lived and we soon found by inquiry which had the bridle, for several persons they passed had noticed it. We found we could not overtake them on the road, but we reached our man's house just after he dismounted at his home in the mountains south of Abingdon. I told the others to keep near and close together so the absence of arms would not be noticed. We were now in the midst of the mountains and in the centre of the nest of rascals. Trotting up to the man, I presented my pistol and ordered him to return the bridle he stole from me near Abingdon. The fellow was completely cowed and begged I would not shoot him, and handed over the bridle. I then told him I was satisfied, and would let him off this time but he had better be careful in the future. It was now sundown and we returned more quietly, for we had been riding hard. Some weeks after, these men stole some horses from a field in which I happened to have a horse, and I was rather surprised to find mine the only horse left. But I found out afterwards they had taken mine out but came back and returned him, for, said they to my informant: "If Colonel Blackford will ride ten miles after a *bridle*, my God! how far would he go after a *horse.*"

Not long after this I was riding alone from the Salt Works where I had been on a visit. I had heard much talk about bands of negroes passing through the country going down to Tennessee for work, and of some cases where they had committed acts of lawlessness, and I was destined to be the means of effectually putting a stop to this. Just as I reached Morell's Mill a violent storm came on and I galloped up to Morell's stable, dismounted and led my horse in. I still wore my Confederate uniform, and, always in those troubled times, my big army revolver, and owing to this I had not been recognized, as we shall see. Just as I entered the stable, the rain came down in torrents, so hitching my horse in a stall, I sat down on a sill to await fair weather. I then heard sounds of a voice, back in a farther stall, praying in low tones but with great earnestness, and my curiosity being aroused, I walked towards the place. As I approached, the prayer became more and more earnest, and louder and louder. "O Lord! O Lord! hab mercy! Jesus Marster! Blessed Jesus! Blessed Jesus!" This, repeated over and over again, seemed all the person in trouble could say. Then I came to the stall from which the sounds proceeded, and there on his knees was a negro I recognized as belonging to the place, who held up his clasped hands to me and begged for mercy. "Why," said I, "Albert, what is the matter with you? Don't you know me?" And the fellow came forward much relieved and, recognizing me, said he thought I was one of the party who had been robbing his master's house. That a gang of about twenty-five or thirty "niggers" had been there and for all he knew were there now, for he had run over to the stable to hide when they came.

I went at once to the house and found Mr. Morell and his family in great terror, or rather the ladies were, but the old gentleman was in rage not demonstrative but deep. When they found who I was they were delighted, for they, like their man, had not recognized me at first and took me for an officer of the gang of negroes who had passed themselves off as soldiers of the Yankee army. I then learned from them that this party had entered the house in the most insolent manner, had gone into every room taking what they fancied, and had eaten and carried off all the provisions and delicacies they took a fancy to, demanding the keys to the smokehouse, the storeroom and the dairy, and had left there only a few moments before the storm, going towards Tennessee on a road which would take them through Abingdon nine miles distant. I at once said they must be captured and old Mr. Morell agreed with me most heartily. I told him then that he must come on to town with me and go to a gentleman who had been a magistrate in Confederate times and get out his warrant for their arrest, which would be sufficient to protect us from trouble, and then I would undertake to execute it, for I knew I could get plenty of men to join me there. This Mr. Morell agreed to do, but under no circumstances would he start until I had some dinner. Then after dinner he mounted a fine, powerful horse and I was riding my thoroughbred Lilly, named by General Stuart after Miss Lilly Dandridge of the Bower, and away we went. On reaching Abingdon the negroes had still an hour's start of us, and we were delayed a little there, but finally I got off with four or five men who happened to have their horses on the street while others were preparing to follow in hot haste, and before we had gone three miles from town I had a party of thirty or forty. It was necessary to overtake these men before they reached the Tennessee line twelve miles distant, for then my warrant, such as it was, was no good and I might get into trouble. But on nearing Colonel Preston's, nine miles from town, my scout reported "the enemy" close ahead and I cut the party into two bodies. I with the first was to push on and head them, while the others would close up as soon as I did so, and by this means we hoped to capture all. By inquiring from Mr. Morell, I had found that most of these fellows were unarmed and the greater part were instigated to their course by a few among them, so I was anxious to avoid taking any lives if it could be helped, and yet it was very important that they should all be captured, for the sake of the example.

Upon getting as near as we could before they saw us I gave the order to charge and then there was a perfect fox chase. How it happened none of them were hit, I can't imagine, for there must have been several hundred pistol shots fired, but none were hit and we captured every one. It was amusing to see how those captured scanned their party and told if anyone was missing, and which way they had seen him going last. We took them back to town and the streets were lined with people to see the procession enter. After a night in jail all but three or four were turned loose on promise to clear out, and in a few days these were set at liberty in the same way: there being no law in the land at that time either to try or to punish anyone for anything. The effect of this affair, however, was most salutary both on itinerant negroes and those of the country.

APPENDIX

(AS COMPILED BY THE AUTHOR)

Roster of Stuart's Staff
Roster of First Engineer Troops, C.S.A., 1864-65
Roster of two companies, 2nd Engineers Regiment
Dates of the Author's Commissions in the Army

ROSTER OF STUART'S STAFF

Major Gen. J. E. B. Stuart, Commander of Cavalry Corps, Army of Northern Virginia.
Wounded at Yellow Tavern near Richmond on May 11th, 1864, and died in Richmond the following day

Capt. L. T. Brien, Adj't. Gen.
Maj. N. R. Fitzhugh, Adj't Gen. — Prisoner; Verdiersville, Aug. 18th, 1862.
Maj. R. C. Price, Adj't. Gen. — Killed; Chancellorsville, May 1st, 1863.
Maj. H. B. McClellan, Adj't. Gen.
Maj. J. Pelham, Chief of Horse Artillery. *— Killed; Kelly's Ford, Mar. 17th, 1863.*
Maj. H. Von Borcke, Inspector. — Wounded; Upperville, June 19th, 1863.
Maj. A. R. Venable, Inspector. — Prisoner, Wounded; Escaped in Philadelphia, wounded June 3rd, 1863.
Maj. L. Terrill, Inspector. *— Died in service.*
Maj. J. T. W. Hairston, Inspector.
Maj. G. Freaner, Inspector.
Lieut. Col. St. L. Grenfel, Inspector. *— Prisoner; Died while prisoner.*
Capt. W. W. Blackford, Corps of Engineers. *— Wounded; Near Upperville, Nov. 3rd, 1862.*
Lieut. F. S. Robertson, Corps of Engineers.
Lieut. T. R. Price, Jr., Corps of Engineers.
Capt. J. E. Cooke, Ordnance.
Capt. C. Grattan, Ordnance.
Lieut. J. E. Webb, Ordnance. — Wounded; Near Belfield, Dec. 1864.
Maj. S. H. Hairston, Quartermaster.
Maj. M. Hanger, Quartermaster.
Maj. D. Ball, Commissary.
Maj. W. S. Johnson, Commissary.
Dr. T. Eliason, Med. Director.
Dr. J. B. Fontaine, Med. Director. *— Killed; near Petersburg in 1865.*
Capt. J. H. Stuart, Signal Officer. *— Killed; 2nd Manassas, Aug. 29th, 1862.*
Capt. R. E. Frayser, Signal Officer.
Capt. R. Burke, Aide-de-Camp. *— Killed; Fauquier co., 1862.*
Lieut. W. D. Farley, Aide-de-Camp. *— Killed; Fleetwood, June 9th, 1863.*
Lieut. B. S. White, Aide-de-Camp. *— Wounded; Fleetwood, June 9th, 1863.*
Lieut. T. S. Garnett, Jr., Aide-de-Camp.
Lieut. C. Dabney, Aide-de-Camp.
Lieut. W. Q. Hullihen, Aide-de-Camp. — Wounded; Chancellorsville, May 2nd, 1863.

Lieut. R. H. Goldsborough, Aide-de-Camp. — Prisoner; Fleetwood, June 9th, 1863 — Killed; April 6th, 1865, during retreat from Richmond.

Lieut. J. S. Mosby, Aide-de-Camp. — *Prisoner; Beaver Dam, July 1862.*

Lieut. Thos. Turner, Aide-de-Camp. — Killed; while Capt., of Co. in Col. Mosby's command.

Lieut. H. Hagan, Aide-de-Camp.

Lieut. G. M. Ryals, Provost Marshal.

*

The Staff comprised usually:

1 Adjutant General
2 Assistant Adjutant Generals
2 Inspectors
2 Aides-de-Camp
1 Surgeon General
1 Signal Officer
1 Quartermaster
1 Commissary
2 Engineer Officers
1 Ordnance Officer
14 Total Staff

ROSTER OF 1ST REGT. ENGINEER TROOPS C.S.A. 1864-5

During Siege of Petersburg and Retreat to Appomattox

FIELD OFFICERS

Colonel T. M. R. Talcott
Lieut. Colonel Wm. W. Blackford
Major Peyton Randolph

STAFF OFFICERS

Quartermaster Capt. H. C. Fairfax
Quartermaster Capt. D. A. Parker
Quartermaster Capt. G. N. Eakin
Adjutant Lieut. McH. Whitaker; Chapman Maupin, acting Adjutant in 1865
Surgeon Dr. Paul Carrington
Surgeon Dr. Russell Murdock
Asst. Surgeon Dr. Chas. W. Trueheart
Asst. Surgeon Dr. J. S. Conrad
Commissary Capt. L. E. Harvie

COMPANY A

Captain J. J. Conway
Captain D. S. Hessey
2nd Lieutenant C. E. Young
2nd Lieutenant Charles Minor

COMPANY B

Captain J. M. Baldwin
1st Lieutenant C. W. Babbitt

2nd Lieutenant R. H. Griffin
2nd Lieutenant Jno. M. Hood
2nd Lieutenant C. R. Venable

COMPANY C

Captain T. M. Topp
1st Lieutenant H. H. Harris
2nd Lieutenant J. H. Gilmer
2nd Lieutenant W. R. Abbot

COMPANY D

Captain H. C. Derrick
1st Lieutenant R. M. Sully
2nd Lieutenant Wm. Glenn
2nd Lieutenant J. M. Beckham

COMPANY E

Captain G. C. Dickinson
1st Lieutenant R. A. Styles
2nd Lieutenant C. M. Bolton

COMPANY F

Captain H. T. Douglas
Captain W. G. Williamson
1st Lieutenant E. N. Wise
2nd Lieutenant C. F. Smith
2nd Lieutenant Jno. S. Morson
2nd Lieutenant Chapman Maupin
2nd Lieutenant W. W. Dallan

COMPANY G

Captain W. R. Johnson
1st Lieutenant [Name missing]
2nd Lieutenant W. A. Gordon
2nd Lieutenant E. B. Meade

COMPANY H

Captain John Bradford
1st Lieutenant T. J. Moncure
2nd Lieutenant R. W. Peatross
2nd Lieutenant C. M. Davis

COMPANY I

Captain W. Ballard Bruce
1st Lieutenant S. Howell Browne
2nd Lieutenant Chapman Maupin
2nd Lieutenant P. G. Scott

COMPANY K

Captain G. W. Robertson
1st Lieutenant G. P. C. Rumbough
2nd Lieutenant D. C. Woodruff
2nd Lieutenant J. J. Norwood
2nd Lieutenant B. S. Long

NON-COMMISSIONED STAFF

Sergeant Major W. Roane Ruffin
Sergeant Major J. P. Cowardin
Q. M. Sergeant R. F. Hyde
Q. M. Sergeant J. W. Smith
Orderly Sergeant V. M. Flemming
Hospital Steward G. Storr

ROSTER OF TWO COMPANIES 2ND ENGINEER REGT.

Attached to 1st Regt. during Siege of Petersburg and during Retreat to Appomattox

COMPANY G

Captain B. M. Harrod
1st Lieutenant J. E. Roller
2nd Lieutenant F. Harris

COMPANY H

Captain John Howard
1st Lieutenant W. P. Walch
2nd Lieutenant C. N. Berkeley Minor
Note: Where the name of more than one officer appears they were appointed to fill vacancies.

DATES OF MY COMMISSIONS IN THE ARMY

1st Lieut. of Cavalry, Virginia State Troops, April 28th, 1859.
Appointed Adjutant of 1st Regt. Va. Cav. by Lieut. Col. J. E. B. Stuart, commanding, on battlefield of 1st Manassas, July 21st, 1861.
Captain of Cavalry in 1st Regt. Va. Cavalry, October 3rd, 1861.
Captain — Engineer Corps (on Stuart's staff), May 26th, 1862.
Major of 1st Regt. Engineer Troops, February 19th, 1864.
Lieut. Colonel of 1st Regt. Engineer Troops, April 1st, 1864.

Made in the USA
Columbia, SC
22 September 2019